India after Vikramāditya

Also by the author:
Vedic Physics: Scientific Origin of Hinduism
India before Alexander: A New Chronology
India after Alexander: The Age of Vikramādityas

India after Vikramāditya
The Melting Pot

Raja Ram Mohan Roy, Ph.D.

Mount Meru Publishing

Published in 2015 by:
Mount Meru publishing
P.O. Box 30026
Cityside Postal Outlet PO
Mississauga, Ontario
Canada L4Z 0B6
Email: mountmerupublishing@gmail.com

ISBN 978-0-9684120-8-4

Dedicated to Dr. Kailash Nath Sharma,
Professor of Sociology, IIT Kanpur,
whose two courses on Indian Civilization
provided the foundation for my research.

CONTENTS

Preface ix

1. When the Sun Sets 1
   1.1 The Land of the Śakas 2
   1.2 The Śālivāhana Śaka Era 4
   1.3 The Sātavāhana and Śaka Chronology 6
2. The War Elephants of Kaliṅga 15
3. The Nomads of Central Asia 28
   3.1 The Kuṣāṇa Chronology 33
   3.2 The Emperor of Persia 36
4. Rider of the Seven-Headed Horse 49
   4.1 The Journey Begins 50
   4.2 The Official Genealogy 51
   4.3 Displaced in Time 63
   4.4 The Sacking of Vallabhī 67
   4.5 The Saga Continues 68
   4.6 The Princess of Persia 70
   4.7 Mistaken Identities 73
5. The Rise of the Gurjaras 76
   5.1 Background 76
   5.2 The Gurjara Chronology 87
   5.3 False Contemporaries 90
   5.4 The Sword of the Gurjaras 96
6. The Beasts of War 101
   6.1 The Last Empire of Persia 102
   6.2 An Emperor Par Excellence 113
   6.3 The Barbaric Hūṇas 119
   6.4 The Urban Decay 122
   6.5 The Axis of Evil 125

7. The Prowess of the Panthers 130
    7.1 The Maukharis 131
    7.2 The Later Guptas 134
    7.3 The Battle for Supremacy 141
    7.4 The Battle of Korūr 144
    7.5 Timeline 149
8. The Roar of the Lions 154
9. The Children of Hāriti 162
10. The Fall of Persia 180
    10.1 When the Curtain Falls 180
    10.2 The Persian Genocide 189
    10.3 A Home Away from Home 191
Bibliography 204
Index 211
About the author 215

PREFACE

Attending the Indian Institute of Technology (IIT), Kanpur for my undergraduate degree in Metallurgical Engineering, I found that the engineering curriculum allowed for some elective courses during the course of study. One of the elective courses I chose, in 1988, was titled "Indian Society and Culture". It was taught by Professor Kailash Nath Sharma. It was during this course that I learnt a phenomenal amount about my culture, religion, and history. I had not expected a Professor at IIT Kanpur to be so well-versed in Indian scriptures. Professor Sharma would sometimes jokingly say that all he needed was a saffron robe to become a religious Guru. I believed him totally. There are not many Hindu Gurus in India who know more than him about Hinduism. I learnt more about Hinduism in that one semester than what I had learnt listening to religious discourses over many years since my childhood. He also showed me the path which I would follow to discover the true history of India.

I have presented my reconstruction of Indian history starting from Buddha and Mahāvīra to the death of Emperor Vikramāditya in my books, "India before Alexander: A New Chronology", and "India after Alexander: The Age of Vikramādityas". While writing these two books, I also started gathering source materials for the current book, third in the series. When I started conceptualizing this book, I had planned to cover the period from the death of Emperor Vikramāditya in 57 BCE to the death of Emperor Harṣavardhana in 647 CE. Beyond that I had only a vague idea of what would be the content of the book. All I had was my hunch that the clues to the reconstruction of this part of history lie hidden in the works of colonial era scholars. Fortunately, Google has made a vast number of books and journals from the colonial era available on the internet. As I searched through these resources, the picture started to get clear and thoughts started to crystallize. It has taken a lot of deliberation to come up with the chronology presented in this book. However, without access to the resource materials made available by Google it would have been extremely difficult, if not impossible, to reconstruct the part of history after the demise of Emperor Vikramāditya. I would like to sincerely thank Google for taking this initiative to electronically preserve the knowledge base of humanity and making the resource materials available for research. I would also like to express my sincere gratitude to Prof. Ramesh Rao for editing the book.

Raja Ram Mohan Roy
Mississauga, Ontario, Canada
August 2015

TRANSLITERATION GUIDE

अ	a	आ	ā		
इ	i	ई	ī		
उ	u	ऊ	ū	ऋ	ṛ
ए	e	ऐ	ai		
ओ	o	औ	au		
अं	ṃ	अः	ḥ		
क	k	ख	kh		
ग	g	घ	gh	ङ	ṅ
च	ch*	छ	chh*		
ज	j	झ	jh	ञ	ñ
ट	ṭ	ठ	ṭh		
ड	ḍ	ढ	ḍh	ण	ṇ
त	t	थ	th		
द	d	ध	dh	न	n
प	p	फ	ph		
ब	b	भ	bh	म	m
य	y	र	r		
ल	l	व	v		
श	ś	ष	ṣ	स	s
ह	h	क्ष	kṣ	त्र	tr
ज्ञ	jñ	श्र	śr		

*Slightly different from International Alphabet of Sanskrit Transliteration scheme.

dharma eva hato hanti, dharmo rakṣati rakṣitaḥ ।

tasmāddharmo na hantavyo mā no dharmo hato avadhīt ॥

-- Dharma, when violated, destroys. Dharma, when protected, protects. Therefore Dharma should not be violated else violated dharma will destroy us.

- Manusmṛti 8.15 [1]

1. WHEN THE SUN SETS

When Vikramāditya Yaśodharmā Viṣṇuvardhana passed away in 57 BCE, the empire he had built quickly disintegrated. This provided a golden opportunity for invaders to seize a piece of the empire. While modern historians have made most Indians the descendants of invaders, the native tradition has been quite the opposite. There is no denying that foreigners came to India throughout history, but they came in small numbers and were simply assimilated by the native population. The Indian population was always far greater than the outsiders/invaders. Neither the so-called Aryans nor the Rajputs came to India from outside. According to native Indian traditions, Indians were always in India. This is in perfect agreement with the population density of India, which has always been high due to its temperate climate. The history of India has been written by foreigners, and they have glorified their own accomplishments and hidden or marginalized India's victories and civilizational strengths. To discover the Indian version of events, we need to carefully analyze the native Indian sources as well as the account of the foreigners. We will show in this book that important clues to fixing the chronology of India, during the first millennium, lie in Persia.

1.1 The Land of the Śakas

In Indian tradition, the Śakas were a barbarian tribe in Persia on the borders of India. According to modern historians, the Śakas were Scythians from Central Asia. Indian sources list many tribes on the borders, including the Śakas, as follows [2]:

> *"In the Institutes of Menu are the following verses: "The following races of Kshatriyas, by their omission of holy rites, and by seeing no Brahmans, have gradually sunk among men to the lowest of the four classes: Paundracas, Odras, and Draviras, Kambojas, Yavanas, and Sacas; Paradas, Pahlavas, Chinas, Kiratas, Deradas, and Khasas."*
>
> *But not to stop here, the Vishnu and other Puranas, according to Professor Wilson, add to the enumeration of the tribes which had lost caste, and had become Mlechchhas. At page 374 of the Vishnu Purana, the Haihayas, and Tilajanghas, the Sakas, the Yavanas, Kambojas, Paradas, and Pahnavas, are enumerated. The Bhagavata Purana adds "Barbaras." The Vayu Purana extends the list by the Mahishikas, Chaulas, Dravas, and Khasas. The Brahma Purana includes the Kolas, the Sarpas, and the Keratas. The Hari Vansa extends the enumeration with the Tusharas, the Chinas, Madras, the Kishkindas, the Kauntalas, the Bangas, the Salwas, and the Konkanas. It is quite in keeping with the pretensions of Brahmanism to make Brighu and the Puranas say that these nations were once followers of Brahma, and fell. It is sufficient that they admit the fact, that when they were written, the nations were not followers of Brahma.*
>
> *Professor Wilson explains who these several nations or people of Mlechchhas or outcasts were. The Paundras were the people of Western Bengal, the Odras those of Orissa, the Draviras those of the Coromandel Coast, the Kambojas were a people on the north-west of India, the Paradas and Pahlavas bordering tribes, probably*

in the same direction, the Keratas were mountaineers, the Duradas of the Hindu Koh, the Mahishikas and Chaulas were the people of the Malabar and Coromandel coasts, and the Dravas and the Khasas of the Himalayas. The Kolas were the forest races of Eastern Gondwana, and the Sarpas and the Keratas the people of Malabar. The Madras were people in the Punjab, the Kishkindas in Mysore, the Kauntalas, the people along the Nerbudda, the Bangas were the Bengalis, the Salwas the people in Western India, and the Konkanas inhabitants of the Konkan. The Sakas were the Indo-Scythians, who established themselves about 125 years before Christ along the western districts of India, the Tasharas were the Turks of Tokharistan, the Yavanas were the Ionians or Greeks, and the Chinas were the Chinese."

Among the many tribes outside India such as the Kambojas, Yavanas, Śakas, Pahlavas, Chinas, and Kiratas, it was the Śakas who captured a large part of Western India after the death of Vikramāditya Yaśodharmā Viṣṇuvardhana. The Śakas came from the historical Sistan region, which was named Śakasthāna earlier. Śakasthāna means the land of the Śakas. Sistan or Śakasthāna was spread around the meeting point of Iran, Pakistan and Afghanistan. Śakasthāna was spread over parts of current day Sistan and Baluchestan province in Iran, Nimruz in Afghanistan, and Balochistan in Pakistan. The Śakas may have been Scythians, who came from the land north of Oxus and settled in Śakasthāna, but there is no reason to believe that ancient Indians knew that. To ancient Indians, the Śakas were proper Persians. The migration of Śakas towards India started with the invasion of their land by Alexander, the ancestors of Varāhamihira being one of them. Later, the tyrannical Śaka ruler Mihirakula was defeated by Vikramāditya Yaśodharmā Viṣṇuvardhana. After the death of emperor Yaśodharmā, his empire disintegrated. This gave the Śakas the opportunity to consolidate power in Western India. As the Śakas grew stronger and started to expand their empire, they were challenged by a mighty emperor with his seat of power at

Pratiṣṭhāna, current day Paithan in Aurangabad district in Maharashtra.

1.2 The Śālivāhana Śaka Era

The defeat of the Śakas at the hands of the Sātavāhana emperor Gautamīputra Śātakarṇi in 78 CE is a celebrated event in the native history of India. The Śālivāhana Śaka was instituted to commemorate the uprooting of the Śaka kings by Śālivāhana Gautamīputra Śātakarṇi. Modern historians have given credit to foreign rulers such as the Kuṣāṇa emperor Kaniṣka or the Śaka ruler Chaṣṭana for instituting this era. As in the case of the Vikrama era, they have ignored native traditions. They refuse to acknowledge that "Śaka" in Śālivāhana Śaka means an era and not a foreigner. Doing so will open a can of worms. How did the word "Śaka" originally meaning a certain foreign tribe come to mean an era? When a word acquires additional meaning there is usually a reason for it. In this case it was the use of "Śaka" era by Varāhamihira who started the use of Cyrus Śaka era in India in second century BCE. The Cyrus Śaka era named after Cyrus the Great of Persia had a starting point of 550 BCE, corresponding to the foundation of the Achaemenid Empire. For further details, readers can check the fourth chapter titled, "From Persia with Love" in the first volume in this three-part series, "India before Alexander." Gradually, the word Śaka became equivalent to an era. It is quite obvious by the use of the word "Śakakāraka", which means creator of the Śaka. During the colonial era, every Hindu calendar had the list of six Śakakārakas or creators of the era, three of them past, and three of them still to come. Let us look at the evidence presented in a paper in 1875 by Rāo Sāheb Vishvanāth Nārāyaṇ Maṇḍalik [3]:

> *"Śālivāhana, sometimes called Śātavāhana or Sātavāhana, is the name of the Hindu king after whom the present Śaka era current in Mahārāshṭra is named. … When a Marāṭhā Hindu makes a*

religious determination about anything, he has to repeat the period of time that has elapsed since the advent of the Kali-yuga, the number of the incarnation believed to preside over the destinies of the world, the geographical position occupied by the performer of the ceremony, and the time with reference to the Śālivāhana era in the calendar. This is the era generally observed to the south of the Narmadā. To the north of that river, the Vikramāditya era is observed in most places.

In the popular enumeration of the founders of Śakās or eras, Śālivāhana stands the third. Thus,

Yudhishṭhiro Vikrama Śālivāhanau,
Tato Nṛpaḥ Syādvijayābhinandanaḥ;
Tatastu Nāgārjunabhūpatiḥ Kalau,
Kalkī shaḍete Śakakārakāḥ Smṛtāḥ.

Translation:— In the Kali age (come) Yudhishṭhira, Vikrama, (and) Śālivāhana, afterwards will be the king Vijayābhinandana, then the king Nāgārjuna, (and) the sixth Kalki : these six are stated to be the makers of śakās or eras.

The calculators of the current native almanacs describe the places of these founders, and the duration of their eras. Thus, beginning with the first, Yudhishṭhira, he is stated to have lived at Indraprastha (supposed to be somewhere near Dehli), and the duration of his era to be 3044 years, up to the time of Vikrama of Ujjayinī, whose era is said to have extended to 135 years, until the advent of Śālivāhana at Pratishṭhāna, whose era will, it is said, last 18,000 years. He will be succeeded by the following:—

(4.) The fourth, Vijayābhinandana, at Vaitaraṇī, at the junction of the Indus; his era 10,000 years.

(5.) The fifth, Nāgārjuna, at Dhārātīrtha, in the Gauḍa country; his era 400,000 years.

(6.) The sixth, Kalkin, at Karavīra-pattana [or Kolhāpura], in the Karnāṭaka; his era 821 years.

The Śaka year of Śālivāhana begins on the first day of the first half of Chaitra."

The verse quoted above listing the six creators of eras has also been reproduced in a paper written by Pandit Jwālā Sahāya in 1893 [4]. Thus, there should not be any problem in crediting the Śālivāhana Śaka era to its founder Gautamīputra Śātakarṇi. The establishment of Śālivāhana Śaka era in 78 CE by Gautamīputra Śātakarṇi gives us a chronological marker for the Sātavāhana dynasty.

1.3 The Sātavāhana and Śaka Chronology

The Sātavāhana dynasty is currently known as Āndhra-Sātavāhana dynasty. This is based on the evidence from Purāṇas that list the Sātavāhana rulers as Āndhras. However, Sātavāhana rulers have never referred to themselves as Āndhras in any of their inscriptions. Therefore, there is no reason to believe that Sātavāhanas and Āndhras were the same. The seat of power of the Sātavāhanas was on west coast of South India in present day Maharashtra, while the Āndhras ruled from the east coast. In the inscriptions of Devānāmpriya Priyadarśī or Kumāragupta I, Āndhras have been differentiated from Satiyaputra, which possibly refers to the Sātavāhanas. Chronologically, the Āndhras became a powerful force several centuries earlier than the Sātavāhanas. Modern historians have created the Sātavāhana chronology based on the information contained in the Purāṇas as well as in the inscriptions of the Sātavāhana rulers. There is no unanimity regarding the Sātavāhana chronology. Table 1.1 shows two different versions of the currently accepted Sātavāhana chronology.

As can be seen from Table 1.1, there is a wide difference in the chronology of early Sātavāhana rulers. The Purāṇas list up to 30 Āndhra (Sātavāhana) rulers. Though the Vāyu, Brahmāṇḍa, Bhāgavata, and Viṣṇu Purāṇas say that there were 30 kings, not all of them list all the kings [8]. In addition, only some of the 30 Sātavāhana rulers are known from inscriptions. This has given the historians the leverage to choose how many rulers they consider historical. Also, modern historians have placed the Suṅga and Kaṇva rulers during the two centuries before the Common Era leading to a big gap in the middle of the Sātavāhana chronology. An alternative Sātavāhana chronology is shown in Table 1.2 below. The proposed chronology is based on the complete list of 30 rulers of the Sātavāhana dynasty along with the length of their reign as given in the Purāṇas and placing the beginning of Śālivāhana Śaka era (78 CE) during the reign of Gautamīputra Śātakarṇi.

Table 1.1: Currently accepted Sātavāhana chronology

Kings	**Modern Chronology I**	**Modern Chronology II [7]**
Simuka (Chimuka)	c. 235-212 BCE [5]	c. 52 - c. 30 BCE
Kṛṣṇa (Kanha)	c. 212-195 BCE [5]	c. 29 - c. 12 BCE
Śātakarṇi I	c. 195-193 BCE [5]	c. 12 BCE - c. 44 CE
Vediśrī and Satiśrī	c. 193-166 BCE [5]	
Śātakarṇi II	166-111 BCE [5]	
Hāla	20-24 CE [5]	
Gautamīputra Śātakarṇi	106-130 CE [6]	c. 61-90 CE
Vāsiṣṭhīputra Pulumāvi	130-159 CE [6]	c. 91-118 CE
Vāsiṣṭhīputra Śātakarṇi		c. 119-147 CE
Vāsiṣṭhīputra Śivaśrī Pulumāvi	159-166 CE [6]	c. 148-155 CE
Vāsiṣṭhīputra Skanda Śātakarṇi	167-174 CE [6]	c. 156-170 CE
Gautamīputra Yajñaśrī Śātakarṇi	174-203 CE [6]	c. 171-199 CE
Gautamīputra Vijaya Śātakarṇi	203-209 CE [6]	c. 200-205 CE
Vāsiṣṭhīputra Chaṇḍaśrī Śātakarṇi	209-219 CE [6]	c. 206-215 CE
Vāsiṣṭhīputra Vijaya Śātakarṇi		c. 216-225 CE
Vāsiṣṭhīputra Pulumāvi (Pulomā)	219-227 CE [6]	c. 226-232 CE

Table 1.2: The Sātavāhana chronology (Proposed)

	Name	Years ruled [9]	Reign
1	Simuka	23	c. 281-258 BCE
2	Kṛṣṇa	10	c. 258-248 BCE
3	Śrī -Śātakarṇi	10	c. 248-238 BCE
4	Pūrnotsaṅga	18	c. 238-220 BCE
5	Skandhastambhi	18	c. 220-202 BCE
6	Śātakarṇi	56	c. 202-146 BCE
7	Lambodara	18	c. 146-128 BCE
8	Āpīlaka	12	c. 128-116 BCE
9	Meghasvāti	18	c. 116-98 BCE
10	Svāti	18	c. 98-80 BCE
11	Skandasvāti	7	c. 80-73 BCE
12	Mṛgendra Svātikarṇa	3	c. 73-70 BCE
13	Kuntala Svātikarṇa	8	c. 70-62 BCE
14	Svātivarṇa	1	c. 62-61 BCE
15	Pulomāvi	36	c. 61-25 BCE
16	Ariṣṭakarṇa	25	c. 25 BCE- 1 CE
17	Hāla	5	c. 1-6 CE
18	Mantalaka	5	c. 6-11 CE
19	Purindraṣeṇa	21	c. 11-32 CE
20	Sundara Śātakarṇi	1	c.32-33 CE
21	Chakora Śātakarṇi	0.5	c.33 CE
22	Śivasvāti	28	c.33-61 CE
23	Gautamīputra	21	c.61-85 CE*
24	Pulomā	28	c.85-113 CE
25	Śivaśrī Pulomā	7	c.113-120 CE
26	Śivaskandha Śātakarṇi	3	c.120-123 CE
27	Yajñaśrī Śātakarṇika	29	c.123-152 CE
28	Vijaya	6	c.152-158 CE
29	Chaṇḍaśrī Śātakarṇi	10	c.158-168 CE
30	Pulomāvi	7	c. 168-175 CE

*24 years were used for the period of reign based on inscriptional evidence.

The Śālivāhana Śaka era was instituted to celebrate the extirpation of Kṣaharata Śakas by Gautamīputra Śātakarṇi. The Kṣaharāta Śakas ruled for a short period, with prominent rulers being Bhūmaka, his son Nahapāna, and Nahapāna's son-in-law Uṣavadata (Ṛṣabhadatta). Since Gautamīputra Śātakarṇi extirpated the Kṣaharāta Śakas in the eighteenth year of his reign [10], he ascended the throne in 61 CE and reigned till 85 CE.

After the defeat of the Kṣaharāta Śakas, another branch of Śakas called the Kārdamaka Śakas came into prominence. They ruled for a long period of time. The list of Kārdamaka Śaka rulers along with their known regnal years are shown in Table 1.3. Modern historians have counted these years from the beginning of the Śālivāhana Śaka era (78 CE). Some of them believe that the first Kārdamaka Śaka ruler Chaṣṭana founded the Śālivāhana Śaka era, while others simply count from this era as there is really no other era available to refer to during the period the Kārdamaka Śakas ruled. We know that the native Indian traditions give credit for founding the Śālivāhana Śaka era to Gautamīputra Śātakarṇi, so Chaṣṭana could not have founded this era. According to Indian traditions, the Śālivāhana Śaka era was founded to celebrate the uprooting of the Śakas, and thus it would not make sense to give a Śaka the credit for founding this era. We have two clues to fix the Kārdamaka Śaka chronology: the reference to a ruler named Tiastenes by Ptolemy, and the marriage of Kārdamaka Śaka ruler Rudradāman's daughter with a Sātavāhana ruler. Based on these two pointers, the revised chronology of Kārdamaka Śakas is presented in Table 1.4 along with the currently accepted chronology. The explanation for the proposed chronology is described below.

If we discount the possibility that Chaṣṭana founded the Śālivāhana Śaka era, then we are led to the conclusion that the Kārdamaka Śakas simply counted their regnal years from the date of ascension of their first ruler Chaṣṭana to the throne.

Table 1.3: Kārdamaka Śaka genealogy [11]

Kings	Relation	Title	Years known
Chaṣṭana	Son of Yasamotika	Mahākṣatrapa	52
Jayadāman	Son of Chaṣṭana	Did not rule	
Rudradāman	Son of Jayadāman	Mahākṣatrapa	72
Dāmajadaśrī*	Son of Rudradāman	Mahākṣatrapa	
Jīvadāman	Son of Dāmajadaśrī,	Mahākṣatrapa	100, 119-121
Rudrasiṃha I	Brother of Dāmajadaśrī	Kṣatrapa	102, 110-112
		Mahākṣatrapa	103-110, 113-118
Satyadāman	Son of Dāmajadaśrī,	Kṣatrapa	
Rudrasena I	Son of Rudrasiṃha I	Kṣatrapa	121
		Mahākṣatrapa	122-144
Saṅghadāman	Son of Rudrasiṃha I	Mahākṣatrapa	144-145
Dāmasena	Son of Rudrasiṃha I	Mahākṣatrapa	145-158
Pṛthīvisena	Son of Rudrasena I	Kṣatrapa	144
Dāmajadaśrī II	Son of Rudrasena I	Kṣatrapa	154-155
Vīradāman	Son of Dāmasena	Kṣatrapa	156-160
Yaśodāman	Son of Dāmasena	Mahākṣatrapa	160-161
Vijayasena	Son of Dāmasena	Kṣatrapa	161
		Mahākṣatrapa	161-172
Dāmajadaśrī III	Son of Dāmasena	Mahākṣatrapa	173-177
Rudrasena II	Son of Vīradāman	Mahākṣatrapa	177-198
Viśvasiṃha	Son of Rudrasena II	Kṣatrapa	197-200
Bhartṛdāman	Son of Rudrasena II	Kṣatrapa	200
		Mahākṣatrapa	204-217
Viśvasena	Son of Bhartṛdāman	Kṣatrapa	215-226

*Also spelt as Dāmaysada or Dāmaghsada

Table 1.4: Kārdamaka Śaka chronology

Kings	**Years known**	**Modern Chronology [11]**	**Proposed Chronology**
Chaṣṭana	52	130 CE	c. 100-152 CE
Jayadāman			Did not rule
Rudradāman	72	150 CE	c. 152-175 CE
Dāmajadaśrī			c. 175-200 CE
Jīvadāman	100-120	178-198 CE	c. 200-203 CE, c. 210-213 CE, c. 219-222 CE
Rudrasiṃha I	102-118	180-196 CE	c. 203-210 CE, c. 213-218 CE
Satyadāman			Ruled as Kṣatrapa
Rudrasena I	121-144	199-222 CE	c. 222-244 CE
Saṅghadāman	144-145	222-223 CE	c. 244-245 CE
Dāmasena	145-158	223-236 CE	c. 245-260 CE
Pṛthīvisena	144	222 CE	Ruled as Kṣatrapa
Dāmajadaśrī II	154-155	232-233 CE	Ruled as Kṣatrapa
Vīradāman	156-160	234-238 CE	Ruled as Kṣatrapa
Yaśodāman	160-161	238-239 CE	c. 260-261 CE
Vijayasena	161-172	239-250 CE	c. 261-273 CE
Dāmajadaśrī III	173-177	251-255 CE	c. 273-277 CE
Rudrasena II	177-198	255-276 CE	c. 277-300 CE
Viśvasiṃha	197-200	275-278 CE	Ruled as Kṣatrapa
Bhartṛdāman	200-217	278-295 CE	c. 300-326 CE
Viśvasena	215-226	293-304 CE	Ruled as Kṣatrapa

Since we know that Chaṣṭana was ruling in year 52 of the era instituted by him, we know that he ruled for a long period. A rule of 52 years is not impossible if he started young and ruled till his seventies. He might have been forced to rule longer till his grandson came of age, as we know that his son did not rule possibly because of dying young. The question now is, when did Chaṣṭana start ruling?

Ptolemy wrote "Geographia" between 127-147 CE [12] and he has mentioned that Tiastenes was ruling Ozene (Ujjayinī) and Siriptolemaios (Śrī-Pulomāvi) was ruling Baithana (Pratiṣṭhāna) [13]. Modern historians consider Tiastenes to be a corrupt form of Chaṣṭana. The data could have been collected many years earlier than the actual writing of Geographia. Looking at the proposed Sātavāhana chronology in Table 1.2, we can identify the Siriptolemaios (Śrī-Pulomāvi) mentioned by Ptolemy as Śivaśrī Pulumāvi, who ruled c. 113-120 CE. As Chaṣṭana was his contemporary, according to Ptolemy, he was also ruling during this period.

Chaṣṭana's grandson Rudradāman has claimed in the Junāgarh inscription that he defeated Śātakarṇi, Lord of Dakṣināpath (South India) twice, but did not kill him as he was a close relative. Based on the Kānheri inscription mentioning the marriage of a Kārdamaka Śaka princess to a Sātavāhana king, it can be concluded that Rudradāman's daughter was married to a Sātavāhana king named Śātakarṇi. Looking again at the proposed Sātavāhana chronology in Table 1.2, we can identify the Śātakarṇi, son-in-law of Rudradāman, as Chaṇḍaśrī Śātakarṇi, who ruled between 158-168 CE. This choice is necessitated by the fact that Rudradāman was the grandson of Chaṣṭana, contemporary of Śivaśrī Pulumāvi, and Śātakarṇi was married to the daughter of Rudradāman. Thus, there needs to be a considerable gap between Śivaśrī Pulumāvi, and Śātakarṇi, son-in-law of Rudradāman. As Chaṇḍaśrī Śātakarṇi was the penultimate ruler of the Sātavāhana dynasty, we can conclude that Sātavāhana Empire collapsed following the disastrous defeats suffered by Chaṇḍaśrī Śātakarṇi at the hands of his father-in-law Rudradāman. The Kārdamaka Śaka chronology presented in Table 1.4 is consistent with the points discussed above. It is estimated that Chaṣṭana ascended the throne in c. 100 CE and his descendants kept counting their regnal years from this date. We will conclude the discussion on Sātavāhanas here. We have not discussed the literary and artistic achievements of the Sātavāhana period as the focus of this book is on fixing the chronology.

When the Sātavāhanas were ruling in Western India, a mighty emperor arose in the east and made conquests of faraway lands. We will discuss next the exploits of this mighty emperor rising from the land of the most fearsome warriors.

Notes:

1. The much maligned Manu Smṛti is only one among many Smṛtis such as Aṅgirā, Vyāsa, Gautama, Atri, Uśanā, Yama, Vaśiṣṭha, Dakṣa, Saṃvarta, Śātātapa, Parāśara, Viṣṇu, Āpastamba, Hārīta, Śaṅkha, Kātyāyana, Bhṛgu, Prachetā, Nārada, Yājñavalkya, Baudhāyana, Pitāmaha, Sumantu, Kāśyapa, Vabhru, Paiṭhīnasi, Vyaghra, Satyavrata, Bharadwāja, Gārgya, Kārṣṇājini, Jāvāli, Jamadagni, Laugākṣi, Brahmagarbha, Bṛhaspati, Likhita, Nāchiketa, Skanda, Kāśyapa, Sanatkumāra, Śantanu, Janaka, Jātukarṇya, Kapiñjala, Kanāda, Viśvāmitra, Gobhila, Devala, Pulastya, Pulaha, Kratu, Āgneya, Gaveya, Marichi, Vatsa, Pāraskara, Ṛṣyaśṛṅga, Vaijāvāpa, Budha, Soma, Chhāgaleya, Jābāla, Chyavana, Āśvalāyana, Mārkaṇdeya, Śaunaka, Kaṇva, Upamanyu and Śāṇdilya (compiled from Girija Prasad Dvivedi, "The Manusmriti or Manavadharmashastra", Courtesy of Bābū M. L. Bhargava, Lucknow, 1917, pages 25-28, in Hindi). The existence of so many Smṛtis clearly proves that the law codes were being updated periodically as needed and did not have the sanctity attributed to them. In fact, Hindu scriptures are crystal clear that Smṛtis have no validity if what they say contradicts the Śrutis, i.e. the Vedas. The Vedas do not directly discuss human behavior, and so

what the Vedas say about human behavior is open to different interpretations.

2. Sykes (1841). Quote on pages 426-427.
3. Maṇḍalik (1875).
4. Sahāya (1893).
5. Middleton (2015): 828.
6. Majumdar et al. (2001): 191-216.
7. Shastri (1999): 35.
8. Pargiter (1913): 36.
9. Pargiter (1913): 71-72.
10. Śrivāstava (2007): 298-299.
11. Majumdar et al. (2001): 178-190.
12. Waldman and Mason (2006): 374.
13. Sircar (1971): 227.

vīra bhogyā vasundharā ।

-- The Earth is for the Enjoyment by the Brave.

- A Sanskrit Proverb

2. THE WAR ELEPHANTS OF KALIṄGA

Kaliṅga was an ancient kingdom located in present day Odisha and the northern parts of Andhra Pradesh before its division. Its natural boundaries were the Ganges delta in the north, the mouth of Godavari in the south, Eastern Ghats to the west, and the Bay of Bengal to the east [1].

Alexander Cunningham has provided the following information about Kaliṅga in his book, "The Ancient Geography of India", which starts with the description of Kaliṅga by Xuan Zang (Hiuen Tsiang) [2]:

> *"In the seventh century, the capital of the kingdom of Kie-ling-kia, or Kalinga, was situated at from 1400 to 1500 li, or from 233 to 250 miles, to the south west of Ganjam. Both bearing and distance point either to Rajamahendri on the Godāvari river, or to Koringa on the seacoast, the first being 251 miles to the south-west of Ganjam, and the other 246 miles in the same direction. But as the former is known to have been the capital of the country for a long period, I presume that it must be the place that was visited by the Chinese pilgrim. The original capital of Kalinga is said to have been*

Srikakola, or Chikakol, 20 miles to the south-west of Kalingapatam. The kingdom was 5000 li, or 833 miles, in circuit. Its boundaries are not stated; but as it was united to the west by Andhra, and to the south by Dhanakakaṭa, its frontier line cannot have extended beyond the Godāvari river, on the south-west, and the Gaoliya branch of the Indrāvati river on the north-west. Within these limits, the circuit of Kalinga would be about 800 miles. The principal feature in this large tract of country is the Mahendra range of mountains, which has preserved its name unchanged from the time of the composition of the Mahābhārata to the present day. This range is mentioned also in the Vishnu Purāna, as the source of the Rishikulya river, and as this is the well known name of the river of Ganjam, the Mahendra mountains can at once be identified with the Mahendra Male range, which divides Ganjam from the valley of the Mahānadi.

Rajamahendri was the capital of the junior, or eastern branch of the Chālukya princes of Vengi, whose authority extended to the frontiers of Orissa. The kingdom of Vengi was established about A.D. 540, by the capture of the old capital of Vengipura, the remains of which still exist at Vegi, 5 miles to the north of Ellūr, and 50 miles to the west-south-west of Rajamahendri. About A.D. 750, Kalinga was conquered by the Raja of Vengi, who shortly afterwards moved the seat of government to Rajamahendri.

The Calingae are mentioned by Pliny, as occupying the eastern coast of India below the Mandei and Malli, and the famous Mount Maleus. This mountain may perhaps be identified with the high range at the head of the Rishikulya river, in Ganjam, which is still called Mahendra Male, or the "Mahendra Mountain." To the south, the territory of the Calingae extended as far as the promontory of Calingon and the town of Dandaguda, or Dandagula, which is said to be 625 Roman miles, or 574 British miles, from the mouth of the Ganges. Both the distance and the name point to the great port-town of Coringa, as the promontory of Coringon, which is situated on a projecting point of land, at the mouth of the Godāvari River.

The town of Dandaguda, or Dandagula, I take to be the Dantapura of the Buddhist chronicles, which, as the capital of Kalinga, may with much probability be identified with Raja Mahendri, which is only 30 miles to the north east of Coringa. From the great similarity of the Greek Γ and Π, I think it not improbable that the Greek name may have been Dandapula, which, is almost the same as Dantapura. But in this ease, the Danta, or "tooth relic," of Buddha must have been enshrined in Kalinga as early as the time of Pliny, which is confirmed by the statement of the Buddhist chronicles, that the "left canine tooth" of Buddha was brought to Kalinga immediately after his death, where it was enshrined by the reigning sovereign, Brahmadatta. Dantapura, also, is said to have been situated on the northern bank of a great river, which can only be the Godāvari, as the Kistna was not in Kalinga. This fact alone would be sufficient to fix the position of Dantapura at the old capital of Rajamahendri, which is situated on the north-eastern bank of the Godāvari. The name of Mahendri is perhaps preserved in the Pitundra Metropolis of Ptolemy, which he places close to the Maisolos, or Godāvari, that is, to the river of Masuli-patam.

A still earlier name for the capital of Kalinga was Sinhapura, which was so called after its founder, Sinha-bahu, the father of Vijaya, the first recorded sovereign of Ceylon. Its position is not indicated, but there still exists a large town of this name on the Lalgla river, 115 miles to the west of Ganjam, which is very probably the same place.

In the inscriptions of the Kālachuri, or Haihaya dynasty of Chedi, the Rajas assume the titles of "Lords of Kalanjjarapura and of Tri-Kalinga. Kālanjar is the well-known hill-fort in Bundelkhand; and Tri-Kalinga, or the "Three Kalingas," must be the three kingdoms of Dhanaka, or Amaravati, on the Kistna, Andhra or Warangol, and Kalinga, or Raja Mahendri. The name of Tri-Kalinga is probably old, as Pliny mentions the Macco-Calingae and the Gangarides-Calingae as separate peoples from the Calingae, while the Mahābhārata names the Kalingas three separate times, and each time in conjunction with different peoples. As Tri-Kalinga thus corresponds with the great province of Telingana, it seems probable that the name of Telingana may be only a slightly contracted form of Tri-Kalingana, or the "Three Kalingas." I am aware that the name is usually derived from Tri-Linga, or the "Three Phalli" of Mahadeva. But the mention of Macco-Calingae and Gangarides-Calingae by Pliny, would seem to show that the "Three Kalingas" were known as early as the time of Megasthenes, from whom Pliny has chiefly copied his Indian Geography. The name must therefore be older than the Phallic worship of Mahadeva in southern India. Kalinga is three times mentioned in the Khandagiri inscription of Aira Raja, which cannot be later than the second century B.C., and at a still earlier date, during the lifetime of Sakya-Muni, it was noted for its manufacture of fine muslins, and at his death, the king of Kalinga is said to have obtained one of the teeth of Buddha, over which he built a magnificent stupa."

As stated above, the ancient capital of Kaliṅga was at Dantapuram, which is about 20 km from Srikakulam (Chicacole, during colonial rule) in Andhra Pradesh. Kalingapatnam at the east coast is about 27 km from Srikakulam. After the parinirvāṇa of the Buddha, a Buddhist monastery was made at Dantapuram, where the left canine tooth of the Buddha was enshrined by the reigning king of Kaliṅga. During the seventh century, the capital of Kaliṅga was at Rajahmundry (Rajamahendri) in Andhra Pradesh, which is about 70 km from Coringa/Korangi at the east coast.

Kaliṅga finds mention in Mahābhārata at several places. When Arjuna went on pilgrimage, he visited the prominent pilgrimage centres and temples of Aṅga, Vaṅga and Kaliṅga [3]. Later, king of Kaliṅga attended the Rājasūya sacrifice performed by Yudhisṭhira after an invitation was sent to him [4]. Still later, his warriors fought along with Kauravas during the Mahābhārata war. Though they fought along the losing side, they were praised as excellent elephant warriors [5]. During the time of the Mahābhārata war, Kaliṅga was outside the cultural sphere of Vedic Aryans.

Gradually as the Vedic culture spread to the east, Kaliṅga also came under it influence.

When the Nandas came to power during 11th to 10th century BCE, Kaliṅga came under the rule of the Nandas, who were the followers of Jainism, and who during their rule brought a Jina image to Magadha from Kaliṅga. After the rule of the Nandas came to an end following a coup, Kaliṅga came under the rule of the Mauryas, who were also followers of Jainism except for Aśoka, who became a Buddhist. Sometime after the rule of the Mauryas, when the central authority of Magadha weakened, Kaliṅga became independent. In time, Kaliṅga became a very powerful kingdom with a formidable reputation.

The might of Kaliṅga was noticed by Megasthenes, who made observations about the residents of Kalinga in his book "Indica". The book is not available now, but fragments of it are available in the works of other Greek writers. McCrindle has presented them in his book "Ancient India as Described by Megasthenes and Arrian". In Fragment XX.B, the following is said about Kaliṅga [6]:

> *"The, tribes which dwell by the Ganges are the Calingae, nearest the sea, and higher up the Mandei, also the Malli, among whom is Mount Mallus, the boundary of all that region being the Ganges."*

To this McCrindle has added the following footnote about Calingae, the residents of Kaliṅga [7]:

> *"A great and widely diffused tribe settled mainly between the Mahānadī and the Godāvarī. Their capital was Partualis (called by Ptolemy Kalligra), on the Mahānadī, higher up than the site of Katak. The name is preserved in Koringa, a great port at the mouth of the Godāvarī."*

In Fragment LVI, further information has been provided about Kaliṅga as follows [8]:

"The tribes called Calingae are nearest the sea, and higher up are the Mandei, and the Malli in whose country is Mount Mallus, the boundary of all that district being the Ganges. This river, according to some, rises from uncertain sources, like the Nile, and inundates similarly the countries lying along its course; others say that it rises on the Skythian mountains, and has nineteen tributaries, of which, besides those already mentioned, the Condochates, Erannoboas, Cosoagus, and Sonus are navigable. Others again assert that it issues forth at once with loud roar from its fountain, and after tumbling down a steep and rocky channel is received immediately on reaching the level plains into a lake, whence it flows out with a gentle current, being at the narrowest eight miles, and on the average a hundred stadia in breadth, and never of less depth than twenty paces (one hundred feet) in the final part of its course, which is through the country of the Gangarides. The royal city of the Calingae is called Parthalis. Over their king 60,000 foot-soldiers, 1,000 horsemen, 700 elephants keep watch and ward in 'procinct of war' ".

To this McCrindle has added the following footnote [9]:

"The common reading, however "Gangaridum Calingarum. Regia," &c., makes the Gangarides a branch of the Kalingae. This is probably the correct reading, for, as General Cunningham states (Anc. Geog. of Ind. pp. 518-519), certain inscriptions speak of 'Tri-Kalinga,' or 'the Three Kalingas.' "The name of Tri-Kalinga," he adds, "is probably old, as Pliny mentions the Macco-Calingae and the Gangarides-Calingae as separate peoples from the Calingae, while the Mahābhārata names the Kalingas three separate times, and each time in conjunction with different peoples." (H. H. Wilson in Vishṇu, Purāṇa, 1st ed., pp.185, 187 note, and 188.) As Tri-Kalinga thus corresponds with the great province of Telingana, it seems probable that the name of Telingana may be only a slightly contracted form of Tri-Kalingana, or 'the Three Kalingas.' "

As pointed above, the name Telingana has developed from Tri-Kalingana or the three Kalingas. With its massive army of 60,000 foot-soldiers, 1,000 horsemen, and 700 war elephants, Kaliṅga was a formidable challenge to any conqueror. When Samudragupta went on his conquest of India, he decided to leave Kaliṅga alone. Kumāragupta-I, grandson of Samudragupta, attacked Kaliṅga to make it a part of the Imperial Gupta Empire. This turned out to be the most important event of his life. Kumāragupta-I ascended the throne in 213 BCE and he attacked Kaliṅga during the eighth year of his rule. Therefore, Kaliṅga was attacked in 206 BCE. Kaliṅga was inhabited by fierce warriors, who engaged Kumāragupta's army bravely. As war raged on, more fighters were added to the Kaliṅga army. Kumāragupta-I managed to win the war, but the cost of this war was far beyond what he had anticipated. Kaliṅga lost 100,000 people and another 150,000 were deported, according to the rock edicts of Kumāragupta-I. The magnitude of the loss of lives in the battlefield and the sorrows of people affected by the war transformed Kumāragupta, who became a Buddhist and assumed the title of Devānāmpriya Priyadarśī. Currently, it is assumed that Aśoka Maurya was Devānāmpriya Priyadarśī of the famous rock edicts.

The next important event in the history of Kaliṅga was the rule of King Khāravela. He was a mighty warrior, who had made wide conquests. The source of information for the rule of King Khāravela is the Hathīgumphā inscription [10]:

> *"(Line 1) Salutation to the Arhats (Arihats = lit. 'Conquerors of Enemies,' i.e., Jinas). Salutation to all the Siddhas. By illustrious* ***Khāravela****, the* ***Aira*** *(Aila), the Great King, the descendant of* ***Mahāmeghavāhana****, the increaser (of the glory) of the* ***Cheti*** *(Chedi)* ***dynasty****, (endowed) with excellent and auspicious marks and features, possessed of virtues which have reached (the ends of) the four quarters, overlord of* ***Kaliṅga****,*

*(L. 2) for fifteen years, with a body ruddy and handsome were played youthsome sport; after that (by him who) had mastered (royal) correspondence, currency, finance, civil and religious laws (and) who had become well-versed in all (branches) of learning, for nine years (the office of) Yuvarāja (heir apparent) was administered. Having completed the twenty-fourth year, at that time, (he) who had been prosperous (**vardhamāna**) since his infancy (?) and who (was destined) to have wide conquests as those of **Vena**,*

(L. 3) then in the state of manhood, obtains the imperial (mahārājya) coronation in the dynasty of Kaliṅga. As soon as he is anointed, in the first (regnal) year (he) causes repairs of the gates, the walls and the buildings (of the city), (which had been) damaged by storm; in the city of Kaliṅga (he) causes the erection of the embankments of the lake (called after) Khibīra Ṛshi, (and) of (other) tanks and cisterns, (also) the restoration of all the gardens (he) causes to be

*(L. 4) done at (the cost of) thirty-five-hundred-thousands, and (he) gratifies the People. And in the second year (he), disregarding **Sātakaṃni**, despatches to the western regions an army strong in cavalry, elephants, infantry (nara) and chariots (ratha) and by that army having reached the **Kānha-beṃṇā**, he throws the city of the **Musikas** into consternation. Again in the third year,*

*(L. 5) (he) versed in the science of the Gandharvas (i.e., music), entertains the capital with the exhibition of dapa, dancing, singing and instrumental music and by causing to be held festivities and assemblies (samājas); similarly in the fourth year, 'the **Abode of Vidyādharas**' built by the former Kaliṅgan king(s), which had not been damaged before ... with their coronets rendered meaningless, with their helmets (?) (bilma) cut in twain (?), and with their umbrellas and*

*(L. 6) bhiṅgaras cast away, deprived of their jewels (i.e., ratana, Skt. ratna, precious objects) all the **Raṭhikas** and **Bhojakas** (he) causes to bow down at his feet. Now in the fifth year he brings into the capital from the road of Tansauliya the canal excavated in the*

*year one hundred-and-three of **King Nanda** .... Having been (re-)anointed (he while) celebrating the Rājasūya, remits all tithes and cesses,*

*(L. 7) bestows many privileges (amounting to) hundreds of thousands or the City-Corporation and the Realm-Corporation. In the seventh year of his reign, his famous wife of **Vajiraghara** obtained the dignity of auspicious motherhood … Then in the eighth year, (he) with a large army having sacked **Goradhagiri***

*(L.8) causes pressure on **Rājagaha** (Rājagṛha). On account of the loud report of this act of valour, the **Yavana** (Greek) **King Dimi[ta]** retreated to **Mathurā** having extricated his demoralized army and transport … (He) gives … with foliage*

(L. 9) Kalpa (wish-fulfilling) trees, elephants, chariots with their drivers, houses, residences and resthouses. And to make all these acceptable (he) gives at a fire sacrifice (?) exemption (from taxes) to the caste of Brāhmanas. Of Arhat ...

*(L. 10) ... (He) causes to be built … a royal residence (called) the **Palace of Great Victory** (Mahāvijaya) at the cost of thirty-eight hundred thousands. And in the tenth year (he), following (the threefold policy) of chastisement, alliance and conciliation sends out an expedition against **Bharatavasa** (and) brings about the conquest of the land (or, country) .... and obtains jewels and precious things of the (kings) attacked.*

*(L.11) ... And the market-town (?) **Pīthuṃḍā** founded by the **Ava King** he ploughs down with a plough of asses; and (he) thoroughly breaks up the confederacy of the **T[r]amira** (Dramira) countries of one hundred and thirteen years, which has been a source of danger to (his) Country (Janapada). And in the twelfth year he terrifies the kings of the **Utarāpatha** with ... thousands of*

*(L.12) ... And causing panic amongst the people of Magadha (he) drives (his) elephants into the **Sugaṃgīya** (Palace), and (he) makes the King of Magadha, **Bahasatimita**, bow at his feet. And (he) sets*

*up (the image) 'the **Jina of Kaliṅga**' which had been taken away by **King Nanda** ... and causes to be brought home the riches of **Aṅga** and **Magadha** along with the keepers of the family jewels of ...*

*(L. 13) ... (He) builds excellent towers with carved interiors and creates a settlement of a hundred masons, giving them exemption from land revenue. And a wonderful and marvellous enclosure of stockade for driving in the elephants (he) ... and horses, elephants, jewels and rubies as well as numerous pearls in hundreds (he) causes to be brought here from the **Pāṇḍya King**.*

*(L. 14) ... (he) subjugates. In the thirteenth year, on the **Kumārī Hill** where the Wheel of Conquest had been well-revolved (i.e., the religion of Jina had been preached), (he) offers respectfully royal maintenances, China clothes (silks) and white clothes to (the monks) who (by their austerities) have extinguished the round of lives, the preachers on the religious life and conduct at the Relic Memorial. By Khāravela, the illustrious, as a layman devoted to worship, is realised (the nature of) jīva and deha*

*(L. 15) ... bringing about a Council of the wise ascetics and sages, from hundred (i.e., all) quarters, the monks (samaṇas) of good deeds and who have fully followed (the injunctions) ... near the Relic Depository of the Arhat, on the top of the hill, ... with stones ... brought from many miles (yojanas) quarried from excellent mines (he builds) shelters for the **Siṃhapatha Queen Sindhula**. ...*

(L. 16) ... Paṭalaka(?) ... (he) sets up four columns inlaid with beryl ... at the cost of twenty-five hundred thousands; (he) causes to be compiled expeditiously the (text) of the seven-fold Aṅgas of the sixty-four (letters). He is the King of Peace, the King of Prosperity, the King of Monks (bhikshus), the King of Religion (Dharma), who has been seeing, hearing and realising blessings (kalyāṇas)-

(L. 17) ... accomplished in extraordinary virtues, respector of every sect, the repairer of all temples, one whose chariot and army are irresistible, one whose empire is protected by the chief of the empire

(himself), descended from the family of the Royal Sage ***Vasu****, the* ***Great conqueror****, the King, the illustrious* ***Khāravela****."*

According to this inscription, King Khāravela was born in Chedi dynasty. He was the descendant of Mahāmeghavāhana, who established the Chedi dynasty in Kaliṅga. There have been various dates proposed for the reign of King Khāravela. According to the translation of Khāravela's inscription by Jayaswal reproduced above, Khāravela brought into the capital the canal excavated in the year 103 of King Nanda. This line is alternatively read to mean that Khāravela extended the canal into the capital when 300 years had passed since King Nanda. Since modern history makes King Nanda a contemporary of Alexander the Great, there is a consensus about King Khāravela ruling during the second half of the first century BCE. It is considered that the date of 49 BCE for becoming crown prince, and 40 BCE for becoming king is consistent with the available information [11]. According to Konow, the canal was built 103 or 300 years after King Nanda, which was extended to the capital by Khāravela [12]. Thus this information has no bearing on the dating of Kharavela, whose reign must be determined by other information provided in his inscriptions -- such as the kings he encountered during his military expeditions. As King Khāravela was a contemporary of King Sātakarṇi, we can look at Table 1.2 in Chapter 1 to see which Sātakarṇi king was the contemporary of King Khāravela. We would like to identify the Sātakarṇi king with Sundara Śātakarṇi, and accordingly the time of King Khāravela can be fixed circa 33 CE. According to Table 1.2, Sundara Śātakarṇi ruled for only one year, and his successor Chakora Śātakarṇi ruled for only six months. We can conclude that their careers were cut short by the attacks of the mighty King Khāravela.

King Khāravela made wide conquests in all three directions he could go by land -- west, north and south. Besides being a great conqueror, he was a great builder too. He brought back the image of Jina from Magadha to Kaliṅga that was taken away by the Nandas. Knowing the military genius that King Khāravela was, it seems plausible that he started building the naval power of Kaliṅga, which later resulted in the colonization of faraway lands by people of Kaliṅga using the naval route.

Being on the east coast, Kaliṅga had many ports for trading with faraway lands, which brought prosperity to the people. The full moon day of Kārttika month (October-November) after the end of the rainy season was considered very auspicious for starting the sea voyage. The people of Odisha still celebrate the memory of those days as they take a bath early in the morning on the full moon day of the Kārttika month and float miniature paper boats with small lamps burning inside them in the ponds and rivers of the region.

King Vijay, who established the first kingdom in Ceylon according to Buddhist texts, was the grandson of the daughter of the king of Kaliṅga. There was a kingdom called Kalingga in the Central Java region of Indonesia during the sixth and seventh centuries, which was established by people from Kaliṅga. Native Malaysian and Indonesian people still use the word "Keling" to refer to the people of Indian origin.

Kaliṅga was the land of the warriors, who dominated the state of affairs on the eastern coast for a long time. Like the rest of India, Kaliṅga also finally fell to the invaders, but this happened much later than the western parts of India. It was the western part of India that bore the brunt of invaders one after the other. After the fall of the Śakas, it was the turn of another set of invaders to dominate the affairs of north-western India, the Kuṣāṇas.

Notes:

1. Skinner (2005): 28.
2. Cunningham (1871): 515-519.
3. Mahābhārata, Ādi Parva, 214.9-10, Gītā Press edition.
4. Mahābhārata, Sabhā Parva, 34.11, Gītā Press edition.
5. Mahābhārata, Karṇa Parva 22.3, Gītā Press edition.
6. McCrindle (1877): 63.
7. McCrindle (1877): 63.
8. McCrindle (1877): 134-136.
9. McCrindle (1877): 135-136.
10. Jayaswal (1933).
11. Skinner (2005): 83.
12. Konow (1923).

aśvaṃ naiva gajaṃ naiva

vyāghraṃ naiva cha naiva cha |

ajāputraṃ baliṃ dadyāt

devo durbalaghātakaḥ ||

-- Not horse, not elephant and not even tiger. It is the son of goat that gets sacrificed. Even God kills the weak.

- A Sanskrit proverb

3. THE NOMADS OF CENTRAL ASIA

In this chapter, we are going to discuss the chronology of the Kuṣāṇas. The origin of Kuṣāṇas as described in modern history books is based on Chinese sources. The following account gives the details of the movement of the Kuṣāṇas before they came to India, according to the currently accepted view [1]:

> *"It is to Chinese sources that we must turn for an account of the tribes which overthrew Graeco-Bactrian rule, and were a constant thorn in the side of the Parthian Empire. These sources, with faint sidelights thrown on an obscure period by allusions to be found in classic authors, enable us to bridge a gap of several centuries replete with events which exercised a lasting influence on the history of Central Asia.*
>
> *The Chow dynasty ruled from B.C. 1122 to B.C. 250. After its fall China split up into a vast number of nearly independent*

principalities, and the reigning sovereign enjoyed but little power. The Tsin succeeded in gaining the foremost rank as feudatories, and finally restored the authority of the central power. Their aim was not achieved without a desperate struggle with their rivals. In the course of the resulting civil war Tsin Chi Hwang-ti began his reign. He was the Louis XI of the Chinese monarchy, and brought force and stratagem by turns to bear on the task of restoring the imperial prestige.

When he found himself master at home, he turned his attention to the task of protecting his frontier from aggressors. Of these, the Hiung-nu, a Tartar tribe whose habitat was Eastern Mongolia, were the most troublesome. He carried the war into the enemy's camp by despatching an army across the great Gobi Desert, with orders to establish a strong place at Hami. In B.C. 250 he commenced a work which had a more lasting effect in repressing their invasion. This was the Great Wall of China, which starts from the Shan-hi Pass and ends at the Chin-Yü barriers, a distance of not less than 1500 miles. The Hiung-nu, like their kinsmen the Mongols of Chingiz and of Timūr, fought on horseback, and their plan of campaign was simply a succession of raids followed by speedy retreats. This stupendous barrier intimidated them, and turned westwards the tide of their migration. Thus the Great Wall, which it is the fashion to decry as a monument of misplaced labour, was a most important factor in the history of Central Asia. At this epoch the Sakas were settled in Hexapolis, to the east of the Pamirs; while the Usuns dwelt on the southern side of Lake Lob, separated from the Sakas by the Uïghūrs. About B.C. 300 the empire of the Yué-Chi who were a branch of the Tung-nu, or Eastern Tartars, extended most probably from the Muztagh Mountains on the north to the Kuen-lun Mountains on the south, and from the Upper Hoang-ho in Shan-si on the east to Koché and Khotan on the west.

About B.C. 200 a war broke out between the Tung-nu and the Hiung-nu (the Western Tartars or Huns), their neighbours. Mothé, the chief of these latter, falling on the Eastern Tartars unawares, utterly defeated them and drove the Yué-Chi from their kingdom. The latter fled to the banks of the Ili River, while Mothé pushed his conquests as far as the Volga on the west and the border provinces of China eastwards. The Emperor Kao-tsu (B.C. 202—194), founder of the famous Han dynasty, who had achieved the subjugation of the whole of China, was alarmed at the progress of Mothé, and marched against him. His troops were, however, surrounded by Mothe's colossal hordes in the north of the province of Shan-si, and only escaped destruction by the employment of a ruse. On the departure of the Chinese army Mothé set out for Tartary. For upwards of fifty years the power of Hiung-nu sustained no check. They continued to press down on the Yué-Chi, who, after suffering a further crushing defeat, broke into separate hordes. The lesser division, or "Little Yué-Chi," passed into Tibet. The "Great Yué-Chi's" first movement was westwards to the banks of the Ili, but finding the Usun too strong for them, they wandered in a southerly direction, and finally descended upon Kāshghar, Yarkand, and Khotan, whence they displaced the Sakas (B.C. 163). The latter, on their expulsion from Soghdiana, invaded Bactria, and from this period until the fall of the Graeco-Bactrian kingdom the Greeks had to deal with both Sakas and Parthians. It would seem that the latter were alternately friends and foes. This intercourse possibly accounts for the Parthian characteristics found on the early Saka coins of India.

The Sakas were driven towards the Pamirs and the Tien-shan. One branch of them fled to Zungaria, while the majority remained in Hexapolis and intermixed with the Uïghūrs, who had been for a long period masters of that country. A third branch turned their steps towards the upper valleys of the Yarkand Darya. Some of these fugitives established themselves in the little Iranian States of Serikūl and Shugnān, where appreciable traces of their language still survive. Others crossed the Karakorum, and invaded the north-east of India.

At this epoch the Chinese obtained a glimpse of the position of Western Asia through the medium of prisoners taken from the Hiung-nu. From them they learned that the Yué-Chi had suffered defeat at the hands of the Huns, and been compelled to migrate far from their ancient abode. They had, however, become very powerful in Bactria and Transoxiana, and had conquered Ta-hia (Khorāsān), establishing themselves finally there in spite of the Parthian resistance. The Emperor Wu-ti eagerly desired an alliance with the Yué-Chi against their common enemy the Hiung-nu. With this view he sent his general Chang-Kien on an embassy to the prince, accompanied by a suite of a hundred attendants. The envoy, however, had the misfortune to fall into the hands of the Huns while traversing their territory, and escaped only after a ten years' imprisonment. On joining the Yué-Chi, he found them employed in driving the Sakas out of Soghdiana. He accompanied them on a victorious expedition, and then returned to China, with two followers, sole survivors of his cortege. The emperor expressed his appreciation of the intelligence brought by Chang-Kien regarding Central Asian events, by elevating him to an important post. These events led to the establishment of direct commercial intercourse between China and the West, which, however, the Huns did their utmost to interrupt.

A collation of the Chinese annals, the classic authors, and the coins which have come down to us, would render it tolerably certain that the Greeks lost their hold on Soghdiana in B.C. 163; that a little later they were deprived of Bactria by the Sakas, and of Margiana by the Parthians. From this period their dominion was limited to the southern slopes of the Indian Caucasus. That the Graeco-Bactrian Empire had attained a high degree of natural civilisation, and, indeed, of artistic culture, is evidenced by the purity of design and the excellence of workmanship displayed by the later coins.

The Bactrians displaced by the Sakas fled eastward, and settled in the confines of Bokhārā, and the surrounding countries. But the dominion of their opponents in Bactria was not destined to be of long duration, for in B.C. 120 the Yué-Chi, who had already overrun the ancient territory of the Sakas, began to pour into Bactria. ... Their invasion of India was directly due to the usurpation of their country by the Yué-Chi. The latter parcelled Bactria out among their five clans. Each had its own capital, but the only Yué-Chi headquarters which has been identified is Bamian, at the foot of the northern slope of the Hindu Kush.

The partition continued in force for nearly a century, during which repeated collisions occurred between the Yué-Chi and the Parthians. In B.C. 30 the chief of one of the clans, the Kwei-shuang, subdued the rest, and assumed sovereignty over the whole race. They became thenceforward known by the name of the conquering clan, which in course of time was modified to Kushan, and appears so inscribed on their coins."

This is the summary of the history of Kuṣāṇas from the above account: Hiung-nu (the Huns) defeated Yué-Chi and drove them away around 200 BCE. As Hiung-nu continued to press down on the Yué-Chi, they broke into separate hordes. The lesser division, or "Little Yué-Chi," went to Tibet, while the "Great Yué-Chi's" moved first westwards and then in a southerly direction. Around 163 BCE, the Great Yué-Chi expelled the Śakas from Sogdiana, which was the land between the rivers Oxus and Jaxartes, north of Bactria. Sogdiana was the area around Samarkand in current day Uzbekistan. The displaced Śakas moved south to Bactria, the area around current day Balkh in northern Afghanistan. Around 120 BCE, the Great Yué-Chi started pouring into Bactria, and the expelled Śakas invaded India. At this point, the Yué-Chi consisted of five clans. Around 30 BCE, the Kwei-shuang clan subdued the rest of the clans and assumed sovereignty. The Yué-Chi then became known as Kwei-shuang or Kuṣāṇa.

It is an interesting story, but it may have nothing to do with the Kuṣāṇas. There are good reasons to believe that the Kuṣāṇas were of Turkish descent, and not Mongols. Bhandarkar has summarized the argument for Turkish descent of the Kuṣāṇas as follows [2]:

> *"Kalhaṇa's Rājataraṅgiṇī speaks of Kanishka as sprung from the Turushka race which corresponds to the modern Turks. Again, Al Biruni tells us a legend which makes Kanika, i.e. Kanishka, a descendant of the Turk family called Shāhiya, founded by Barhatakīn, whom it describes as wearing "Turkish dress, a short tunic open in front, a high hat, boots and arms." And this is clearly attested by the royal figures on the coins, notably of Wema-Kadphises and Kanishka. About the costume and features of Wema-Kadphises, Kanishka's predecessor, H. H. Wilson makes the following remarks: "He wears a conical cap turned up at the sides, a tunic close to the body over which is a sort of strait coat: boots are invariably worn. The features are not those of the Mongal but of the Turk tribe." Thus Kalhan's statement, the legend mentioned by Al Biruni and the figures on the coins of Wema-Kadphises and Kanishka so thoroughly corroborate one another as to leave no doubt that in regard to the Turk extraction of Kanishka."*

Thus, from both literary and numismatic evidence, it stands to reason that the Kuṣāṇas were of Turkish descent.

3.1 The Kuṣāṇa Chronology

History books since the colonial times have been teaching that the Kuṣāna emperor Kaniṣka-I was the founder of the Śalivāhana Śaka era, which started in 78 CE. However, Kaniṣka was a Kuṣāna and not a Śaka. Modern historians have justified it by saying that the term Śaka was used by Indians for any foreigner. Recent research by Professor Harry Falk has demolished this theory. He has shown that according to the Yavanajātaka, by Sphujidhvaja, the Kuṣāna era started 149 years after the Śaka era, i.e. in 227 CE [3]. However, Falk has proposed the starting date of 127 CE by taking a hundred years off from this straightforward calculation with no ambiguity in the meaning of the text. The problem he faces in accepting the evidence of Yavanajātaka is that modern history has placed the Imperial Guptas in fourth century CE and the rule of the Kuṣāṇas has to end before the Imperial Guptas start ruling their territories. This makes the starting date of 227 CE for Kuṣāṇa era too late in the framework of currently accepted Indian chronology. In the chronological framework that we have developed, the time of the Imperial Guptas is several centuries before the Kuṣāṇas, and the Kuṣāṇa era can begin in 227 CE in accordance with the Yavanajātaka. Loeshner has considered three different starting dates for the accession of Kaniṣka I to the throne -- 78 CE, 127 CE, and 227 CE [4]. Table 3.1 shows the three versions of Kuṣāṇa chronology based on these three dates.

Table 3.1: Kuṣāṇa chronology [4]

	Modern chronology I [1]	**Modern chronology II**[2]	**Modern chronology III**[3]
Kujula Kadphises	c. 20 BCE – 20 CE	c. 20 – 60 CE	c. 50 – 125 CE
Wima Takto	c. 20 – 55 CE	c. 60 – 95 CE	c. 125 – 180 CE
Wima Kadphises	c. 55 – 77 CE	c.95 – 126 CE	c. 180 – 226 CE
Kaniṣka I	77/78 – c. 102 CE	126/127 – 152 CE	226/227 – 252 CE
Huviṣka	c. 102 – 142 CE	c.152 – 191 CE	c. 252 – 291 CE
Vasudeva I	c. 142 – 180 CE	c. 191 – 230 CE	291 – 330 CE
Kaniṣka II	c. 180 – 195 CE	c. 230 – 245 CE	c. 330 – 345 CE
Vasiṣka	c. 195 – 210 CE	c. 245 – 260 CE	c. 345 – 360 CE
Kaniṣka III	c. 210 – 227 CE	c. 260 – 290 CE	c. 360 – 370 CE
Vasudeva II	c. 227 – 260 CE	c. 290 – 320 CE	c. 370 – 375 CE
Shaka	c. 260 – 295 CE	c. 320 – 355 CE	c. 375 – 390 CE
Kipunadha	c. 295 – 320 CE	c. 355 – 375 CE	c. 390 – 400 CE

[1]Kaniṣka era starting in 78 CE
[2]Kaniṣka era starting in 127 CE
[3]Kaniṣka era starting in 227 CE

Modern chronology I is the version based on the assumption that the Kuṣāna emperor Kaniṣka I was the founder of the Śalivāhana Śaka era. Modern chronology II has been gaining ground recently and is based on the work of Falk, who considers the Kuṣāna era to have begun in 127 CE with the accession of Kaniṣka-I. Modern chronology III has not become acceptable yet.

One of the important events to have taken place during the reign of Kaniṣka-I was the convening of the fourth Buddhist council in Kashmir. Under the patronage of Kaniṣka-I, Buddhist monk Pārśva played an important role in organizing the Fourth Buddhist Council, in which 500 monks participated. Xuan Zang (Hiuen Tsiang) has given the following background about the organization of this council [5]:

> *"In the four-hundredth year after the Nirvāṇa of Tathāgata, Kanishka, king of Gandhāra, having succeeded to the kingdom, his kingly renown reached far, and he brought the most remote within his jurisdiction. During his intervals of duty he frequently consulted the sacred books of Buddha; daily he invited a priest to enter his palace and preach the law, but he found the different views of the schools so contradictory that he was filled with a doubt, and he had no way to get rid of his uncertainty. At this time the honoured Pārśva said, "Since Tathāgata left the world many years and months have elapsed. The different schools hold to the treatises of their several masters. Each keeps to his own views, and so the whole body is torn by divisions."*
>
> *The king having heard this, was deeply affected and gave way to sad regrets. After a while he spoke to Pārśva and said, "Though of no account personally, yet, thanks to the remnant of merit which has followed me through successive births since the time of the Holy One till now, I have come to my present state. I will dare to forget my own low degree, and hand down in succession the teaching of the law unimpaired. I will therefore arrange the teaching of the three pitakas of Buddha according to the various schools." The*

> *honourable Pārśva replied, "The previous merit of the great king has resulted in his present distinguished position. That he may continue to love the law of Buddha is what I desire above all things."*

As the council took place during the reign of Kaniṣka-I, it must have been during 227–252 CE. During this council the Buddhist scriptures were organized, and the great commentary on the Abhidharma was produced. Puruṣapura, current day Peshawar in Pakistan, was the main capital of Kaniṣka-I's vast empire, which extended from Bactria to Bihar. When Kaniṣka-I attacked and defeated the king of Magadha, he asked for a huge sum of money as indemnity, which the king of Magadha could not afford. Kaniṣka-I was instead offered a begging bowl used by the Buddha, and the services of Buddhist philosopher Aśvaghoṣa, which he accepted. Aśvaghoṣa then came to Puruṣapura with Kaniṣka-I and became his spiritual counsellor. Thus we can date Aśvaghoṣa to the second quarter of the third century CE.

Now that we are in the process of building the correct chronology of Indian history, we can begin exploring the interactions between the sister civilizations of India and Persia to confirm the links that have been established by historians from pre-British era but denied by modern historians.

3.2 The Emperor of Persia

Ancient Indian and Persian civilizations were sister civilizations, both of them arising from the common source, the Indus Valley Civilization (IVC). When the IVC cities became inhospitable around 1900 BCE, the Vedic Aryans migrated in different directions. Some clans moved east and south towards India, while some other clans moved west towards Iran and then continued towards Europe. While Vedic Indians were able to completely preserve the Vedas due to their herculean effort unparalleled in history, ancient Persians were able to keep the Vedic wisdom more intact than the rest of Indo-European tribes due to their close proximity to the source of Vedic knowledge. Persians turned out to be great empire builders, and over time Persians had to face the same forces that tried to subjugate Indians as well. One of those deadly forces was the Hūṇas, who tried to overrun both of these civilizations. When the Kuṣāṇas were ruling Northwestern India, Persia was being ruled by the emperors of the Sasanian dynasty. We turn to the article "Analysis of Eastern Works – No. 1 - The Rozat al Sofa" for an overview of the Sasanian dynasty [6]:

> *"With the history of the race of Sassan, founded by Ardashir Babegan, the Persian annals begin to take an authentic form, and exhibit a considerable agreement with the rival historians of the West. At the same time they add numberless minute traits of character and graphic incidents—a peculiarity which gives Oriental history much of the charm of biography. Ardashir was first noticed by a viceroy of Ardavan, the last king of the Ashganian family. This nobleman had heard of Ardashir's wonderful talents, and sent for him to his court, where he grew into such favour as to be entrusted with the government of the province during the absence of his patron. Encouraged by dreams and the predictions of astrologers, Ardashir invades and conquers Azerbijan, and writes to his father Babek to rebel against the governor of Fars, and procure his death. The old man so far complies, but confers the sovereignty of the conquered province on his eldest and favourite son, Shahpour. Shahpour summons his brother to court on the death of their father, and on his refusal to obey the invitation, marches a large army against him to compel his obedience. Betrayed by his dependants, he is taken prisoner by his brother, who gradually extends the conquests thus begun over the provinces of Persia. Ardavan, who in the first instance attempts intimidation, and subsequently an amicable arrangement, is at length routed and slain, and the son of Babek assumes the crown of all Persia, with the title of Shahinshah, 'king of kings.' For the preservation of this dignity in his own*

family we are told he provided, by crowning his son Shahpour during his life-time.

A romantic story of the birth and education of this prince occurs in this part of our narrative. Ardashir, after destroying as far as possible the male and female progeny of the "kings of the tribes," was struck with the beauty of a young maiden, who by degrees gained a great ascendancy over him. One day she accidentally revealed to him that she was of the Ashkanian family. Now it had been prophesied to him that his crown should pass into the hands of a descendant of that family, and to defeat this prophecy he had had recourse to the barbarous policy of putting to death the whole race, as far as they were in his power, and thus he delivered the lady to his vizir, with an injunction to put her to death. Moved, however, to compassion by her unfortunate condition, and by her plea of pregnancy, the vizir spared her life, and brought up her son in all points as a prince. A querulous complaint of the old monarch, that he was leaving his kingdom to strangers, emboldened the vizir to confess the fraud he had practised, and the king received with joy a son whom he imagined had perished with his unhappy mother, and whom he found grown in appearance and character worthy of himself, and of the throne which he had to bequeath to him.

As Shahpour grew to manhood, he distinguished himself by the bravery, generosity, and justice, of which his earlier years had given promise. One of the memorable actions of his reign was the reduction of Khadr, a strong hold of Mesopotamia, in the possession of the Arabs. This fortress was betrayed to him by the daughter of the governor, who had fallen in love with him, and whom he subsequently married. Some time afterwards, the lady complained of a severe pain, which was found to arise from her having slept, like the Sybarite, on a crumpled rose-leaf, and this extraordinary sensibility of feeling she explained to arise from the delicacy with which her father had brought her up. "Were you treated thus kindly by your father, and could you betray him?" said the indignant king;

and he punished the cruel treason by a more cruel death: the fair traitress was dragged limb from limb by wild horses.

The cruel policy which had induced Ardashir to attempt the murder of Shahpour's mother, had led to the proscription of the family of Mahrek, an Ashkanian nobleman. His daughter made her escape from this tyranny, and lived for some time in the family of a herdsman, where she was seen by the young Shahpour when out on a hunting excursion. He loved and married her, and learning from her the fatal fact of her descent, he promised to keep this secret from his father, and even to conceal from him their marriage. Accident, however, revealed to Ardashir his son's alliance and the parentage of his wife: but far from taking the violent measures his son had dreaded, the monarch was delighted to find thus harmlessly fulfilled the dreaded prophecy that his crown should pass to a descendant of the Ashkanians. Hormuz, the successor of Shahpour, was the fruit of this marriage. During the life-time of Shahpour, his courtiers endeavoured with success to prejudice him against his son, and to persuade him that he entertained treasonable designs against his father's crown. Hormuz heard of this, and cutting off his right hand, sent it to his father: for this mutilation, according to the law of Persia, incapacitated him from reigning. Shahpour, not less admiring the generosity of his son than shocked at this mark of it, declared that the prince should succeed him, in spite of this disqualification; and kept his word.

Of the reign of Hormuz our author relates little, but that he was distinguished for his good qualities, and his wise and just government. The succeeding sovereigns are dismissed with a very brief notice, until we reach the reign of Bahram. ...

A series of brief and uninteresting notices of subsequent reigns brings us to that of Shapour, remarkable in European history for his conquest of the emperor Valerian, and the indignities he heaped upon him. The Persian history states that this was a reprisal for similar indignities inflicted upon Shapour. That he was recognized, whilst at Constantinople in disguise, from his resemblance to his picture painted by Mani, and obliged to witness the destructive progress of the imperial arms through his country; and that, having at length made his escape, he defeated Valerian's army, took him prisoner, and detained him until the damage done by his troops had been repaired, and a sum of money paid as a ransom for the Persian bloodshed in the campaign. Shapour was called Zulektaf ('lord of the shoulder-blades'), from his breaking the shoulder-blades of his Arabian captives.

Between this prince and Bahram Gour, four kings intervene, of whom little is related but the length of their reigns. Bahram is one of the most renowned monarchs in Persian history. His romantic bravery, his spirit of adventure, his love of the chase, of music, and of the fine arts, have all contributed to render him famous in eastern history, while oriental fable has made him the hero of some of her most delightful stories. His brothers had all died early, which induced his father, Yezdejird, to send him to Arabia, under the care of a friendly prince of that nation. To this education, amongst a romantic and hardy people, may be ascribed, in part, his bravery, his adventurous spirit, and that love of field-sports which has passed into a proverb. On the death of his father, another prince of the royal family was raised to the throne by the Persian nobles, and Bahram only obtained his right after a terrible struggle, which is thus described:

After much speaking and disputing on one side and the other, it was decided, with the concurrence of Bahram, that the royal diadem should be placed between two hungry lions, and that the kingly power should be given to him who should snatch it from between them. Then the commander of the forces brought into an enclosed space two furious lions and the Kaianian diadem; and Bahram said to Cosroe, "Step forward and take up the diadem." But Cosroe thought in himself,

The splendid diadem, when such a mortal fear is in the way to it, Is, indeed, a heart-stirring ornament, but it is not worth the loss of the head.

So he said to Bahram, "I am the actual possessor of crown and throne, and thou the pretender to them: it is thou that must venture first for the acquisition of them. "The lion-hearted prince, on this, stepped towards the diadem, and was assailed by one of the lions. The young hunter leaped upon him, and struck him on the head with a stone; and when the second lion approached, he seized him by the ears, and smote together the heads of the two, so that their brains were dashed out of their skulls and through their ears, and by the blows of the prince they were driven into the thicket of destruction; then he took the crown and placed it upon his head.

The mildness, justice, and benevolence of his administration, and his own fondness for elegant amusements, seem to have afforded the leisure and encouraged the taste for such pleasures, which became general amongst his people. Finding a deficiency of musicians amongst his own subjects, he sent for them from India; and from the great number of persons of this class who then came into Persia and settled, a class of men are supposed to descend who hold much the same anomalous position there as the gipsies in our own country. An irruption of Tatars interrupted for a while this universal festivity. The Khacan crossed the Jihoun with an immense army, laid waste the country as he advanced, and saw Bahram retire before him, leaving both the enemy and his own nobles and people under the impression that he had fled from terror of the invader. But when the barbarian leader was thus lulled into perfect security, he was surprised by a night attack from Bahram, who had returned with a chosen band of his bravest warriors, "men who would fearlessly place their foot in the lion's mouth, and advance into the jaws of the crocodile." Each carried on his horse's neck the dried skin of a bullock, filled with stones; and the suddenness of the attack, the extraordinary noise thus produced, and the daring valour of the little band and their heroic leader, spread a panic through the

> *immense Tatar host, and many of them were slaughtered. Bahram killed the Khacan with his own hand, and the kingdom was wholly delivered from its northern invaders by this bold manoeuvre of her monarch.*
>
> *A long and romantic story is then told of a journey taken by this monarch in disguise into India. He is there said, single-handed, to have slain an enormous elephant, which had long kept the inhabitants of the metropolis in terror, and wholly taken possession of the road between the jungle it inhabited and the city."*

During the reign of the Sasanian kings, Persia was attacked by Central Asian invaders, who are called "Khacan" in this narrative. We will explore the invasion of Persia and India by "Khacan" further in Chapter 6. Right now, let us pay attention to the connection of Persian emperor Bahram with India. According to well-established Persian traditions, Bahram had married an Indian princess during his visit to India. We find further details about this in "The Hindoos" [7]:

> *"According to the Persian historians of India, the whole country fell, after the death of Vicramāditya, into confusion and anarchy, each great vassal of the crown seizing upon the province over which he had been placed, and assuming the state and appellation of sovereign; so that the very memory of the emperors or mahārājas was quickly lost. It is little to be regretted that history has not preserved from oblivion the petty wars which must necessarily have arisen in such a state of society. It much more imports us to know that the commerce which India already carried on with Arabia and Egypt, and through those channels with all the western world, had even at this early period, reached a high degree of prosperity. Hippalus, or Annius Plocamus, according to Pliny, had, by the discovery of the monsoon winds, greatly facilitated the intercourse of the western nations with India; and the Romans, who from conquerors had now become merchants, engaged in this traffic as the rivals of the Egyptians and Arabs.*

Here the Brahmins, who speak with so much familiarity of Satyavrata and the Deluge, find their historical documents suddenly fail them. During a space of three hundred years they know not who reigned, who was murdered, or who died in his bed. Even tradition, which frequently amuses with probabilities where history has no truths to offer, is here dumb. All we know of this long period of darkness is, that in the reigns of Trajan and Antoninus, ambassadors from some part of India traversed the Roman empire to the capital, awakening, at least in the former of these princes, the vain regret that he could not, like Alexander, carry his victorious arms into that remote country. At the expiration of three hundred years Basdeo appeared, who, having subdued Bahar and Bengal, was saluted by his subjects with the title of Mahārājah, and restored the faded splendour of Cauouj. It is said, that during the reign of this prince, Bahram, king of Persia, visited India in the disguise of a merchant, with the intention of studying, in this condition, the government and religion of the country. An accident revealed his rank. Walking one day in the environs of the Canouj, he was attacked by an enraged elephant. Bahram, practised in the use of arms, immediately threw a javelin at the animal, with so much force and dexterity that the weapon pierced its forehead, and killed it on the spot, which being related to the emperor, he commanded the merchant to be conducted into his presence. No sooner was Bahram introduced than he was recognized by a Rajah, who had formerly visited Persia. Upon this Basdeo descended from his throne and embraced the stranger, who, on confessing the truth, was entertained with the greatest magnificence. In order to cement their friendship still further, Basdeo bestowed his daughter in marriage on the Persian monarch."

As described above, the period after the death of Vikramaditya is a dark period of history as North India was overrun by invaders. There were trade contacts with Rome as ambassadors from Roman emperors Trajan and Antoninus came to India. Roman emperor Trajan reigned between 98-117 CE, while Antoninus Pius reigned between 138-161 CE. Unfortunately, we do not know whose court these ambassadors visited. What we do know is that a Persian emperor named Bahram came to India and married the daughter of Indian emperor Basdeo. There is not only literary but also numismatic proof to this effect from Persia as described below by Prinsep [8]:

> *"One confirmation of a historical fact from numismatic aid has been remarked in the discovery of the name of Vāsa Deva or Bas Deo on a Sassanian coin. Ferishta states, that Bas Deo, of Kannauj, gave his daughter in marriage to Behram of Persia, A.D. 330:- the coin marks exactly such an alliance; but the Hindu chronicles admit no such name until, much later, one occurs in the Malwa catalogue of Abul Fazl."*

Prinsep again mentions this marriage in the genealogical table of Kanauj where he says that Basdeo (Vasudeva) revived the Kanauj dynasty and his daughter married Bahram Sassan of Persia in 390 CE, according to Ferishtah [9]. Fergusson has made the following comments in 1870 CE regarding the coins with Vasudeva written on one side and an image of a Sassanian king on other side [10]:

> *"There is still another group of coins called Indo-Sassanian, which, however, have only been imperfectly read. The typical example of the class is one originally drawn by Prinsep, and produced by Thomas (vol. i, pl. vii., fig. 6.). It represents a Sassanian king on one side; on the other, another who may be an Indian with a distinctly legible inscription in Sanskrit characters, which reads Śrī Vasudeva. While the other inscriptions are undecyphered, it is too hazardous even to suggest that this may be the father-in-law of Bahram Gour; but the number of these Indo-Sassanian coins which are found in India, extending even beyond Hegira, prove a close intercourse between the two countries at the period we are now speaking about, and when thoroughly investigated, will, I fancy, throw more light on the political and religious changes that took place in India about the sixth century, than anything else which has yet come to light."*

The possibility of the marriage of an Indian princess, daughter of King Vasudeva, with Persian emperor Bahram is denied by modern Indian historians. There was no king named Basdeo in India when Bahram ruled in Persia, according to these historians. To show that this indeed was possible, we have compiled the list of rulers of Sasanian dynasty along with their regnal periods as shown in Table 3.2 [11]. To this, we have added the list of Kuṣāṇa monarchs along with their regnal periods according to Modern Chronology III based on the accession of Kaniṣka-I to the throne in 227 CE (rightmost column in Table 3.1). Looking at this Table, we have to choose from a multitude of possibilities, instead of having no possibility at all. We have five Persian monarchs named Bahram and two Kuṣāṇa monarchs named Vasudeva, which is the equivalent of Basdeo in Persian stories.

Table 3.2: Sasanian and Kuṣāṇa chronology

Sasanian rulers	**Reign periods [11]**	**Kuṣāṇa rulers**	**Modern chronology III [4]**
Ardashir I	224 – 241 CE	Kujula Kadphises	c. 50 – 125 CE
Shapur I	241 – 272 CE	Wima Takto	c. 125 – 180 CE
Hormizd I	272 – 273 CE	Wima Kadphises	c. 180 – 226 CE
Bahram I	273 – 276 CE	Kaniṣka I	226/227 – 252 CE
Bahram II	276 – 293 CE	Huviṣka	c. 252 – 291 CE
Bahram III	293 CE	Vasudeva I	291 – 350 CE
Narseh	293 – 302 CE	Kaniṣka II	c. 330 – 345
Hormizd II	302 – 309 CE	Vasiṣka	c. 345 – 360 CE
Shapur II the great	309 – 379 CE	Kaniṣka III	c. 360 – 370 CE
Ardashir II	379 – 383 CE	Vasudeva II	c. 370 – 375 CE
Shapur III	383 – 388 CE	Shaka	c. 375 – 390 CE
Bahram IV	388 – 399 CE	Kipunadha	c. 390 – 400 CE
Yazdegerd I	399 – 421 CE		
Bahram V	421 – 438 CE		

According to the Persian historians, it was Bahram V also known as Bahram Gor or Gūr, who married an Indian princess. It will then make Vasudeva II as the Indian emperor, who gave his daughter in marriage to Bahram Gor. Bahram Gor reigned between 421 to 438 CE, Vasudeva II ruled between c.370-375 CE according to Modern Chronology III based on the accession of Kaniṣka-I to the throne in 227 CE. This brings the regnal period of Vasudeva II close to that of Bahram Gor, but there is a gap of about 45 years between the two rulers. Why do we have this gap, if the Persian traditions are so clear about the marriage alliance between Bahram Gor and Vasudeva II? To find the reason, we have to look at Table 3.1 again carefully.

Since Modern Chronology II is based on the accession of Kaniṣka-I to the throne in 127 CE and Modern Chronology III is based on the accession of Kaniṣka-I to the throne in 227 CE, one would expect a difference of 100 years between Modern Chronology II and Modern Chronology III. This clearly is not so for the last four rulers, and here is the reason. Modern historians have the Imperial Guptas reigning during the fourth and fifth century and therefore they are forced to wrap up the Kuṣāṇa dynasty before the Imperial Guptas have expanded into what is considered Kuṣāṇa territory. With no such restriction in the proposed chronology, later Kuṣāṇa rulers can be allowed a few decades more than what is allowed by Modern Chronology III. Accordingly, it is entirely possible that Vasudeva II was still ruling when Bahram Gor visited India. In fact, we know this based on the numismatic evidence presented in this chapter. Based on this consideration, a revised chronology is proposed for Kuṣāṇa rulers starting with Kaniṣka-I as shown in Table 3.3, which affirms the marriage of Sasanian Emperor Bahram V with the daughter of Kuṣāṇa emperor Vasudeva II.

Table 3.3: Kuṣāṇa chronology

	Modern chronology II [4]	**Modern chronology III [4]**	**Proposed chronology**
	Kaniṣka era starting in 127 CE	Kaniṣka era starting in 227 CE	Kaniṣka era starting in 227 CE
Kaniṣka I	126/127-c. 152 CE	226/227 – c. 252 CE	227 – c. 252 CE
Huviṣka	c. 152 – 191 CE	c. 252 – 291 CE	c. 252 – 291 CE
Vasudeva I	191 – c. 230 CE	291 – c. 330 CE	291 – c. 330 CE
Kaniṣka II	c. 230 – c. 245 CE	c. 330 – 345 CE	c. 330 – 345 CE
Vasiṣka	c. 245 – c.260 CE	c. 345 – c. 360 CE	c. 345 – c. 360 CE
Kaniṣka III	c. 260 – c.290 CE	c. 360 – c. 370 CE	c. 360 – c.390 CE
Vasudeva II	c. 290 – c. 320 CE	c. 370 – c. 375 CE	c. 390 – c. 435 CE
Shaka	c. 320 – c. 355 CE	c. 375 – c. 390 CE	c. 435 – c. 455 CE
Kipunadha	c. 355 – c. 375 CE	c. 390 – c. 400 CE	c. 455 – c. 475 CE

Having affirmed the marriage between Bahram Gor and the princess of India, let us explore another link between Persian and Indian civilizations, this time the marriage of an Indian emperor with the princess of Persia. To establish this connection, we will need to reconsider the history of a celebrated kingdom called Vallabhī.

Notes:

1. Skrine (1899): 14-19.
2. Bhandarkar (1902).
3. Falk (2001).
4. Loeschner (2008).
5. Beal (1906a): 151-152.
6. Analysis of Eastern Works (1838).
7. The Hindoos (1835): 327-329.
8. Thomas (1858): 221.
9. Thomas (1858): 258.
10. Fergusson (1870).
11. http://www.cais-soas.com/CAIS/History/Sasanian/sasanid.htm.

hato vā prāpsyasi svargam jitvā vā bhokṣyase mahīm |

tasmāduttiṣṭha kaunteya yuddhāya kṛtaniśchayah | |

-- If you are killed, you will go to heaven. If you win, you will enjoy the earth. Therefore, O Son of Kuntī, make up your mind and get ready to fight.

- Gītā 2.37

4. RIDER OF THE SEVEN-HEADED HORSE

As North-west India fell to invaders, Vallabhī, a kingdom in present day Gujarat, became the beacon of hope for Hindu-Jain culture. A chain of events in the kingdom of Vallabhī brought into prominence the most celebrated clan of the Rajputs, the clan of Sisodias. The fascinating history of the rise of Sisodias has been denied by modern historians. Now is the time to reclaim the lost history of the ancestors of Sisodias, and in order to do that we need to establish the proper chronological framework of the history of Vallabhī.

Sisodias, who ruled from Mewar, belonged to the solar line of the kings and traced their ancestry to Lord Rama. They were the most exalted among the Rajput clans, and were called the "Sun of the Hindus" (Hindu Suraj). In this clan were born such great warriors and proud sons of the soil as Bappa Rawal, after whom the city of

Rawalpindi in Pakistan is named, Maharana Pratap, and Kshatrapati Shivaji.

4.1 The Journey Begins

The fascinating story of the Sisodias begins with the arrival of Kanaksen, founder of this clan, to Saurashtra region in present day Gujarat in 145 CE, as described by Tod [1].

> *"At least ten genealogical lists, derived from the most opposite sources, agree in making Kanaksen the founder of this dynasty; and assign his emigration from the most northern of the provinces of India to the peninsula of Saurashtra in S. 201, or A.D. 145. We shall, therefore, make this the point of outset; though it may be premised that Jai Singh, the royal historian and astronomer of Amber, connects the line with Sumitra (the fifty-sixth descendant from the deified Rama), who appears to have been the contemporary of Vikramaditya, A.C. 56."*

Saurashtra was earlier named Surāṣṭra, meaning good country, from the prefix Su meaning good, and Rāṣṭra meaning country. The ancestors of Kanaksen had stayed at current day Lahore in Pakistan before Kanaksen moved to Dwarka in Saurashtra [2]:

> *"Rama had two sons, Lava and Kusa: from the former the Rana's family claim descent. He is stated to have built Lahore, the ancient Lohkot; and the branch from which the princes of Mewar are descended resided there until Kanaksen emigrated to Dwarka. … Sen seems to have been the martial termination for many generations: this was followed by Dit, or Aditya, a term for the 'sun.' The first change in the name of the tribe was on their expulsion from Saurashtra, when for the generic term of Suryavansi was substituted the particular appellation of Guhilot. This name was maintained till another event dispersed the family, and when they settled in Ahar, Aharya became the appellative of the branch. This continued till loss of territory and new acquisitions once more transferred the dynasty to Sesoda, a temporary capital in the*

> *western mountains. The title of Ranawat, borne by all descendants of the blood royal since the eventful change which removed the seat of government from Chitor to Udaipur, might in time have superseded that of Sesodia, if continued warfare had not checked the increase of population; but the Guhilot branch of the Suryavansi still retain the name of Sesodia."*

Vijayasen, a descendant of Kanaksen after four generations, rose to prominence and founded the celebrated city of Vallabhī [3]:

> *"By what route Kanaksen, the first emigrant of the solar race, found his way into Saurashtra from Lohkot, is uncertain: he, however, wrested dominion from a prince of the Pramara race, and founded Birnagara in the second century (A.D. 144). Four generations afterwards, Vijayasen, whom the prince of Amber calls Nushirwan, founded Vijayapur, supposed to be where Dholka now stands, at the head of the Saurashtra peninsula. Vidarba was also founded by him, the name of which was afterwards changed to Sihor. But the most celebrated was the capital, Valabhipura, which for years baffled all search, till it was revealed in its now humbled condition as Walai, ten miles west of Bhaunagar. The existence of this city was confirmed by a celebrated Jain work, the Satrunjaya Mahatmya. The want of satisfactory proof of the Rana's emigration from thence was obviated by the most unexpected discovery of an inscription of the twelfth century, in a ruined temple on the tableland forming the eastern boundary of the Rana's present territory, which appeals to the 'walls of Valabhi' for the truth of the action it records."*

4.2 The Official Genealogy

Sometime after Vijayasen, the kingdom was passed on to Bhaṭārka from whom the genealogy is commenced in the inscriptions of the rulers of Vallabhī. Alina copper plate inscription of Śilāditya VII gives the genealogy of Vallabhī rulers as follows [4]:

"Om! Hail! From the victorious camp located at the famous town of ***Ānandapura****:-In unbroken descent from the most devout worshipper of (the god) Maheśvara, the illustrious* ***Bhatārka****,-who was possessed of glory acquired in a hundred battles fought with the large armies, possessed of unequalled strength, of the* ***Maitrakas****, who had by force bowed down (their) enemies; (and) who acquired the goddess of royalty through the strength of the array of (his) hereditary servants, who had been brought under subjection by (his) splendour, and had been acquired by gifts and honourable treatment and straightforwardness, and were attached (to hint) by affection,-(there was) the most devout worshipper of (the god) Maheśvara, the illustrious* ***Guhasena****,-whose sins were all removed by doing obeisance to the waterlilies that were the feet of (his) parents; whose sword was verily a second arm (to him) from childhood; the test of whose strength was manifested by clapping (his) hands on the temples of the rutting elephants of (his) foes; who had the collection of the rays of the nails of (his) feet interspersed with the lustre of the jewels in the locks of hair on the tops of the heads of (his) enemies who were made to bow down by his prowess; whose title of 'king' was obvious and suitable, because he pleased the hearts of (his) subjects by preserving the proper rites of the path prescribed by all the traditionary laws; who in beauty, lustre, stability, profundity, wisdom, and wealth, surpassed (respectively) (the god) Smara, the moon, (Himālaya) the king of mountains, the ocean, (Bṛhaspati) the preceptor of the gods, and (the god) Dhaneśa; who, through being intent upon giving freedom from fear to those who came for protection, was indifferent to all the (other) results of his vigour, as if they were (of as little value as) straw; who delighted the hearts of learned people and (his) friends and favourites, by giving (them) wealth greater (even) than their requests; (and) who was, as it were, the personified happiness of the circumference of the whole earth.*

(Line 7.) - His son, whose sins were all washed away by the torrent of the waters of (the river) Jāhnavī spread out by the diffusion [of

the rays] of the nails of his feet, (was) the most devout worshipper of (the god) Maheśvara, the illustrious ***Dharasena (II.)****, whose riches were the sustenance of a hundred thousand favourites; who was with eagerness, as if from a desire for (his) beauty, resorted to by (all) the virtuous qualities of an inviting kind; who astonished all archers by the speciality of (his) innate strength and (skill acquired by) practice; who was the preserver of religious grants bestowed by former kings; who averted calamities that would have afflicted (his) subjects; who was the exponent of (the condition of being) the one (joint) habitation of wealth and learning; whose prowess was skilful in enjoying the goddess of the fortunes of the compact ranks of (his) enemies; (and) who possessed a spotless princely glory, acquired by (his) prowess.*

(L. 10.) - His son, who meditated on his feet, (was) the most devout worshipper of (the god) Maheśvara, the illustrious ***Śilāditya (I.)****, who acquired the second name of* ***Dharmāditya*** *by the pursuit of wealth, happiness, and riches, illumined by conformity with religion,-who pervaded all the regions with the excess of (his) wonderful good qualities that gladdened all mankind; who supported the great burden of weighty desires on a cushion that was (his) shoulder, radiant with the lustre of (his) scimetar that was possessed of the brilliance of victory in a hundred battles; who, though (his) intellect was pure through mastering the endmost divisions of the limits of all the sciences, was easily to be gratified with even a small amount of good conversation; who, though (his) heart possessed a profundity that could be fathomed by no people, yet had a most agreeable disposition that was displayed by the excess of (his) good actions; (and) who acquired an eminent reputation by clearing out the blocked-up path (of the good behaviour) of the kings of the Kṛta age.*

(L. 14.) - His younger brother, who meditated on his feet, (was) the most devout worshipper of (the god) Maheśvara, the illustrious ***Kharagraha (I.)****,-who possessed a wealth [of vigour] that was not worn out, either with fatigue or with pleasurable enjoyment, when,*

bearing the yoke as if he were a most choice bullock, he was carrying on (his) shoulders, with the sole object of fulfilling his commands, the goddess of sovereignty, even while she was still an object to be longed for by (his) elder (brother) who, excessively full of respect (for him), (behaved) as if he were (the god Indra) the elder (brother) of ***Upendra****; who, though (his) footstool was covered over with the lustre of the jewels on the heads of a hundred kings subdued by (his) wealth of power, had a disposition that was not embued with the sentiment of haughtiness (induced) by contempt for other people; by (whose) enemies, even though renowned for manliness and pride, no remedy, except the performance of obeisance alone, could be successfully employed; the collection of whose pure virtues effected the happiness of the whole world; who forcibly destroyed all the specious procedure of (this wicked) Kali age; whose very noble heart was not tainted by any of the faults that assert an ascendancy over inferior people; who was renowned for manliness; who excelled in knowledge of the sacred writings; (and) who manifested (his) attainment of being accounted the first among heroes, by being spontaneously chosen (as her lord and husband) by the goddess of the fortunes of the assembled hostile kings.*

(L. 19.) - His son, who meditated on his feet, (was) the most devout worshipper of (the god) Maheśvara, the illustrious ***Dharasena (III.)****,-who, by mastering all the sciences, produced an excess of joy in the minds of all learned people; who, with (his) goodness and wealth and liberality, and with (his) heroism, broke the chariot-axles that were the thoughts of (his) enemies who, occupied in intense reflection (upon his might), lost the power of acting in concert (against him); who, though thoroughly well conversant with the devious divisions of the many sacred writings and the arts and sciences and the proceedings of mankind, still had a nature that was of the most gracious kind; who, though possessed of innate affability, was (still further) decorated with the grace of modesty; who destroyed the display of pride of (his) opponents by the staff of (his) arm that was uplifted in the act of capturing banners of*

victory in a hundred battles; (and) whose commands were hailed with joy by the whole array of kings whose pride, induced by (their) skill in the use of weapons, was subdued by the power of his own bow.

(L. 22.) - His younger brother, who meditated on his feet, (was) the most devout worshipper of (the god) Maheśvara, the illustrious ***Dhruvasena (II.)****, whose famous second name of* ***Bālāditya*** *was established as one of appropriate meaning, through the (whole) world being pervaded by the affection of mankind that was produced by (his) rising,-who surpassed all previous kings in excellent achievements; who was the accomplisher of objects, even such as were hard to be attained; who was, as it were, the very personification of manhood; who, as if he were Manu, was spontaneously resorted to by (his) subjects, the action of whose thoughts excelled in affection for (his) great good qualities; who mastered all the arts and sciences; who, in beauty, put to shame the moon, which (lustrous as it is, still) is marked with spots; who pervaded with (his) great brilliance all the intermediate spaces between the points of the compass; who destroyed the mass of darkness; who, being a sun that was always risen, was (ever) conferring upon (his) subjects confidence of the highest kind, that was fully justified, (and) was the result of the very various objects with which he busied himself (for their welfare), (and) was filled out with (constant) augmentation; who, being clever (on the one side) in determining peace and war and reconciliation (and on the other) in settling the euphonic joining of letters and the analysis of words and composition, was thoroughly well versed even in both the rituals of sovereignty and of* ***Śālāturīya****, (the text-books on the one side) of those who give commands suitable to the rank (of their subordinates) (and on the other side) of those who apply substituted grammatical forms suitable to the places (that they are to fill), (and on the one side) of those who are eminent in refinement effected by the employment of an increase of virtue, (and on the other side) of those who excel in the perfection of language effected by the*

employment of the guna and vriddhi changes of vowels; who, though naturally valorous, possessed a heart that was tender through compassion; who, though well acquainted with sacred learning, was free from pride; who, though beautiful, was full of tranquillity; (and) who, though firm in friendship, repudiated people pervaded with faults.

(L. 28.) - His son, whose forehead, resembling a portion of the moon, had on it a spot that was the mark caused by rubbing against the earth in performing obeisance to the waterlilies that were his feet, (was) the most devout worshipper of (the god) Maheśvara, the Paramabhattāraka, Mahārājādhirāja, Parameśvara, and Chakravartin, the glorious ***Dharasena (IV.)****,-who, in very childhood, had a speciality of sacred learning that was as pure as the beauty of the pearl-ornaments worn in (his) ears; who had the waterlilies that were (his) fingers besprinkled with the stream of (constant) liberality; who intensified the happiness of the earth by the lenient levying of taxes, as if he were intensifying the happiness of a maiden by tenderly taking (her) hand (in marriage); who, as if he were (the very personification of) the science of archery of bowmen, perceived at once all objects that should be aimed at; (and) whose commands were like the jewels in the locks of hair worn on the heads of all the chieftains who bowed down before (him).*

(L. 32.) - Of the son of the illustrious ***Śilāditya (I.)****, who was the (elder) brother of his father's father (****Kharagraha I.****), (and) who was, as it were, (the god) Śāmgapāṇi,-(viz.) of the illustrious* ***Derabhaṭa****, who performed obeisance with (his) limbs bowed down through attachment; whose head was always rendered pure, as if by (the river) Mandākinī, by the very dazzling lustre, proceeding from the waterlilies that were his feet, of the jewels that were the nails of (his) feet; who, as if he were Agastya, was a royal saint, displaying courtesy on all sides; who with the exceedingly white circle of (his) fame, that adorned the points of the compass, formed an entire halo round the moon in the sky; (and) who was the lord of the earth which has (the mountains) Sahya and Vindhya for (its) lovely*

breasts, the nipples of which are (their) summits that are made of a dark-blue colour by the clouds (resting upon them),-the son (was) the most devout worshipper of (the god) Maheśvara, the illustrious ***Dhruvasena (III.)****,-who accepted in marriage the goddess of royalty, just as if she were longing to choose (him) of her own accord, from the assemblage of kings, full of affection (for him) (and) wearing fine garments that were (their) resplendent reputations, which offered (her to him); who relied upon (his) heroism, which was never exerted in vain, as if upon a scimetar which bowed down the array of (his) fierce enemies; who in the autumn season, according to proper custom levied taxes from (his) enemies' lands, the quiet state of which was upset by (his) bow, the arrows of which were forcibly drawn out to the full; who, having (his) ears already decorated with an excess of sacred learnings, radiant with a variety of topics, had them (still further) adorned with the embellishment of jewels, as if it were (with that sacred learning) repeated again and again; (and); who,-holding up a fore-arm which, (covered) with gleaming bracelets and wings of beautiful insects and rays of jewels, was as it were a fresh sprout of a śaivala-plant looking charming in the waters that were (his) ceaseless gifts,-embraced the (whole) earth with (his) arms which, wearing great jewelled bands, behaved as if they were the banks of the shores of the ocean.*

(L. 39.) - His elder brother (was) the most devout worshipper of (the god) Maheśvara, the illustrious ***Kharagraha (II.)****, who, in a very clear and suitable manner, had the second name of* ***Dharmāditya****-whose slender body was embraced in a very public fashion by the goddess of fortune herself, who was minded, as it were, to destroy the pollution of the touches of other kings; who surpassed all (other) kings by the greatness of (his) exceedingly brilliant achievements, who had the waterlilies that were (his) feet studded with the rays of the jewels in the locks of hair on the tops of (their) heads of the whole assemblage of chieftains who bowed down when they had been subdued by the violence of (their) excessive affection (for him); who broke the pride of the multitude of (his) enemies with the large*

and lofty staff of (his) arm; who scorched the whole race of (his) foes with (his) very hot brilliance that spread itself abroad; who delivered over (all his) wealth to the ranks of (his) favourites; who had a mace that he hurled, and a nice-looking discus that he threw; who discarded childish sports; who never treated the twice-born with contempt; who acquired the (whole) surface of the earth by (his) prowess alone; who approved not of making his couch among stupid people; who was one of the best of men of a kind that was unprecedented; who, as if he were the personification of religion, properly regulated the practices of the different castes and stages of life; whose lofty and excellent white banner of religion was hailed by the three worlds that were gladdened by (his) collecting together, in the joy of (his) very upright disposition, and then assenting to (the continuance of the enjoyment of), even those grants to gods and Brāhmans that had been confiscated by previous kings, who were made avaricious by a little greed; who glorified his own lineage; (and) who, having done worship to the gods and Brāhmans and spiritual preceptors, filled all the circuit of the regions with the continuity of (his) excellent reputation acquired by (their) satisfaction produced by (his) settlement of liberal grants of the udraṅga and other (rights) which were ceaselessly made (by him) according to the merits (of the recipients.)

(L. 47.) - Of his elder brother, the illustrious ***Śilāditya (II.)****,-who made all the regions white with (his) fame, as if with the light of the full-moon that makes the beauty of the waterlilies to develop itself; (and) who was the lord of the earth, the bulky breasts of which are the Vindhya mountains of a dark-blue colour like cakes of ointment made of pounded aloe-bark,-the son (was) the Paramabhattāraka, Mahārājādhirāja, and Parameśvara, the glorious* ***Śilādityadeva (III.)****,-who by day by day increased (his) circle of accomplishments, like the new cold-rayed (moon) day by day increasing (its) digits; who adorned the goddess of sovereignty, like a young lordly lion adorning a forest on a mountain; who, like (the god Kārttikeya) who has the banner of a peacock, was adorned with a beautiful lock*

of hair on the top of the head, and was possessed of excessively great energy and majesty; who was [full of glory (and) possessed ample treasures], like the approach of autumn, [which is full of warmth (and) causes the waterlilies to bloom]; who used to part asunder in battle the elephants of (his) enemies, just as the young sun, hot (even) in (its) rising, parts asunder the clouds]; [who used to steal in war the lives] of (his) enemies; who was a most devout worshipper of (the god) Maheśvara; (and) who meditated on the feet of the Paramabhattāraka, Mahārājādhirāja, and Parameśvara, (his) glorious uncle.

(L. 51.) - His son (was) the Paramabhattāraka, Mahārājādhirāja, and Parameśvara, the glorious ***Śilādityadeva (IV.)***, *-[who achieved] supreme lordship [by engaging in the creation of another world]; the diffused fire of whose great prowess played about on the temples of (his) enemies' elephants, which were split open by the blows of (his) sword that was drawn in anger; who acquired a firm position on the earth by encircling it about with a rampart; whose umbrella was constituted by the canopy of (his) fame, white as the clusters of foam of the ocean of milk when it was stirred about by the shaking of the churning-stick, which hung out from a mighty staff that was his own arm, (and) which enveloped the whole circumference of the earth; who was a most devout worshipper of (the god) Maheśvara; (and) who meditated on the feet of the Paramabhattāraka, Mahārājādhirāja, and Parameśvara, (his) glorious father.*

(L. 53.) - [His son] (was) the Paramabhattāraka, Mahārājādhirāja, and Parameśvara, the glorious ***Śilādityadeva (V.)***, *-the waterlilies of whose feet were tinted by being covered over with the rays of the jewels in the locks of hair on the tops of the heads of all the chieftains, who did obeisance through the affection (produced) by (his) splendour; who was a most devout worshipper of (the god) Maheśhvara; (and) who meditated on the feet of the Paramabhattāraka, Mahārājādhirāja, and Parameśvara, (his) glorious father.*

(L. 55.) - [His son] (was) the Paramabhattāraka, Mahārājādhirāja, and Parameśvara, the glorious ***Śilādityadeva (VI.)****,-who allayed the pride of the strength of (his) enemies; who was the auspicious asylum of great victory; whose breast dallied with the embraces of the goddess of fortune; whose unrestrained energy exceeded (even) that of (the god Vishṇu) who assumed the form of the man-lion; who effected the protection of the whole earth by eradicating the hostile kings; who was the best of men; who tinted the faces of all the women that are the distant regions with the rays of the nails of (his) feet shining with the rubies in the tiaras of the powerful princes who bowed down before (him); who was a most devout worshipper of (the god) Maheśvara; (and) who meditated on the feet of the Paramabhattāraka, Mahārājādhirāja, and Parameśvara, (his) glorious father.*

(L. 58.) - Victorious is his son, the glorious ***Dhrūbhaṭa****, born in a lineage of supreme kings of kings and supreme lords, (and) possessed of great happiness,-who is renowned for an abundance of heroism that is hard to be resisted; who is the abode of the goddess of fortune; who has striven to destroy hell; who has made it (his) sole resolve to save the earth; whose fame is as pure as the rays of the full-moon;-who is full of virtue through his knowledge of the three (Vedas); who has conquered the ranks of (his) enemies; who is possessed of happiness . . . ; who always confers happiness; who is the abode of knowledge; who is a protector of the world whom all people applaud; who is attended by learned men; who is praised far and wide on the earth;-who is resplendent with jewels; who has a beautiful person; who is a very pile of jewels that are virtuous qualities; who is endowed with the choicest virtues of lordship and prowess; who is always employed in conferring benefits on living creatures; who, as if he were (the god) Janārdana incarnate, humbles the pride of wicked people;-who is always most skilful in disposing the array of elephants in war; who is the abode of religious merit; (and) whose great prowess is sung over the (whole) earth.*

(L. 63.) - [And he], the most devout worshipper of (the god) Maheśvara the Paramabhattāraka, Mahārājādhirāja, and Parameśvara, the glorious ***Śilādityadeva (VII.)****, who meditates on the feet of the Paramabhattāraka, Mahārājādhirāja, and Parameśvara, (his) glorious father, issues a command to all people:-*

(L. 64.) - Be it known to you that, for the purpose of increasing the religious merit of (my) parents and of myself, (and) in order to obtain a reward both in this world and in the next, the ***village named Mahilabalī****, in the* ***Uppalaheṭa*** *pathaka in the famous* ***Kheṭaka*** *āhāra,-with the udraṅga (and) the uparikara; with (the right to) forced labour as the occasion arises; with the revenue of the bhūta and vāta; with (the fines for) the ten offences; with (its) enjoyments and shares; with the grain, and gold, and ādeya; (with the privilege that it is) not to be (even) pointed at with the hand (of undue appropriation) by any of the king's people; (and) with the exception of previously-given grants to gods and Brāhmaṇs,-is given by me, with copious libations of water, on the terms of a grant to a Brāhmaṇ, in accordance with the rule of bhūmichchidra,-to endure for the same time with the moon, the sun, the ocean, the earth, and the mountains; (and) to be enjoyed by the succession of sons and sons' sons,-to the Bhaṭṭa Ākhaṇḍalamitra, the son of the Bhaṭṭa Vishṇu, an inhabitant of the famous town of Ānandapura, belonging to the community of Chaturvedins of that (place), a member of the Śārkarākshi gotra, and a student of the Bahvṛcha (śākhā),-for the maintenance of the rites of the bali, charu, vaiśvadeva, agnihotra, and atithi sacrifices, and other (ceremonies).*

(L. 69.) - Wherefore, no one should behave so as to cause obstruction to this person in enjoying (it) in accordance with the proper conditions of a grant to a Brāhmaṇ (and) cultivating (it), (or) causing it to be cultivated, or assigning (it to another).

(L. 70.) - (And) this Our gift should be assented to and preserved by future pious kings, whether born of Our lineage or others, bearing in mind that riches do not endure for ever, that the life of man is

uncertain, and that the reward of a gift of land belongs in common (both to him who makes it and to him who continues it).

(L. 72.) - And it has been said by Vyāsa, the arranger of the Vedas:- The earth has been enjoyed by many kings, commencing with Sagara; whosoever at any time possesses the earth, to him belongs, at that time, the reward (of this grant that is now made, if he continue it)! These chattels, made into altars of religion, which have been formerly given here (on earth) by (previous) kings, (are) like the remains of offerings to gods, and like food that is vomited up; verily, what good man would take them back again? The giver of land abides in heaven for sixty thousand years; (but) the confiscator (of a grant), and he who assents (to an act of confiscation), shall dwell for the same number of years in hell! Those who confiscate a grant of land, are born as black serpents, dwelling in the hollows of dried-up trees in the Vindhya mountains, destitute of water!

(L. 75.) - The Dūtaka in this matter (is) the Mahāpratihāra, . . . the Mahākṣhapatalika, a member of the king's household, the illustrious ***Siddhasena****, the son of the illustrious Śarvata; and (this charter) has been written by his deputy, the Pratinartaka, the high-born Amātya* ***Guha****, the son of Hembaṭa, who was deputed by him (to write it).*

(L.77.)-In four centuries of years, increased by forty-seven; on the fifth lunar day of the bright fortnight of (the month) Jyeshṭha; (or) in figures, the year 400 (and) 40 (and) ***7****; (the month) Jyeshṭha; the bright fortnight; (the lunar day) 5. (This is) my sign-manual."*

This inscription mentions that Guhasena was born in the line of Bhaṭārka. The son of Guhasena was Dhārasena (II), who was followed by his son Śīlāditya (I) Dharmāditya. He was followed by his younger brother Kharagraha (I), who was followed by his son Dharasena (III). Dharasena (III) was followed by his younger brother Dhruvasena (II) Bālāditya, who was followed by his son Dharasena (IV). Dharasena (IV) bore the imperial titles Paramabhattāraka, Mahārājādhirāja, Parameśvara, and

Chakravartin. The kingdom then passed on to the line of Śilāditya (I), who was the (elder) brother of Kharagraha (I), grandfather of Dharasena (IV). Derabhaṭa was son of Śilāditya (I). Son of Derabhaṭa, Dhruvasena (III), became king next. He was followed by his elder brother Kharagraha (II) Dharmāditya, who in turn was followed by his elder brother Śilāditya (II). After him the rule of Vallabhī passed from father to son successively in the following order: Śilāditya (III), Śilāditya (IV), Śilāditya (V), Śilāditya (VI) and Śilāditya (VII). All of these rulers bore imperial titles of Paramabhattāraka, Mahārājādhirāja, and Parameśvara.

Maliya copper plate inscription of Mahārāja Dharasena II of the year 252 provides the missing genealogy from Bhaṭārka to Guhasena [5]. There was illustrious Senāpati Bhaṭārka, whose son was Senāpati Dharasena (I). His younger brother was Mahārāja Droṇasingh, whose younger brother was Mahārāja Dhruvasena (I). Mahārāja Dharapaṭṭa was the younger brother of Mahārāja Dhruvasena (I). Son of Mahārāja Dharapaṭṭa was Mahārāja Guhasena, whose son was Mahārāja Dharasena (II).

4.3 Displaced in Time

The Alina copper plate inscription of Śilāditya VII was written in the year 447, which modern historians have taken to refer to the Vallabhī era. This has placed the last Vallabhī ruler Siladitya VII in 766 CE. This creates a peculiar situation that Bappa Rawal, who according to very well-established traditions was a descendant of Śilāditya VII, was born before Śilāditya VII in the framework of modern chronology. As we have seen above, the inscriptions of Vallabhī rulers specify only the year but not the era. We will show in the next chapter that the early Gurjaras, who were neighbours of Vallabhī rulers, used the Śaka era. It therefore stands to reason that Vallabhī rulers were also using the Śaka era. Also, the region of Vallabhī and the surrounding areas were once under the rule of Sātavāhana kings. As the Śaka era was instituted by the

Sātavāhana king Gautamīputra Śātakarṇi to commemorate the extirpation of Śakas, it became popular in the areas ruled by Sātavāhana kings. Once we take this into account by applying the Śālivāhana Śaka era to the Vallabhī inscriptions, we can reconstruct the history that does justice to the well-established traditions.

Based on the assumption that Vallabhī rulers were using the Śaka era, Table 4.1 shows the proposed chronology of Vallabhī rulers. We have added the names of Kanaksen and Vijayasen before Bhaṭārka as discussed earlier, and added the name of Goha after Śilāditya VII. Figure 4.1 shows the genealogy of the Vallabhī dynasty to illustrate the information presented in Table 4.1. The continuation of the bloodline after Śilāditya VII will be discussed a little later in this chapter. We have also added all the known years of the Vallabhī rulers that we have been able to find in the second column of Table 4.1. The reason we cannot be comprehensive is that the inscriptions of Vallabhī rulers have not been compiled in a volume and many inscriptions have gone missing. There are only two inscriptions of the Vallabhī rulers in Volume 3 of the Corpus Inscriptionum Indicarum, which ideally should have contained all the inscriptions found till the date of its publication in 1888. This volume contains the inscriptions that used the Gupta/Vallabhī era in the editor's opinion. To make matters worse, many inscriptions of the Vallabhī rulers have not seen the light of day. Bhandarkar had written the following in 1872 [13]:

> *"Dr. Bhau Dāji gives, in one place, the dates of five copper plate grants of this dynasty, whilst in another he mentions seven dates professedly derived from copper plates. But he does not say when or by whom so many grants of the Vallabhī kings were discovered, nor who deciphered and translated them, or where the plates of their transcripts and translations are to be found."*

Table 4.1: Chronology of Vallabhī dynasty

Kings	Years known	Accepted chronology	Proposed chronology
Kanaksen			144 CE
Vijayasen			c. 204 CE
Bhaṭārka			c. 224 CE
Dharasena I			c. 244 CE
Droṇasingh		502 CE [10]	c. 261 CE
Dhruvasena I	207 [6], 216 [7]	525-545 CE [10]	284-304 CE
Dharapaṭṭa			
Guhasena	240, 248 [8]	556-567 CE [10]	315-326 CE
Dharasena II	252, 269, 270 [8]	571-590 CE [10]	330-349 CE
Śilāditya I Dharmāditya	286 [8]	606-612 CE [10]	365-371 CE
Kharagraha		615 CE [11]	374 CE
Dharasena III		623 CE [12]	382 CE
Dhruvasena II Bālāditya	310 [8]	629-640 CE [11]	388-399 CE
Dharasena IV	326, 328, 330 [8]	645-650 CE [11]	404-409 CE
Derabhaṭa			
Dhruvasena III	332 [8]	651 CE	410 CE
Kharagraha II Dharmāditya	337 [8]	656 CE	415 CE
Śilāditya II			
Śilāditya III Vajrāta	342[6], 348 [8], 352 [9], 356 [9]	662-684 CE [11]	420-443 CE
Śilāditya IV			
Śilāditya V	441 [8]	760 CE	519 CE
Śilāditya VI Dhrubhaṭa	447 [8]	766 CE	525 CE
Śilāditya VII	447 [4]	766 CE	525-543 CE
Goha/Guhāditya			Born 544 CE

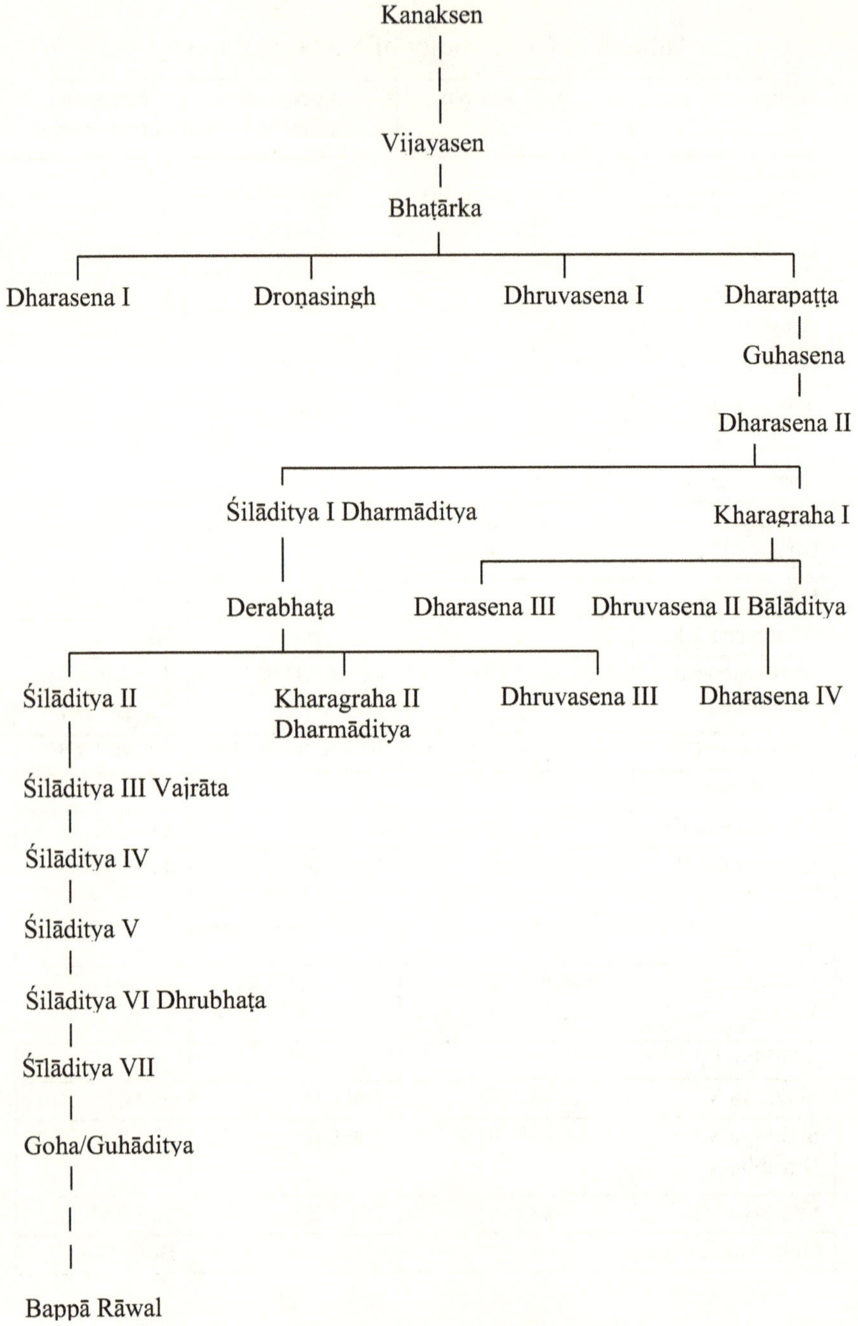

Figure 4.1: Genealogy of Vallabhī dynasty

Based on the reference provided by Bhandarkar, we have been able to find the set of five years mentioned by Bhāu Dāji on Vallabhī plates as 310, 332, 346, 347 and 376 [14]. It is certainly a matter of concern that some of these copper plates have simply vanished. It stands to reason that all inscriptions were vetted by British authorities and only those inscriptions have survived that in the eyes of the colonial authorities did not directly contradict the official chronology. If, somehow, some inscriptions escaped their attention and later proved to pose a challenge to the official chronology, these inscriptions were declared forgeries, as we will see in the case of the Gurjara kings (Chapter 5), who were neighbours of the Vallabhī kings.

4.4 The Sacking of Vallabhī

The last known ruler of Vallabhī was Śilāditya VII, as per the inscriptions. According to well-established traditions of the Sisodias, Vallabhī was sacked during the reign of Śilāditya. The sacking of Vallabhī is described by Tod [15]:

> *"And a work written to commemorate the reign of Rana Raj Singh opens with these words: 'In the west is Sorathdes, a country well known: the barbarians invaded it, and conquered Bal-ka-nath; all fell in the sack of Valabhipura, except the daughter of the Pramara.' And the Sandrai roll thus commences: 'When the city of Valabhi was sacked, the inhabitants fled and founded Bali, Sandrai, and Nadol in Mordar des.' These are towns yet of consequence, and in all the Jain religion is still maintained, which was the chief worship of Valabhipura when sacked by the 'barbarian.' The records preserved by the Jains give S.B. 205 (A.D. 524) as the date of this event. ... One of the poetic chronicles thus commences: 'The barbarians had captured Gajni. The house of Siladitya was left desolate. In its defence his heroes fell; of his seed but the name remained.' "*

As the tradition remembers Śilāditya as the ruler when Vallabhī was sacked, and the last named ruler of Vallabhī based on the inscriptions was Śilāditya VII, we can safely conclude that Vallabhī was sacked during the rule of Śilāditya VII. There is an interesting legend about Śilāditya that tries to explain why Śilāditya lost to the invaders [16]:

> *"There was a fountain (Suryakunda) 'sacred to the sun' at Valabhipura, from which arose at the summons of Siladitya (according to the legend) the seven-headed horse Saptasva, which draws the car of Surya, to bear him to battle. With such an auxiliary no foe could prevail; but a wicked minister revealed to the enemy the secret of annulling this aid, by polluting the sacred fountain with blood. This accomplished, in vain did the prince call on Saptasva to save him from the strange and barbarous foe: the charm was broken, and with it sunk the dynasty of Valabhi."*

The royal line of Vallabhī was all but wiped out along with multitudes of its people, but as luck would have it, the son of Śilāditya VII was safe, far away from Vallabhī.

4.5 The Saga Continues

Let us continue with what happened after the sacking of Vallabhī by the barbarians [17]:

> *"Of the prince's family, the queen Pushpavati alone escaped the sack of Valabhi, as well as the funeral pyre, upon which, on the death of Siladitya, his other wives were sacrificed. She was a daughter of the Pramara prince of Chandravati, and had visited the shrine of the universal mother, Amba-Bhavani, in her native land, to deposit upon the altar of the goddess a votive offering consequent to her expectation of offspring. She was on her return, when the intelligence arrived which blasted all her future hopes, by depriving her of her lord, and robbing him, whom the goddess had just granted to her prayers, of a crown. Excessive grief closed her pilgrimage. Taking refuge in a cave in the mountains of Malia, she was*

delivered of a son. Having confided the infant to a Brahmani of Birnagar named Kamlavati, enjoining her to educate the young prince as a Brahman, but to marry him to a Rajputni, she mounted the funeral pile to join her lord. Kamlavati, the daughter of the priest of the temple, was herself a mother, and she performed the tender offices of one to the orphan prince, whom she designated Goha, or 'cave-born.' The child was a source of perpetual uneasiness to its protectors: he associated with Rajput children, killing birds, hunting wild animals, and at the age of eleven was totally unmanageable: to use the words of the legend, "How should they hide the ray of the sun?"

At this period Idar was governed by a chief of the savage race of Bhil; his name, Mandalika. The young Goha frequented the forests in company with the Bhils, whose habits better assimilated with his daring nature than those of the Brahmans. He became a favourite with the Vanaputras, or 'children of the forest,' who resigned to him Idar with its woods and mountains. The fact is mentioned by Abu-1 Fazl, and is still repeated by the bards, with a characteristic version of the incident, of which doubtless there were many. The Bhils having determined in sport to elect a king, the choice fell on Goha; and one of the young savages, cutting his finger, applied the blood as the tika of sovereignty to his forehead. What was done in sport was confirmed by the old forest chief. The sequel fixes on Goha the stain of ingratitude, for he slew his benefactor, and no motive is assigned in the legend for the deed. Goha's name became the patronymic of his descendants, who were styled Guhilot, classically Grahilot, in time softened to Gehlot.

We know very little concerning these early princes but that they dwelt in this mountainous region for eight generations; when the Bhils, tired of a foreign rule, assailed Nagaditya, the eighth prince, while hunting, and deprived him of life and Idar. The descendants of Kamlavati (the Birnagar Brahmani), who retained the office of priest in the family, were again the preservers of the line of Valabhi. The infant Bappa, son of Nagaditya, then only three years old, was

> *conveyed to the fortress of Bhander, where he was protected by a Bhil of Yadu descent. Thence he was removed for greater security to the wilds of Parasar. Within its impervious recesses rose the three-peaked (trikuta) mountain, at whose base was the town of Nagindra, the abode of Brahmans, who performed the rites of the 'great god.' In this retreat passed the early years of Bappa, wandering through these Alpine valleys, amidst the groves of Bal and the shrines of the brazen calf."*

Thus, according to well-established traditions, it is clear that the great Bappa Rawal was a direct descendant of Śilāditya VII and was separated from him by eight generations. It will be appropriate at this point then to make a few remarks regarding the chronology of Vallabhī rulers. Modern historians have used Vallabhī era to date the Vallabhī inscriptions, which makes Śilāditya VII rule in the year 766 CE. This has completely muddied the well-preserved traditions of Mewar and the genealogy maintained by the Rajputs. As quoted above, Jain traditions maintain that Vallabhī was sacked in 524 CE. If we assume that Vallabhī rulers were using the Śaka era, the last known date of Śilāditya VII would fall in 525 CE as shown in Table 4.1. These two dates differ by only one year, which is quite tantalizing. Thus, the assumption that Vallabhī rulers were using the Śaka era is in line with well-established traditions. Obviously, there will be objections to this thesis by the modern historians. Before we take up those objections, there is another fascinating aspect of the history of the Guhilots and Sisodias, which we will present now.

4.6 The Princess of Persia

When the real history of India is written, the Sisodias will appear in golden letters in the pages recounting their rule. The Sisodias became the most exalted of all the Rajput clans and true to their honour, they kept fighting for their motherland, when the rest of the Rajputs gave up to the blackmailing of the Turko-Mongol invader Akbar, and his descendants. Akbar, who slaughtered 30,000 civilians when Mewar fell to his designs, has been proclaimed as great in modern history books. To add to the insult, his blackmailing of Rajput kings to offer their daughters as a condition of their capitulation and humiliation has been eulogized into a policy of promoting communal harmony by biased historians. If communal harmony by marriage alliance was the policy of Akbar, then how many of Turko-Mongol princesses were married to Rajputs? There were none. The Rajput princesses sacrificed their honour to protect their loved ones and save their motherland from plunder by the invaders. They were abandoned by their families as they were considered to have become impure by the alliance. They never saw their family again after the marriage. Their eldest brothers were held hostage by the Turko-Mongols to prevent Rajputs from revolting. Some of the Rajput princesses committed suicide under the depressing conditions of their lives. It is a travesty of history and insult to the supreme sacrifices made by Rajput princesses to glamorize their condemned lives post-marriage into imaginary love stories. If Akbar's intentions were so noble, Rajput women would not have committed *jauhar* to save their honour, when Mewar fell. Mewar was the only Rajput kingdom that did not yield to the blackmail of the Turko-Mongols, because for them their honour was dearer than their lives. The ancient name of Mewar, Medapāṭa, bears the testimony of the sacrifices made by the Guhilots and the Sisodias in protecting their motherland from invaders. Medapāṭa is the combination of the words "Meda" meaning body fat and "Pāṭa" meaning covered with. Thus Medapāṭa received its name from being covered with the (blood and) fat of the fallen warriors and invaders. In view of the extraordinary valour shown by the Sisodias of Mewar, there is great interest in discovering their origins. Readers are referred to two excellent articles by Shah for exploring this subject further [18-19]. Here, we will focus on the Persian connection, as mentioned by Abul Fazl [20], court historian of Akbar. This gives us the opportunity to look at the bigger picture.

> *"The chief of the state was formerly called Rāwal, but for a long time past has been known as Rānā. He is of the Ghelot clan and pretends a descent from Noshirwān the Just."*

To this, a footnote is added by H.S. Jarrett, who had translated Ain-I-Akbari [21]:

> *"It is asserted that a daughter of Noshirwān, whose queen was a daughter of Maurice of Constantinople married into the Udaipur royal family."*

These statements have not been taken seriously so far, as the accepted timelines did not match. King Noshirwān the Just, referred to by Abul Fazl, was a ruler of Persia belonging to the Sasanian dynasty. He ruled from 531-579 CE. He is better known as Khosrow I, and is also called Anushirvan the Just or Adil Nashirwan. Jarrett seems to have confused Khosrow I with Khosrow II, as it was Khosrow II who married the daughter of the Byzantine emperor Maurice. Khosrow I was born in 501 CE. Considering that Vallabhī was sacked in 524 CE, according to Jain traditions, and the last known date of Śilāditya VII would be 525 CE according to Śaka era, the timelines now match, and the statement by Abul Fazl can be given serious consideration. The sacking of Vallabhī in 524 CE is a little bit too early as at that time Khosrow I was only 23 years old and could not have had a daughter of marriageable age. Also, we know that Śilāditya VII was still ruling in 525 CE, while according to tradition he was killed when Vallabhī was sacked.

At this point, we would like to introduce another piece of evidence, the Battle of Korūr, a famous battle that was fought in 544 CE. We will make a case later in this book that the Battle of Korūr was fought in the aftermath of the sacking of Vallabhī. Thus it seems that Vallabhī was sacked closer to 544 CE, nearly 20 years later than the Jain records. Considering what Hindus and Jains have gone through during the past thousand years, a mismatch of just 20 years can be considered quite reasonable. Śilāditya VII would have married the princess of Persia, the daughter of Anushirvan the Just, in circa 541 CE, when Anushirvan the Just was about 40 years old. The reason for this marriage is easy to understand. Both of them were facing a ruthless enemy, the Hūṇas, and what better way than a matrimonial alliance to fight a common enemy? A number of books were brought from India during the rule of Anushirvan the Just and translated into Pahlavi. This close interaction also corroborates the statement of Abul Fazl that the Sisodias traced their ancestry to Anushirvan the Just. Alarmed with this development, the Hūṇas conducted a surprise attack on Vallabhī. Śilāditya VII was caught unprepared and Vallabhī fell. We now have good evidence that is consistent with literary traditions and inscriptional evidence. Therefore, let us work out some obvious objections to this thesis.

4.7 Mistaken Identities

According to modern historians, the Vallabhī king Dhruvasena II Bālāditya was married to the daughter of emperor Harṣavardhana. This is based on the testimony of Xuan Zang (Hiuen Tsiang). How is this possible in the proposed chronology where we show that Dhruvasena II Bālāditya was ruling towards the end of fourth century CE and Harṣavardhana ruled in the first half of the seventh century CE? In fact, there is no proof that the name of the Vallabhī ruler who was married to the daughter of emperor Harṣavardhana was Dhruvasena or Bālāditya. To prove that we need to know exactly the name that Hiuen Tsiang has mentioned. This information is provided by Bühler as follows [22]:

> *"The remarks of Hiuen Tsiang leave no doubt that it was Dhruvasena II, who had to fly before the armies of the great king of Kanauj. He says, Siyuki, II. p. 267 (Beal), in his account of*

> *Valabhi, "the present king is of the Kshatriya caste, as they all are. He is the nephew of Śilāditya rāja of Mālava, and son-in-law of the son of Śilāditya [i.e. Śrīharsha] the present king of Kanyākubja. His name is Dhruvabhaṭa (Tu-lu-ho-po-tu). He is of a lively and hasty disposition, his wisdom and state-craft are shallow."*

The name given by Hiuen Tsiang of the Vallabhī king married to the daughter of emperor Harṣavardhana was "Tu-lu-ho-po-tu". How did modern historians come to the conclusion that "Tu-lu-ho-po-tu" is Dhruvabhaṭa? They did so simply by checking who was ruling Vallabhī during the time of Harṣavardhana, according to the accepted chronology. Since the last part of the name of Dhruvasena didn't sound anywhere close to the last part of "Tu-lu-ho-po-tu", they changed the name of Dhruvasena to Dhruvabhaṭa. If we look at it objectively, there is no similarity between "Tu-lu-ho-po-tu" and Dhruvasena or Dhruvabhaṭa. In fact, we can challenge these historians and ask them why neither Dhruvasena II Bālāditya nor any of his successors mention that Dhruvasena II Bālāditya was married to the daughter of emperor Harṣavardhana. They should have been happy about it, but they fail to mention it even once though they continued to rule for more than a century after this supposed marriage had taken place.

The next obvious objection to the proposed chronology is that Gurjara king Dadda II, whom modern historians place in seventh century CE, had protected Vallabhī king Dhruvasena II Bālāditya from emperor Harṣavardhana, which doesn't fit the proposed chronology. To answer that, we will need to fix the chronology of the Gurjara kings, a task that we will take up next.

Notes

1. Tod (1920): 251.
2. Tod (1920): 252.
3. Tod (1920): 253.
4. Fleet (1888): 171-191.
5. Fleet (1888): 164-171.
6. Bühler (1876).
7. Bühler (1875).
8. Bühler (1878a).
9. Bühler (1882).
10. Majumdar et al. (1997): 60-63
11. Agnihotry (2010): A-416.
12. Śrivāstava (2007): 452-453.
13. Bhandarkar (1872).
14. Dāji (1872).
15. Tod (1920): 253-255.
16. Tod (1920): 257.
17. Tod (1920): 258-260.
18. Bipin R. Shah, "Bappa Rawal, Rana Kumbha, Sisodiya-Guhilots-Maitrakas of India", https://www.academia.edu/4500576/Bappa_Rawal_Rana_Kumbha_Sisodiya-Guhilots-Maitrakas_of_India.
19. Bipin R. Shah, "Rise of Maitraka's Dynasty of Vallabhipura-Saurashtra, India", https://www.academia.edu/8606918/Rise_of_Maitraka_s_Dynasty_of_Vallabhipura-Saurashtra_India.
20. Jarrett (1891): 268.
21. Jarrett (1891): 268, Footnote 5.
22. Bühler (1888).

mitrasangraheṇa balam sampaddāte |

-- Your strength is increased by your friends.

- Chāṇakya

5. THE RISE OF THE GURJARAS

Gurjaras have a very special place in the history of India. The state of Gujarat, from where they originated, is named after them. One of their clans, the Pratihāras, defended India from invaders for many centuries. Currently, the early Gurjaras have been placed during the time period spanning from sixth to eighth century. In this chapter we will attempt to fix the chronology of the early Gurjaras, and in the process provide concrete proof of how genuine grants have been declared forgeries in order to support the faulty chronology that is considered sacrosanct right now.

5.1 Background

To reconstruct the Gurjara chronology, we will take the help of an excellent paper on Gurjara Inscriptions by Bühler in 1888 CE [1]. Let us start by going into the details of how the current chronology of early Gurjaras was developed [1]:

> *"The name of the Gurjaras first became known through Dr. Burns' four **Kheḍā plates** which mention (I) the illustrious Sāmanta or feudal baron Dadda I, (2) his son the illustrious Jayabhaṭa*

Vītarāga, and (3) his son the illustrious Dadda II or Praśāntarāga, all of whom were worshippers of the sun or adherents of the Saura sect.

Their dates, Saṃvat 380 and 385, were taken to refer to the so-called Vikrama era, until a third grant, Dr. Bhandarkar's ***Ilāo plates****, was discovered. The latter names likewise three princes, (1) the illustrious Dadda I, (2) the illustrious Jayabhaṭa Vītarāga, and the illustrious supreme king of great kings Dadda II Praśāntarāga. Relying on the identity of the names and of the birudas, Dr. Bhaṇḍārkar assumed that the princes of* ***I.*** *were the same persons as those mentioned in* ***Khe. I and II****. But, as the date of* ***I.*** *was clearly the year 417 of the Śaka era and as the eclipse of the sun, stated to have occurred on the new-moon day of the month of Jyaishṭha, corresponded, according to Professor Kero Lakshmaṇ's calculation, to that of June 8, 495 A.D., he transferred the three Gurjara princes from the fourth to the fifth century and assumed that the dates of* ***Khe. I and II*** *referred to the same era.*

I accepted these combinations in my articles on the ***Kāvī and Umetā grants****, which next came to light. The historical contents of the latter fully agree with those of* ***I.*** *Its date, full-moon day of Vaiśākha, Śaka Saṃvat 400, fitted in well with those already known, which apparently lay between the years 380 and 417 of the same era.* ***Kā.****, of which only the second part has been preserved, names only one prince, the illustrious lord of feudal barons Jayabhaṭa, who vanquished a king of Valabhī. I identified him with the Jayabhaṭa of the other grants and referred the date, Saṃvat 486, tenth day of the bright half of Āshāḍha, a Sunday, to the Vikrama era, and thus arrived at the year 429 A.D., which was not too early for the father of Dadda II."*

We take note that the dates on the copper plates of the grants are either in the Śaka era or simply state Saṃvat, which means year and could be in any era. For the Kheḍā plates, initially the dates were taken to be in the Vikrama era and the Gurjara ruler Dadda II was placed in the first half of the fourth century. Later when **Ilāo plates** were discovered, all dates were assumed in the Śaka era and Gurjara rulers were placed in the fifth century as the information in the plates was found to be consistent if all the plates were dated in the Śaka era. This remained the official position for many years till matters took an unexpected turn, as described below [1]:

> *"These views were considered to be right for several years and were utilised by Mr. Fleet in his article on the Indian eras, pp. 48-49. But matters changed when Dr. Bhagvānlāl published his important* ***inscription from Nausāri****. This document mentions four princes,-(l) the illustrious Dadda I; (2) his son the illustrious Jayabhaṭa I; (3) his son the illustrious Dadda II-Bāhusahāya, an ardent devotee of Siva; and (4) his son the illustrious Jayabhaṭa II, an ardent devotee of Siva. Of Dadda I, it narrates that he protected a prince of Valabhi against the supreme lord (parameśvara) Śrīharshadeva. Its date is Monday or Tuesday, the full-moon day of Māgha, Saṃvat 436, at the time of an eclipse of the moon. The mention of the supreme lord Śrīharshadeva and the lucky discovery of some grants of the Chālukyas of Gujarāt with dates according to two different eras enabled Dr. Bhagvānlāl to offer an altogether new theory regarding the Gurjaras of Broach and their inscriptions. He very naturally identified Śrīharshadeva with Śrīharsha-Harshavardhana, the famous king of Thānesar and Kanauj, who ruled from 606 to 648 A.D. over the greater part of Northern and Western India. If this identification was to stand, the reign of the first Dadda, mentioned in Na, must fall in the first half of the seventh century A.D. The possibility of proving this was given by the inscriptions o three nephews of Pulikeśin II of Bādāmī (610-634 A.D.), viz. Śīlāditya, Maṅgalarāja and Pulakeśin, sons of Jayasiṃhavarman, who ruled over southern Gujarat as feudatories of the Western Chālukyas. Their grants being dated Saṃvat 421, Saṃvat 443, Śaka-Saṃvat 653 and Saṃvat 490, it followed that an era, simply marked by the word Saṃvat and beginning shortly before 250 A.D., was used in Gujarāt during the seventh and eighth centuries. Fixing*

its initial date conjecturally in 244-45 or 245-46, and assuming that the date of ***Na.****, Saṃvat 456, referred to it, Dr. Bhagvānlāl obtained for the latter the year 700 or 702 A.D., and thereby the probability that the first Dadda, the third ancestor of the donor of* ***Na.****, reigned between 600-625, or even somewhat later. As* ***Khe. I, Khe. II and Kā.*** *likewise bear dates simply marked Saṃvat, it became probable that the era intended was the same as that of* ***Na.*** *With this supposition Saṃvat 380 corresponded to 624-626 A.D. and Saṃvat 385 to 629-631 and it appeared that the donor of the* ***Khédā*** *grants, Dadda II-Praśāntarāga, was the same person as the first Dadda of* ***Na.*** *The* ***Kāvi*** *date, Saṃvat 486, on the other hand, being now equal to 730-731 A.D., its Jayabhaṭa, the lord of great feudal barons, had to be considered as identical with the donor of* ***Na.*** *By means of these highly ingenious combinations, the probability of which Dr. Bhagvānlāl believed to be increased by epigraphic arguments, he obtained the following pedigree of the Gurjara dynasty: (1) Dadda I., the feudal baron, (2) Jayabhaṭa I-Vītarāga, (3) Dadda II- Praśāntarāga, Saṃvat 380-385, or 621-631 A.D., a contemporary of king Śrīharsha,600 -648 A.D., (4) Jayabhaṭa II, (5) Dadda III-Bāhusahāya, (6) Jayabhaṭa III, Saṃvat 456-486, or, 700-2 to 730-2 A.D. As the statements of* ***U.*** *and* ***I.*** *which placed Dadda II- Praśāntarāga in the fifth century, did not seem to agree with these results, Dr. Bhagvānlāl declared them to be spurious and contended that they must be forgeries, (1) because* ***U. and I.*** *in spite of the alleged interval of seventeen years resemble each other so much that they must have been written by the same person, (2) because they closely resemble a spurious grant of Dharasena II of Valabhī, which has been fabricated by the same forger, (3) because it is alleged that* ***I.*** *has been written by the same writer Reva, who drew up* ***Khe. I and II****. He thought it, however, not impossible that the spurious grants might contain correct dates for the reign of Dadda II., if it might be assumed that the forger had only made a mistake with respect to the era."*

Let us note the important points. Gurjara rulers are named after their grandfathers, and as such they are alternately named Dadda and Jayabhaṭa. Grants do not specify whether we are dealing with I, II, III or IV, as they simply name them Dadda or Jayabhaṭa. Historians have added I, II, III or IV based on their interpretation of the inscriptions. The most important point from the **Nausāri** inscription is that one of the Gurjara rulers named Dadda protected a prince of Vallabhī against the supreme lord (parameśvara) Śrīharṣadeva. Bhagvānlāl identified this Śrīharṣadeva with Harṣavardhana, the famous North Indian emperor during first half of the seventh century. To justify this assumption, he contended that the inscriptions are to be dated in an era that began shortly before 250 CE. As this was inconsistent with **Umetā and Ilāo plates**, which give the dates in the Śaka era, Bhagvānlāl declared them forgeries and cooked up some reasons to justify his theory. As the theory of Bhagvānlāl gained ground, more frivolous reasons were concocted to bury the inconvenient truth [1]:

> *"A portion of Dr. Bhagvānlāl's conjectures was apparently confirmed by a discovery of Sir A. Cunningham, which Mr. Fleet published in a postscript to the article. The nearness of Dr. Bhagvānlāl's initial date 244-246 A.D. to 249-50 A.D., the supposed beginning of the Chedi era which the Kulachuri or Haihaya kings of Tripura used, led Sir A. Cunningham to suspect that the latter might be the Saṃvat occurring in the Gurjara and Chālukya inscriptions. Calculating on this supposition the date of* ***Na.****, "Monday or Tuesday, 15th day of the bright half of Māgha of Saṃvat 456, at the time of an eclipse of the moon," he found that it corresponded to February 2, 706 A.D., a Tuesday, on which date an eclipse of the moon actually happened. On the same supposition the week-day of* ***Kā.*** *had been given correctly, For Chedi-Saṃvat 486, 10th day of the bright half of Āshāḍha, corresponds to June 24, 736, which was a Sunday. Sir A. Cunningham also calculated the date of* ***I.*** *on the supposition that Śaka-Saṃvat had been written erroneously for Chedi- Saṃvat. The result was that though no*

> *eclipse happened in the month of Jyaishtha of the exactly corresponding year 666, this was the case in the preceding one, 665 A. D., when the new moon of Jyaishtha fell according to the Purṇimānta reckoning on April 21. Hence the possibility that the date of* ***I.*** *was, as Dr. Bhagvānlāl thought, a genuine one, could not be denied. In his later article on the* ***Ilāo*** *grant, Mr. Fleet added two new arguments against the genuineness of* ***V. and I.*** *to those brought forward by Dr. Bhagvānlāl. First he pointed out that the description of Dadda I given in* ***Khe. I and II*** *agrees literally with that of Dadda II in* ***V. and I.****; and that the latter grants show some corrupt readings not occurring in the former. Hence he inferred that the author of* ***V. and I.*** *must have known the* ***Kheḍā*** *plates and have copied from them. As the* ***Kheḍā*** *plates had been shown to belong to the seventh century,* ***V. and I.*** *could not possibly have been written in Śaka-Saṃvat 400 and 417, or 478 and 495 A.D. Secondly, he remarked that no weight could be attached to the apparently correct mention of the solar eclipse of June 8, 495 A.D., in* ***I.****, because it was not visible in India and for this reason would not be noticed by an Indian astronomer."*

As the establishment historians proceeded to bury the genuine inscriptions of **Umetā and Ilāo plates**, another grant inscription identified as the **Bagumrā plates** was discovered by Bühler, which also gave the date in the Śaka era. When we say "burying the evidence", in this case it is literally true. The two parts of Corpus Inscriptionum Indicarum, Volume 4 are supposed to list and present all inscriptions belonging to Early Gurjara rulers, whether considered genuine or forged, but the inscriptions of **Bagumrā**, **Umetā and Ilāo plates** are not found in this volume. Bühler made a valiant attempt to show that the three grants dated in Śaka era were genuine [1]:

> *"The subjoined inscription is engraved on two copper plates, found some years ago at* ***Bagumrā****, in the Palsāṇa Tālukā of the Nausāri District in the Baroda State. ... it shows, like those of the*

published grants of the same king from ***Umetā and Ilão****, the legend Śrī Dada and a square emblem the character of which is not clear. (Footnote: In order to save space I call in the sequel the Umetā grant, U., that from Ilão, I, and the new one, B.)...*

The contents of this new grant are as follows:-The 'supreme king of great kings,' the illustrious Dadda II, who had obtained the five mahāshabdas and who was the son of the illustrious Jayabhaṭa and the grandson of the illustrious Dadda I, presents the village of TathāUmbarā to a Brāhmaṇ on the occasion of an eclipse of the sun, which happened on the new-moon day of the month Jyaishṭha, when 415 years of the Śaka king had elapsed. The village was situated in the āhārādvalisha or district of TathāUmbarā. Its boundaries were, to the east the village of Ushilathaṇa, to the south Ishi, to the west Saṃkiya, and to the north Jaravadra. The donee was Bhaṭṭa Govinda, the son of Bhaṭṭa Mahīdhara, who belonged to the community of the Chaturvedins of Kanyakubja, i.e. to the Kanojiā Brāhmaṇs of Gujarāt, to the Kauśika-gotra, and to a school of the adherents of the Chhandoga-Śākhā. He received the village in order to defray the expenses of the five so-called great sacrifices and of other religious ceremonies. The conditions of the grant are the usual ones. The charter was written by the royal servant Revādita, or, as the correct form of the name would be, Revāditya, the son of Dāmodara. Like the other two grants, it is dated from the victorious camp or cantonment (vikshepa), situated at the gates of the town of Bharukachchha.

The date and the geographical names are the only new points contained in the inscription, which require further remarks. The former seems to contain a mistake in the name of the month. According to Dr. Schram's calculations the new-moon day of Jyaishṭha, Śaka-Saṃvat 415, corresponds to May 31, 493 A.D. On that day there was no eclipse of the sun which, as the inscription asserts, occurred on the day when the grant was made.

More important even than this result is the fact that ***the discovery of B. permits us to assert with full confidence the genuineness of V. and I.****, which has been disputed by Dr. Bhagvānlāl and by Mr. Fleet. But before I try to show the bearing of B. on this question, it seems to me advisable to subject the arguments, brought forward against V. and I., to a careful consideration. It seems to me that they are by no means so strong as the two eminent epigraphists suppose, and that a good deal may be said against them, even without extraneous assistance. … Dr. Bhagvānlāl's remaining inference, that V. and I. are forgeries, seems to me untenable. His first argument, the assertion that their perfect agreement in characters and form shows them to have been written by one and the same person, rests, it seems to me, on an insufficiently accurate comparison of the two documents. It is no doubt true that they are very similar. But their resemblance is just such a one as might be expected in the case of two grants written by a father and son in an archaic alphabet, not in daily use. The main features mostly agree, but in the details various small differences are observable.*

The same remarks apply to Dr. Bhagvānlāl's second argument, that the plates must be forgeries, because they closely resemble the admittedly forged grant of Dharasena II., dated Śaka-Saṃvat 400, and have been evidently fabricated by the forger of the spurious Valabhi inscription. …

With respect to the eclipse of the sun, I cannot agree with Mr. Fleet in his opinion that a Hindu astronomer or astrologer would not notice an invisible eclipse. The great majority of the eclipses mentioned in the inscriptions were no doubt visible, and the reason is that on the occasion of a visible eclipse fasting, bathing and gifts are according to the Brāhmaṇical law highly meritorious, nay absolutely necessary. On the occurrence of a calculated eclipse of the sun which falls in India before sunrise, or of an eclipse of the moon which falls in India before sunset, these observances are not required. … The restriction of obligatory gifts to visible eclipses, however, does not preclude the possibility that kings who wished to make gifts chose intentionally, in case no visible eclipse was close at hand, the day of an invisible one, and that they still believed to have secured for themselves the great rewards promised for a gift made grahaṇaparvaṇi. In such a case the invisible eclipse would of course be entered in the grants.

These remarks will suffice to show that ***the arguments, brought forward against the genuineness of I. and V. are by no means conclusive. On the other hand, there are various reasons which speak against the assumption that they are forgeries.*** *(1) The characters in which they are written are certainly ancient. (2) The statement that the first was written by Mādhava, the son of Gilaka, and the second by Ṛeva, the son of Mādhava, is of some importance. A Hindu forger would hardly think of such a collateral circumstance. And (3) their historical contents, taken by themselves, are perfectly believeable. There is no reason why we should deny the existence of a Gurjara kingdom during the fifth century A.D., and the interval of seventeen years, at which they are stated to have been issued, is not too long for the reign of one king. If Dr. Bhagvānlāl felt unable to reconcile their contents with those of Khe. I. and II. his difficulty was, I think, merely a self-created one."*

With these arguments, Bühler proceeded to create a chronology of Gurjara kings that in his view was consistent with all available evidence. Bühler's reconstruction of early Gurjara chronology is as follows [1]:

"Though both sets of documents name three homonymous kings, two of which receive also the same birudas, it by no means follows that the same persons are meant. The pedigree of the Gurjaras which Dr. Bhagvānlāl gave, ante, Vol. XIII. p. 73, according to the ***Kheḍā and Nausāri*** *grants, and which I too consider to be correct, shows that these kings during six generations contented themselves with the two names, Dadda and Jayabhaṭa. Dr. Bhagvānlāl also gave the correct explanation of this curious fact. He added that the*

Hindus very commonly name the grandson after the grandfather. I see no reason why we should deny that this practice had prevailed for a longer time, and that in the fifth and sixth centuries each Dadda was succeeded by a Jayabhaṭa and each Jayabhaṭa by a Dadda, as regularly as during the seventh and eighth. ...

Under these circumstances it seems impossible to suspect the information, conveyed by the Gurjara plates, that one Dadda-Praśāntarāga, the son of a Jayabhaṭa-Vītarāga, ruled in the fifth century, while the reign of another prince, who bears the same name and the same honorific title and likewise was the son of a Jayabhaṭa-Vītarāga, fell in the seventh century. This view gains, I think, a great deal more probability by the find of the ***Bagumrā*** *inscription. For, instead of two, we have now three documents which fully agree in their historical contents, which all three show ancient characters and show as close a relationship to each other as may be expected from their belonging to the short period of seventeen years. The larger such a group of grants becomes, the less is it possible to deny their genuineness. For they mutually protect each other, since the contents of the one confirm those of the others. With every additional document, the hypothesis that we have to deal with the works of a forger, requires more and more complicated suppositions and hence becomes more difficult. I believe it to be unnecessary to point out these difficulties in detail; and I turn to the more important task of attempting a systematic arrangement of the historical information which the Gurjara grants yield, and of supplementing it by the statements of some other documents.*
Assuming, as we now must do, the three grants, ***V. B. and I.*** *to be genuine, we obtain from the seven sets of plates, the following pedigree of the Gurjara princes of Breach :—*

Dadda I [circiter 430 A.D.]
Jayabhaṭa I-Vītarāga I [circiter 455 A.D.]
Dadda II- Praśāntarāga I [Śaka-Saṃvat 400]
415, 417, or 478-495 A.D.]

Dadda III [circiter 580 A.D.]
Jayabhaṭa II- Vītarāga II [circiter 605 A.D.]
Dadda IV- Praśāntarāga II [Chedi-Saṃvat 380, 385, or 628-29 to 633-34 A.D.
Jayabhaṭa III [circiter 655 A.D.]
Dadda V-Bāhusahāya [circiter 680 A.D.]
Jayabhaṭa IV [Chedi-Saṃvat 456 to 486, or 706 to 734-35 A.D.]

In fixing the approximate dates of the kings of whose times we have no inscriptions, I go on the assumption that the duration of a generation is about twenty-five years. The gap between Dadda II and Dadda III was probably filled by the reigns of two Jayabhatas and of one Dadda between them."

Despite his best efforts, Bühler's chronology did not gain acceptance as his chronology suffers from the drawback of the repetition of the first three kings. The chronology of Gurjara kings is faulty because modern historians are dating the Gurjara inscriptions in the Chedi-Kalchuri era, while the inscriptions are in the Śaka era. The obvious problem then is how to explain the mention of Harṣavardhana in the Gurjara inscriptions. According to the **Nausāri** inscription, a Gurjara ruler named Dadda protected a ruler of Vallabhī against the supreme lord (parameśvara) Śrīharṣadeva. The point to note is that the Gurjara inscriptions do not explicitly mention Harṣavardhana. They only mention a king named Harṣa. He could not have been Harṣavardhana because Dadda II was the ruler of a small state. Dadda II was in no position to protect the Vallabhī king from Harṣavardhana, a mighty emperor who ruled over most of North India. This fact has been noted by all historians, including Bühler as noted below [1]:

"A great deal more is known about Dadda IV- Praśāntarāga II. The inscriptions ***Khe. I and II*** *shew that he occupied the throne during*

> *the years 628-633 A.D., which as the dates of* ***Kā. and Na.*** *show, fell in the commencement of his reign, and that he was an adherent of the Sauras or worshippers of the Sun.* ***Na.*** *adds that he gained great fame by protecting the ruler of Valabhī against the supreme lord Śrīharshadēva. The latter is, of course, Śrīharsha-Harshavardhana of Thānesar and Kanauj, who ruled over the whole of Northern and Central India during the greater part of the first half of the seventh century 606-648 AD. At first sight it seems difficult to understand how the king of Valabhī whose capital lay west of Broach, could be attacked by a Central-Indian power before Broach had been subdued, and it seems still less intelligible how the ruler of a very small state, a mere Sāmanta, could afford protection against the armies of one of the most powerful kings of India."*

Before we identify the King Harṣa of the Gurjara inscriptions, we will need to reconstruct the Gurjara Chronology.

5.2 The Gurjara Chronology

To reconstruct the Gurjara Chronology, we have prepared a list of all Gurjara grants as shown in Table 5.1. The grants have been listed in order of the years mentioned in the grant, disregarding whether the grants mention Śaka or not.

The rightmost column of Table 5.1 lists the key information contained in the grants. As can be seen from this Table, the information contained in Umetā, Bagumbrā and Ilāo plates is completely consistent with the information contained in the rest of the grants, if we assume that the years given in all grants are in the Śaka era. Based on this assumption, the revised chronology of the early Gurjara kings is presented in Table 5.2.

Table 5.1: Gurjara Grants

Name	Issuer	Year	Key information
Kairā (Kheḍā) Plates [2]	Dadda (II)	Samvatsara 380	Dadda (I) was father of Jayabhaṭa (I). Jayabhaṭa (I) was father of Dadda (II). Jayabhaṭa (I) was named Vītarāga. Praśāntarāga was son of Vītarāga.
Kairā (Kheḍā) Plates [3]	Dadda (II)	Samvatsara 385	Dadda (I) was father of Jayabhaṭa (I). Jayabhaṭa (I) was father of Dadda (II). Jayabhaṭa (I) was named Vītarāga. Praśāntarāga was son of Vītarāga.
Saṅkheḍā Plate [4]	Raṇagraha	Samvatsara 391	Raṇagraha was son of Vītarāga. Grant was sanctioned by Dadda (II)
Saṅkheḍā Plate [5]	Dadda (II)	Samvatsara 392	Dadda (II) was named Praśāntarāga. Praśāntarāga was son of Vītarāga.
Umetā plates [6]	Dadda (II)	Śaka king 400	Dadda (I) was father of Jayabhaṭa (I). Jayabhaṭa (I) was father of Dadda (II). Dadda (II) is called great king of kings. Dadda (II) was named Praśāntarāga, who was son of Vītarāga.
Bagumbrā plates [1]	Dadda (II)	Śaka king 415	Dadda (I) was father of Jayabhaṭa (I). Jayabhaṭa (I) was father of Dadda (II). Dadda (II) is called great king of kings.
Ilão plates [7]	Dadda (II)	Śaka king 417	Dadda (I) was father of Jayabhaṭa (I). Jayabhaṭa (I) was father of Dadda (II). Dadda (II) is called great king of kings. Dadda (II) was named Praśāntarāga, who was son of Vītarāga.
Prince of Wales Museum Plates [8]	Dadda (III)	Samvat 427	Genealogy is traced to Karṇa. Dadda (II) protected the king of Valabhī from Emperor Harṣadeva. Dadda (II) was father of Jayabhaṭa (II). Jayabhaṭa (II) was father of Dadda (III).

Table 5.1: Gurjara Grants (continued)

Name	Issuer	Year	Key information
Navsāri plates [9]	Jayabhaṭa (III)	Samvatsara 456	Genealogy is traced to Karṇa. Dadda (II) protected the king of Valabhī from Emperor Harṣadeva. Dadda (II) was father of Jayabhaṭa (II). Jayabhaṭa (II) was father of Dadda (III). Dadda (III) was named Bāhusahāya. Dadda (III) was father of Jayabhaṭa (III).
Anjaneri plates [10]	Jayabhaṭa (III)	Sa 460	Genealogy is traced to Karṇa. Dadda (II) protected the king of Valabhī from Emperor Harṣadeva. Dadda (II) was father of Jayabhaṭa (II). Jayabhaṭa (II) was father of Dadda (III). Dadda (III) was named Bāhusahāya. Dadda (III) was father of Jayabhaṭa (III).
Kāvī plates [11]	Jayabhaṭa (IV)	Samvatsara 486	First plate is missing. Jayabhaṭa (IV) forcibly vanquished the Tājjikas in the city of Valabhī.
Prince of Wales Museum Plates [12]	Jayabhaṭa (IV)	Samvatsara 486	Same as Kāvī plates. Makes missing information from First Kāvī plate available. Genealogy is traced to Karṇa. Dadda (II) protected the king of Vallabhī from Emperor Harṣadeva. Dadda (II) was father of Jayabhaṭa (II). Jayabhaṭa (II) was father of Dadda (III). Dadda (III) was named Bāhusahāya. Dadda (III) was father of Jayabhaṭa (III). Jayabhaṭa (III) was father of Ahirole. Ahirole was father of Jayabhaṭa (IV). Jayabhaṭa (IV) forcibly vanquished the Tājjikas in the city of Valabhī.

Table 5.2: The Chronology of Early Gurjaras

Kings	Accepted dates [13]	Years known	Proposed dates
Dadda (I)	570-595 CE		c. 410-435 CE
Jayabhaṭa (I) Vītarāga	595-620 CE		c. 435-455 CE
Dadda (II) Praśāntarāga	620-645 CE	380 (458 CE), 385 (463 CE), 392 (470 CE), 400 (478 CE), 415 (493 CE), 417 (495 CE)	c.455-500 CE
Jayabhaṭa (II)	645-665 CE		c. 500-505 CE
Dadda (III) Bāhusahāya	665-690 CE	427 (505 CE)	c. 505-525 CE
Jayabhaṭa (III)	690-715 CE	456 (534 CE), 460 (538 CE)	c. 525-540 CE
(Dadda (IV)) Ahirola	715-720 CE		c. 540-544 CE
Jayabhaṭa (IV)	720-738 CE	486 (564 CE)	c. 544-565 CE

To seriously challenge the currently accepted chronology of the early Gurjaras, we still need to identify King Harṣa, who was the contemporary of Dadda II. Let us do that now.

5.3 False Contemporaries

In the fifth century CE, the Kuṣāṇa Empire had disintegrated under the attack of the Hūṇas. As the Kuṣāṇa Empire disintegrated, two new centres of power emerged in North India, those of the Later Guptas and the Maukharis.

Initially, their relationship was cordial, but they became bitter rivals as they engaged in the expansion of their respective empires. To expand his domain, the Later Gupta king Harṣagupta attacked the kingdom of Vallabhī around 500 CE. The ruler of Vallabhī had to flee, and he was given shelter by the Gurjara king Dadda II.

Harṣagupta retreated in the aftermath of this attack unwilling to engage the joint forces of Vallabhī and Gurjara kings. As noted earlier, if this Harṣa was emperor Harṣavardhana, Dadda II would have been in no position to protect the Vallabhī king. To avoid this obvious difficulty, modern historians have made up a story of Dadda II himself being a feudatory of Pulakeshina II, who was the rival of Harṣavardhana in South India. According to them, it was because of the might of Pulakeshina II behind him that Dadda II could offer protection to the Vallabhī king. There is no evidence to this effect. To the contrary, Xuan Zang (Hiuen Tsiang) mentions that the Vallabhī king was married to the daughter of emperor Harṣavardhana. So, modern historians have developed the fancy theory that Harṣavardhana first attacked the Vallabhī king, who was protected by Dadda II backed by Pulakeshina II, but later Harṣavardhana changed his mind and got his daughter married to Vallabhī king [14].

Because of this muddied and muddled chronology, historians have been forced to brush aside or bury the inconvenient facts. According to their chronology, Vallabhī rulers were issuing grants from the capital of Gurjara territory, while the Gurjaras at that point were independent rulers and did not have an overlord. Let us get back to the excellent paper by Bühler and see what he has said regarding this point, noting again that his Dadda IV is actually Dadda II [1]:

> *"A consideration of other Valabhī inscriptions and of the grants of the Gujarāt Chālukyas, teaches us that the reign of Dadda IV was filled by more events than the Gurjara grants mention. These events were all untoward ones and led to a temporary annihilation and to a permanent weakening of the Gurjara kingdom. The friendly relations with the rulers of Valabhī do not seem to have lasted long. For we possess two grants of Dharasena IV, the son and successor of Dhruvasena II, which were both issued in the autumn of the year 648 A.D., from "the victorious camp situated at Broach." This date*

*leaves no doubt that Dharasena had made war on the king of Broach and had occupied his capital. The silence of **Na.** on this point proves nothing, as Indian inscriptions very rarely confess to a defeat of the princes by whose orders they were made. As the dates of **Khe. I and II** fall in the beginning of the reign of Dadda IV, it is very probable that he in person received this extraordinary return for his kindness to Dhruvasena II. The occupation of Broach by the ruler of Valabhī, however, cannot have lasted long; for **Kā. and Na.** prove the continuance of the Gurjara dynasty and their holding the province of Broach. Moreover a great political catastrophe seems to have happened in Valabhī soon after 648 A.D. The grants of this year are the last which, as far as we know at present, Dharasena IV issued. In Saṃvat 332 or 650-51 A.D., Dhruvasena III, his youngest cousin twice removed, occupied his place. Dharasena IV must, therefore, have died shortly after the issue of the two grants dated from Broach. As the youngest member of another branch of his family succeeded him, it is probable that he lost his life in consequence of an internal revolution. Such an event would, of course, present a favourable opportunity for the Gurjaras to regain their lost possessions."*

So, there we have it in black and white. Dharasena IV was issuing grants from Broach, the capital of the Gurjaras, while the Gurjara ruler Dadda II called himself king of the kings. Of course, modern historians of India have found ways to explain away these inconvenient truths. In this case they have come up with the unsubstantiated theory that the Gurjaras had lost their sovereignty briefly when Dharasena IV issued grants from Broach. Well, it turns out that the ruler of Vallabhī was not the only one issuing grants from Gurjara territory, as the Chālukyas too were doing that. Let us look at the evidence [1]:

"About the same time as the conquest of Broach by Dharasena IV, or perhaps a little earlier, happened the second misfortune which the Gurjaras had to suffer. This was the loss of the southern half of

their dominions to the Chālukyas. We know at present of five Chālukya grants, belonging to the second, third and fourth quarters of the sixth century and to the second quarter of the seventh century, which show that during this long period the districts immediately north and south of the Taptī, the British Tālukā of Olpād and the Gaikwāḍī district of Kamrej and Nausāri, belonged to branches of the great Chālukya dynasty of Bādāmi. These documents are (1) the Kheḍā grant of Vijayarāja or Vijayavarman, dated Saṃvat 394 (2) the Nausāri grants of the Yuvarāja Śīlāditya Śryāśraya, dated Saṃvat 421, (3) the Surat grant of the same prince, dated Saṃvat 443, (4) the Balsār grant of Maṅgalarāja, dated Śaka-Saṃvat 663, (5) the Nausāri grant of Pulakeśivallabha Janāśraya, dated Saṃvat 490. After what has been said by Dr. Bhagānlāl and General Sir A. Cunningham, it may be considered certain that all these inscriptions, excepting the fourth, are dated according to the Chedi era, and that their dates correspond to the years 642-3, 669-70, 691-92, 731, and 738-39 A.D. As regards the family of the donors, Vijayarāja calls himself a Chālukya, and names a Jayasiṃha as his grandfather. His connection with the main line of Bādāmi is not stated. But the date of his grant makes it probable that his grandfather was the Jayasiṃha Dharāśraya who is named in the Nirpaṇ grant, and who was a younger brother of Pulakeśin II of Bādāmi. The donors of the other four grants are brothers and sons of a younger son of Pulakeśin II of Bādāmi, who was also called Jayasiṃha Dharāśraya (see the Pedigree of the Chālukyas of Bādāmi and Gujarāt, on page 199). This Jayasiṃha received, as the grants hint, the province of Gujarāt from his brother Vikramāditya I of Bādāmi, and handed over the administration to his son and heir apparent Śīlāditya Śryāśraya, who, it would seem, died before his father. Afterwards the succession to the Chālukya possessions in Gujarat devolved on Jayasiṃha's second son Maṅgala or Maṅgalarasarāja, surnamed Vinayāditya Yuddhamalla, and later on Pulakeśivallabha Janāśraya. All these kings remained feudatories of the kings of Bādāmi in the Dekhan."

If modern historians had the chronology right, these situations would not arise and they would not need to explain away the inconvenient facts. These historians have been so blinded by the identification of Devānāmpriya Priyadarśī with Aśoka that they have been obfuscating the facts instead of trying to figure out alternative explanations. To show that the chronology developed in this book fits the known facts far better than the accepted chronology, we have prepared two Tables that are presented below. Table 5.3 shows selected Gurjara, Vallabhī and Chālukya rulers according to the accepted chronology.

Table 5.3: Gurjara, Vallabhī and Chālukya chronology: Accepted dates

Vallabhī [15]	**Gurjaras [13]**	**Chālukyas [16]**
Guhasena 556-567 CE	Dadda I 570-595 CE	Pulakeśina I 547-567 CE
Dharasena II 571-590 CE	Jayabhaṭa I Vītarāga 595-620 CE	Kirtivarman I 567-598 CE
Śilāditya I Dharmāditya 606-612 CE	Dadda II Praśāntarāga 620-645 CE	Mangaleśa 598-608 CE
Dhruvasena II Bālāditya 629-640 CE	Jayabhaṭa II 645-665 CE	Pulakeśina II 608-642 CE
Dharasena IV 645-650 CE	Dadda III Bāhusahāya 665-690 CE	Vikramāditya I 655-680 CE
Śilāditya III Vajrāta 662-684 CE	Jayabhaṭa III 690-715 CE	Vinayāditya 680-696 CE
Śilāditya IV-VI 685-766 CE	(Dadda IV) Ahirola 715-720 CE	Vijayāditya 696-733 CE
Śilāditya VII 766 CE	Jayabhaṭa IV 720-738 CE	Vikramāditya II 733-743 CE

According to Table 5.3, when Dharasena IV was issuing grants from Broach, Gurjara king Jayabhaṭa II was ruling. His father Dadda II had already declared himself the king of kings, so starting from him, Gurjara rulers were sovereign and would not allow anyone to issue grants from their capital. The same argument applies to Chālukya rulers issuing grants from Gurjara territory.

Table 5.4 shows selected Gurjara, Vallabhī and Chālukya rulers according to the proposed chronology. *Please note that ruling periods of the Chālukya rulers stay the same in both Tables as the Chālukya rulers have specified their dates in Śaka era, which makes their dating unequivocal.* If we look at Table 5.4 carefully, we will find that contradictions listed above do not arise when we have the correct chronology. When Dharasena IV was issuing grants from Broach, Gurjara kings had not even started their rule. When Chālukya rulers were issuing grants from supposedly Gurjara territory, the rule of Gurjara kings had already come to an end. Let us now try to put the important information obtained from the current analysis in historical perspective.

Table 5.4: Gurjara, Vallabhī and Chālukya chronology:
Proposed dates (Gurjara and Vallabhī)

Vallabhī	**Gurjaras**	**Chālukyas [16]**
Guhasena 315-326 CE	Dadda I c. 410-435 CE	Pulakeśina I 547-567 CE
Dharasena II 330-349 CE	Jayabhaṭa I Vītarāga c. 435-455 CE	Kirtivarman I 567-598 CE
Śilāditya I Dharmāditya 365-371 CE	Dadda II Praśāntarāga c. 455-500 CE	Mangaleśa 598-608 CE
Dhruvasena II Bālāditya 388-399 CE	Jayabhaṭa II c. 500-505 CE	Pulakeśina II 608-642 CE
Dharasena IV 404-409 CE	Dadda III Bāhusahāya c. 505-525 CE	Vikramāditya I 655-680 CE
Śilāditya III Vajrāta 420-443 CE	Jayabhaṭa III c. 525-540 CE	Vinayāditya 680-696 CE
Śilāditya IV-VI 444-525 CE	(Dadda IV) Ahirola c. 540-544 CE	Vijayāditya 696-733 CE
Śilāditya VII 525-543 CE	Jayabhaṭa IV c. 544-565 CE	Vikramāditya II 733-743 CE

When we look at Table 5.4 closely, we find something fascinating. The rise of the early Gurjaras coincides with the change in guard at Vallabhī.

5.4 The Sword of the Gurjaras

We know from the inscriptions of the Vallabhī rulers that after Dharasena IV, the throne of the Vallabhī suddenly went to the bloodline of Śilāditya I Dharmāditya, who was the brother of the Kharagraha I, grandfather of Dharasena IV. The rule of Vallabhī never went back to the line of Dharasena IV. There are two possibilities here. Either there was an attack by the invaders, possibly Hūṇas, or there was an internal struggle for power. The result was the transfer of power to Śilāditya II. The Gurjara ruler Dadda I helped Śilāditya II in gaining control of power and was rewarded by being made a sub-ordinate ruler. The relations between Gurjara rulers and Vallabhī rulers remained cordial based on this mutual gratitude.

When the Later Gupta king Harṣagupta attacked Vallabhī, it was only natural for the Gurjara ruler Dadda II to come to the rescue of his overlord at that point in time. The Vallabhī ruler, who was attacked by Harṣagupta, would be either Śilāditya V or VI. As a token of gratitude, Dadda II was accepted as a sovereign ruler by the Vallabhī king, and Dadda II assumed the title of the king of the kings.

There was peace and prosperity in Vallabhī for over 40 years after the attack by the later Gupta king Harṣagupta. In circa 541 CE, a matrimonial alliance took place between the rulers of Vallabhī and Persia to fight the common enemy, the Hūṇas. Soon, the city of Vallabhī was sacked by the Hūṇas and Turks in a surprise attack. The surprise attack took place in circa 543 CE and Vallabhī was occupied by Tajikas, the name by which Hūṇas and Turks have been referred to in the inscription. Modern historians have identified Tājikas as Arabs [17]. This identification is based on the faulty chronology, which places Jayabhaṭa (IV) in eighth century. This is due to the application of the Kalchuri-Chedi era to the inscriptions of early Gurjaras, while the inscriptions refer to the Śaka era. In light of the revelations made in this chapter, all inscriptions presumed to be dated in the Kalchuri-Chedi era need to be reassessed. There is a lot of fuzziness in the application of Kalchuri-Chedi era to a number of inscriptions [18]. The starting dates of 247-248 CE or 248-249 CE or 250-251 CE are chosen based on what fits the data. On top of that current years are sometimes used, and sometimes expired years are used. Some inscriptions have been judged irregular as they do not fit any of the combinations described above. Coming back to the Tājikas, we can state that they came from Central Asia and not Arabia. There is a country named Tajikistan in Central Asia, which is north of Afghanistan, east of Uzbekistan and west of China. Obviously, Tajikistan has got its name because it is the homeland of Tājikas. Prichard has given the following information about Tājikas in his book, "Researches into The Physical History of Mankind" [19]:

> *"Although the name of the Tājiks is little known to Europe, it has long been in the East the most generally prevalent designation of the native Persian race. Its real origin is unknown. It has been supposed to be derived from the Mongolian language, in which "Tājik" signifies "tillers of the soil." The people in Persia so termed, are, in fact, like the Helots of the Peloponnesus, or the Fellahs of modern Egypt, everywhere a dependent class, in part "glebae ascripti", or a rustic population, in part the traders, or the lower class of the inhabitants of cities. In the times of Tchinggis and of Timūr, the Mongoles and Turks gave the name of Tājiks to people who spoke the Persian language, and who appear to have been spread through various countries beyond the limits of Iran, and to have constituted, in various parts of Tūrkistan, the industrious population of towns. It has been supposed by Klaproth, and other Chinese scholars, that the Tājiks of the Mongolians are the Tiao-tschi, a people celebrated in the annals of the Han dynasty, and in*

the compilation of Ma-tuanlin. The Tiao-tschi are said to have dwelt on the banks of the Si-Hai, or Caspian, and the description of their country in the ancient Chinese books begins with Persia. But the appellation of Tājik is not unknown to the ancient Persians themselves. Hyde recognised Tajyik as an ancient name of Persia. It occurs among other designations of tribes in the Boundehesh. Lastly, a very similar name is found in the works of one classical writer. Dionysius, the geographer, mentions the Τασκοι, *or Taski, among the tribes who inhabited Persia, as dwellers in the neighbourhood of the Pasargadae.*

It has been supposed by some, that the Tājiks are a mixture of various races, who were forced by the conquerors of Iran to adopt Islām; but by Sir John Malcolm and other well-informed writers they are admitted to be the only genuine descendants of the old indigenous population, who, amidst all the conquests and revolutions which the country has undergone, have preserved their ancient language and their original stock. They speak every where an old Persian dialect, which is different from the cultivated Persian of the higher orders, but is much more different from the idioms of the nomadic tribes.

The eastern parts of Iran had been divided, long before the Mohammedan conquest, between mountaineers and the inhabitants of the plains and cities. The mountain tribes were the Affghāns, whom we shall hereafter describe. The people of the plains were, according to Elphinstone, Tājiks. The mountaineers held out against the Arabs, who conquered the plains and forced the inhabitants to embrace Islam. The name of Tājik and Parsewān are now used in discriminately as designative of the native inhabitants throughout Afghānistan and Tūrkistan."

The above quote should make it clear that Tājikas were inhabitant of Central Asia and were of Persian origin, and not Arabs. As seen in the previous chapter, the queen of Vallabhī, daughter of the Sasanian emperor Khosrow I (Anushirvan the Just), survived the attack of the barbarians as she was away on pilgrimage. She could not have gone back as Vallabhī was occupied by the Tajikas. It fell upon the Gurjaras to free Vallabhī from the rule of the barbarians. The Gurjara king Ahirola passed the crown to young Jayabhaṭa IV with the blessing to drive the barbarians away. Jayabhaṭa IV did not act in haste but waited for the right opportunity. When the opportunity came, he attacked the Tājikas with full might of the Gurajras. This attack took place sometime after the sacking of Vallabhī by the Tājikas in 543 CE. Based on an improper reading of Kāvī plates, it was thought earlier that Jayabhaṭa (IV) had attacked the Lord of Vallabhī, a Hindu ruler instead of Tājikas [20]. This error has been rectified after the correct reading was obtained from the Prince of Wales Museum plates. Jayabhaṭa IV inflicted a crushing defeat on the Tājikas and the Tājika survivors fled. On the other side, the Hūṇas were attacked by the Persian emperor Khosrow I to avenge the killing of his son-in-law Śilāditya VII. In the aftermath of these events, hordes of Hūṇas descended on India to pillage and conquer. An epic battle followed in which the Hūṇas were completely routed. This epic battle was etched in the collective memory of the Hindus as the battle of Korūr. In order to identify the hero of this epic battle, we will need to learn more about the Hūṇas, the barbarians who tormented most of the civilized world for centuries before they were gradually civilized and then finally assimilated by the very people they vanquished.

Notes

1. Bühler (1888).
2. Mirashi (1955a): 57-66.
3. Mirashi (1955a): 67-72.
4. Mirashi (1955a): 72-75.
5. Mirashi (1955a): 75-78.
6. Bühler (1878b).
7. Bhandarkar (1871-74).
8. Mirashi (1955b): 617-622.
9. Mirashi (1955a): 82-89.
10. Mirashi (1955a): 90-96.
11. Mirashi (1955a): 96-102.
12. Mirashi (1955a): 102-109.
13. Mirashi (1955a): cxc.
14. Mirashi (1955a): lii-liii.
15. See Table 4.1 in Chapter 4 of this book.
16. Daniélou (2003): 155-159
17. Mirashi (1955a): lvi.
18. Mirashi (1955a): i-xxx.
19. Prichard (1844): 51-53.
20. Mirashi (1955a): lv.

āhāra nidrā bhaya maithunam cha

samānametatpaśubhirnarāṇam |

dharmo hi teṣāmadhiko viśeṣo

dharmeṇa hināḥ paśubhiḥ samānāḥ | |

-- Eating, sleeping, fear and sex are common among animals and human beings. Dharma is the only distinguishing feature of human beings. Those without Dharma are same as animals.

- Hitopadeśa

6. THE BEASTS OF WAR

At the crossroads of civilizations lay a vast expanse now known as Central Asia. Hordes after hordes of barbaric nomads sprung from this land, one after another, and brought to ruin everything that fell in their path. They tried to vanquish the four great civilizations -- Indian, Persian, Roman/Byzantine and Chinese -- that shared their boundaries with the land of barbarians. These civilizations had to fight for survival as their resolve was tested again and again by these Central Asian hordes. It is ironic that this land is currently considered the cradle of civilization from where Indo-Europeans spread in different directions eventually reaching India and Persia. We start our journey through the past by following the trials and tribulations of the Persians under attack from invaders descending from the Central Asian region.

6.1 The Last Empire of Persia

In Chapter 3, we discussed the history of the Sasanian dynasty of Persia from its beginning to the rule of Bahram Gūr. Our focus in that chapter was to affirm the marriage of the Persian emperor Bahram Gūr with an Indian princess, whom we have identified as the daughter of Kuṣāṇa emperor Vasudeva II. In this chapter, our focus will be on the Central Asian invaders that threatened both the Persian and Indian civilizations. We will start with the account of the Sasanian dynasty from the book "The Heart of Asia" [1]:

> *"The history of Central Asia during the earlier centuries of our era is bound up in that of Persia, and its course was moulded by the fortunes of the great dynasty called after the grandfather of its founder, the Sāsānide, which governed the empire from A.D. 219 until the Arab invasion more than four centuries later. In the third century (A.D. 200) of our era the condition of Persia resembled that of France before the power of feudalism was broken by the crafts and iron will of Louis XI. The authority of the reigning dynasty was little more than nominal, and the land was parcelled out among a host of petty tribes whose mountain fastnesses enabled them to bid defiance to the Parthian dynasty. Among the followers of one of their rabble chieftains was a certain Pāpak, a native of a village lying to the east of Shīrāz. With the aid of a son named Ardashīr, he overthrew his master, and usurped authority over the province of Fars. Ardashīr's bold and restless character appears to have inspired his father with some distrust, for on his death he left his dominions to another son, named Shāpūr. The succession was contested by Ardashīr, but when he was about to enforce his claim with the sword, Shāpūr died, in all probability by poison. Ardashīr's thirst for empire now led him to attack his neighbouring potentates. One after another succumbed to his genius; and he became master, in turn, of Kirmān, Susiana, and other eastern States. Then finding himself in a position to strike a blow for the sovereignty of Persia, he bade defiance to Ardavān, the last of the Parthian line. A*

decisive battle was fought between them, probably in Babylonia, in the year 218. Ardavān was slain, and Ardashīr was crowned "king of kings" on the field. His capital was Istakhr, but he chose Ctesiphon (or Madā'in) as a residence. How far Ardashīr's personal conquests actually extended, it is hard to define. Oriental historians have greatly exaggerated the extent of his empire, which they allege to have stretched from the Euphrates on one side, to Khwārazm on the other. Ardashīr was a wise and just ruler, and his career can be compared only with Napoleon's. Without the prestige of birth or fortune he won an empire, and was able to maintain order in extended realms which had for centuries been a prey to anarchy. He died in 241, and was succeeded by his son Shāpūr I. For the first ten years of his reign he was, like his father, engaged in chronic warfare with Rome, which did not terminate till 260, when the Emperor Valerian fell into his hands, dying afterwards in captivity. According to extant coins, Shāpūr I made himself master of the non-Iranian lands to the east of Khorāsān, and to him is ascribed the conquest of Nīshāpūr, and Shāpūr in Northern Persia. In 272 he was succeeded by his son Hormuz, who continued the struggle with the Romans, in which Syria, Asia Minor, and Armenia were alternatively subjects of contention.

The succeeding reigns have little bearing on history until we come to that of Bahrām Gūr, which was signalised by a persecution of the Christians, and a recommencement of warfare with Rome. Bahrām Gūr was worsted in the latter, and entered into a treaty with the Western Empire, which bound the contracting parties to tolerate the Christian and Zoroastrian cults respectively. The Romans further undertook to pay an annual subsidy towards the maintenance of the fortifications on the Dariel Pass in the Caucasus, by which both kingdoms were protected from the inroads of the wild hordes of the North. Bahrām took advantage of his truce with the Romans to make an expedition into Bactria, where he encountered the Ephthalites, or White Huns, whom, according to Persian accounts, he utterly defeated. We are told that the Khākān of the "tribes of Transoxiana," being informed that Bahrām and his court were immersed in luxury and had entirely lost their martial spirit, ventured to cross the Oxus and laid waste the whole of Khorāsān. He was soon undeceived, for Bahrām, at the head of seven thousand men, fell upon the Turks by night, and put them utterly to rout, the Khākān perishing by the king's own hand. Bahrām then crossed the Oxus and concluded a peace with his eastern neighbours. Bahrām died in 438, and was succeeded by his son Yezdijerd II. During his reign of nineteen years his attention was engrossed by Armenia and by Khorāsān, where he suffered many reverses at the hands of the Ephthalites. On his death in A.D. 457 his two sons, Hormuz III and Pīrūz, became rival claimants to the throne. Their father, who preferred the former, but feared a quarrel between the brothers, had given Pīrūz the governorship of a distant province, Sīstān. Pīrūz, on learning that his brother had seized the throne and won the support of the nobility, fled across the Oxus, and implored the chief Khākān of the Ephthalites to espouse his cause. The Huns consented, and sent an army thirty thousand strong to his aid. With this accession of strength, Pīrūz invaded Persia, and defeated his brother in a pitched battle. Hormuz III thus lost his crown, and was put to death together with three of his nearest relatives. The reign of his successful rival was fraught with useful domestic measures. He had to contend against a famine which lasted for seven years; but, so prompt and effectual were the means adopted to combat it, that, if Tabari is to be believed, there was not a single death from starvation. Pīrūz's foreign policy was by no means so praiseworthy: though he owed his crown to the ready help of the Khākān of the Ephthalites, we find him in 480 freely attacking his benefactor's son and successor. This apparent ingratitude is ascribed by Joseph Stylites to the intrigue of the Romans, whose jealousy of the power of Persia induced them to incite the Huns to attack her eastern frontier. Nöldeke suggests as the cause of this rupture the exorbitant nature of the demands made by the Huns as the price of their assistance in placing Pīrūz on the throne. Be this as it may, the struggle was disastrous to the Persian army. After obtaining some trivial successes, Pīrūz was obliged to conclude more than one humiliating treaty with the Huns, the terms of which he did not loyally fulfil. On one occasion his son Kobād was left for two years in their hands as a hostage for the payment of a large indemnity. A little later we find Pīrūz himself a prisoner.

A crisis in his affairs came in 484, when he led an immense force against his inveterate foes, only to suffer a crushing defeat at their hands, and to lose his life; while his daughter was taken prisoner and forced to enter the Khākān's harem. Persia now lay at the mercy of the barbarians whose hordes overran the country, drowning its civilisation in blood. From this anarchy the land was saved by the efforts of a great noble named Sukhrā, or Zermihr. At the time of the Huns' invasion he was essaying to quell one of the periodical revolts in Armenia. Hurrying back to the Persian capital with a considerable force, he established a semblance of order, and placed Balāsh, a brother of Pīrūz, on the throne. The new king bought off the White Huns, probably by undertaking to pay a yearly tribute. But his treasury was empty. He was able to attach no party in the State to his banner, and in 488 he incurred the resentment of the all-powerful priesthood. Falling into their hands, he was deprived of his eyesight, a loss which under the Persian law incapacitated him from ruling. Balāsh was succeeded by his nephew, Kobād, son of Pīrūz. Tabari tells us that before he came to power, even probably on the accession of his brother, he had fled to the Khākān for help to meet his claim. On his way he halted at Nīshāpūr, and took to wife the daughter of a nobleman, who bore him a son, the famous Anūshirawān. He was kept waiting four years for the promised help, but finally, after much entreaty, the Khākān gave him the control of an army, with which he set out for Madā'in. On reaching Nīshāpūr he learnt the news of his brother's death. The first act of his reign was to resign the entire administration to Sukhrā, on the score of his own youth and inexperience. Finding, when he came to man's estate, that the people regarded Sukhrā as their sovereign and ignored his own ancestral claims, he determined to rid himself of a too powerful minister, and had him put to death.

When Kobād had been for ten years on the throne a false prophet arose in the person of a certain Mazdak, who taught that all men were equal, and that it was unjust that one should have more possessions or wives than another. The inference was that there should be an equal division of all property. These tenets appear at first identical with the latest plans of social ethics. But Mazdakism had a side which is not shared by the Socialistic creed. Its founder preached a life of piety and abstinence, and himself practised an extreme asceticism, refraining from the use of animal food. Kobād saw in the new cult an opportunity of eluding the grip of the nobles and clergy, who stifled his aspirations to govern as well as reign. He espoused the reformer's side with ardour, and thereby hastened the anarchy which such doctrines were certain to promote. The followers of Mazdak adopted such of his principles as appealed to their unbridled lust, and ignored the religious teaching with which he sought to hold it in check. The disorders were stemmed by a combination between the nobles and the clergy, who seized and imprisoned Kobād, setting up his brother Jāmāsp in his stead. But Kobād contrived to escape from confinement, and sought shelter with old allies, the Ephthalites. With them he sojourned until 502, when he returned to Persia at the head of a large force, and overthrew his brother, thus regaining sovereignty. The remainder of Kobād's career was as stirring as the commencement had been. Hardly was he reinstated on the throne ere hostilities broke out with Rome, and then began a series of terrible conflicts which reduced the strength of both parties to the lowest ebb, and rendered them a prey to barbaric invasion.

Not until 506 was a truce concluded between the two powers; but it did not bring rest to Kobād's distracted empire. He was soon plunged into hostilities with the Huns,—whether the Ephthalites, or another branch of the race, is uncertain. The result is not recorded, but it must be assumed to have been favourable to his army."

We turn to the article "Analysis of Eastern Works – No. 1 - The Rozat al Sofa" for the continuation of Persian history [2]:

"The reign of Kobad was marked by the prevalence of the heresy of Mazdak, a wretched impostor, who held the doctrine of the community of goods and of wives; and whose followers, acting up to his doctrine, and combining the power with the will to do evil, became the scourge of the unhappy country in which their strange heresy prevailed. Kobad himself embraced the detestable doctrine, and all the earnest remonstrances of the indignant Nushirvan were necessary to prevent his mother from being sacrificed, by her infatuated husband, to the lawless passion of Mazdak. On Nushirvan's accession to the throne, he was obliged, for a while, to temporize with the impostor, till the establishment of his government gave him the power, and the heresiarch's excesses a pretext, to put him to death. His followers were punished by death and confiscation of goods, which were returned, as far as possible, to those from whom they had been forcibly taken away. The number of these sacrifices to offended justice and humanity was very great: a hundred thousand stakes are said to have impaled as many wretched fanatics.

The reign of Nushirvan, though the most prosperous and renowned in the Iranian history, was disturbed by a bitter domestic calamity. His son Noushizad, the child of a Christian wife, rebelled against his father, and seizing the occasion of his absence in Syria, and the report of his death, gathered together a considerable body of Christians, and made a formidable show of opposition. Nushirvan, like David of old, gave strict charges to his generals to preserve the life of his guilty son, and these charges were as inefficient as those of the Jewish monarch. Noushizad's last words were, to desire that he might be buried with Christian rites; and his father was long inconsolable for the scion of his royal house which had thus perished.

This monarch was alike famed for the wisdom of his internal policy, and the extent of his foreign conquests. On the side of Tatary, Arabia, and Syria, he made extensive conquests: he humbled the pride of the Greek emperor in many battles, and raised the Persian empire to a height of power which it had never before attained. He encouraged the arts of life, made the most judicious arrangements for the administration of justice, and, by a division of the Persian provinces into four parts, over each of which he appointed a trusty vicegerent, provided for the more careful supervision of his whole empire.

The reign of his son, Hormuz, who had during his father's life-time acquired much military reputation, commenced under the most happy auspices, and for nearly twelve years of successful administration he sustained the high reputation of his father. But intoxicated, perhaps, by success, he at length lapsed into tyranny: his nobles rebelled against a monarch who had thinned their numbers by his cruelties; his dominions were invaded by the Greeks, the Arabs, and the Tatars ; and his unworthy treatment of his gallant general, Baharam Choubin, who had signalized himself against the last-named enemy, completed his ruin. Baharam rebelled, threw his king into prison, and set up Khosru Parviz, the son of the deposed monarch, as a pageant to favour his own usurpation of the throne. The public voice, however, was for the young prince, who, during the course of these troubles, had taken refuge in the Greek empire: he was recalled, formally crowned, and two of his uncles removed the only impediment to his dominion, by butchering the unfortunate Hormuz in prison—an act for which they were themselves put to death by the young king.

The reign and the personal history of Khosru, like those of Bahram Gour, have furnished many materials for oriental fiction. His unbounded magnificence, the luxury in which he lived, the beauty and romantic history of his fair wife Shirin, have been recorded with all the embellishments of eastern imagination. He extended his conquests widely, too, into the eastern portion of the Greek empire, took Jerusalem, and, as the Persian historian assures us, obtained possession of the holy cross, which was found cased in gold and buried deeply in the ground. His fate, in many respects, resembles that of his father. Reverses of fortune, aggravated by his own supineness and luxury, raised against him the nobles of the kingdom: he was thrown into prison, where he languished till the hand of an assassin, at the direct instigation of his unnatural son, closed a life of unparalleled splendour, by a terrible and retributive death. Shirouiah, the parricide, did not long enjoy the fruits of his crime. He seems to have died under the terrors of remorse, within a few months of his ascending the throne.

The rest of the history of Persia, till its final conquest by the Mohamedan Arabs, is a mere detail of usurpations and depositions, till we reach the reign of Yezdejird, under whom the Persians sustained a signal defeat, in which their monarch was slain, their independence destroyed, and their rich and powerful empire rendered tributary to the soldiers whom they had so lately despised as the naked eaters of lizards of the deserts."

With this background of Persian history, we can try to piece together the fragments of Indian history when the power of the Kuṣāṇas started to wane. To facilitate this process, we have compiled the chronology of the Sasanian dynasty and added some of the important events that took place during this period as shown in Table 6.1. We had seen part of this Table in Chapter 3 up to the reign of Bahram V, as the focus in that chapter was on affirming the marriage between Bahram V and the daughter of Vasudeva II. This important link between Persian and Indian civilizations provided an opportunity to develop a revised chronology of the Kuṣāṇa rulers.

Table 6.1: Sasanian dynasty of Persia

Sasanian rulers	**Regnal period [4]**	**Important events**
Ardashir I	224-241 CE	Founded the dynasty.
Shapur I	241-272 CE	Defeated Roman Emperor Valerian.
Hormizd I	272-273 CE	
Bahram I	273-276 CE	
Bahram II	276-293 CE	
Bahram III	293 CE	
Narseh	293-302 CE	
Hormizd II	302-309 CE	
Shapur II	309-379 CE	Crowned while still inside the womb.
Ardashir II	379-383 CE	
Shapur III	383-388 CE	
Bahram IV	388-399 CE	
Yazdegerd I	399-421 CE	
Bahram V	421-438 CE	Killed Khākān, chief of Hūṇas
Yazdegerd II	438-457 CE	Fought Hūṇas
Hormizd III	457-459 CE	Fought Hūṇas, killed by Piruz
Piruz	459-484 CE	Took help of Khākān, later attacked Khākān, finally killed by Khākān.
Balash	484-488 CE	
Kavadh	488-496 CE	Became king with the help of Hūṇas
Djamasp	496-498 CE	
Kavadh	498-531 CE	Became king again with the help of Hūṇas
Khosrow I*	531-579 CE	Crushed the Hūṇas
Hormizd IV	579-590 CE	
Khosrow II	590-628 CE	
Civil war		
Yazdegerd III	632-651 CE	

*also called Anushirvan the Just or Adil Nashirwan

The focus in this chapter is how the Sasanians dealt with one of the most devastating forces in the history of mankind, the Hūṇas, and how this impacted Indian civilization. Looking at Table 6.1, we find that the attack of the Hūṇas started during the reign of Bahram V (421-438 CE) and ended during the reign of Khosrow I (531-579 CE). It is possible that the Kuṣāṇas shared their western border with the Sasanian Empire, when Bahram V had to face the attack of the Hūṇas. We can see that the marriage of Bahram V with the daughter of Vasudeva II was not a marriage of just two individuals, but had a political motive. Bahram V was not in India just for pleasure, but he was on a reconnaissance mission. He was aware of the deadly forces of the Hūṇas on the north-eastern boundaries of the Persian Empire and was in India to see whether the Kuṣāṇas were aware of the lurking danger and if conducive, seek an alliance with the Kuṣāṇas to fight the Hūṇas. This is precisely what Fergusson had said in his book, "History of Indian and Eastern Architecture," published in 1876 CE. He uses "Guptas" instead of Kuṣāṇas in the following quote as the Imperial Guptas were ruling North India during this time period according to modern Indian history [3]:

> *"But the great point is that it was just about this time that the White Huns broke loose and extended their incursions east and west, so that there is not only no improbability of their being the "foreign invaders" alluded to, but every likelihood they were so. No one, indeed, can, I believe, with the knowledge we now possess, read De Guignes' chapter on the White Huns, without perceiving that it contains the key to the solution of many mysterious passages in Indian history. It is true India is not mentioned there; but from the time of Bahram Gaur in 420, till the defeat of Feroze in 475, the Persians were waging an internecine war with these Huns, and nothing can be more likely than that the varying fortunes of that struggle should force them to seek the alliance of the then powerful Guptas, to assist them against their common foe.*

> *Precisely the same impression is conveyed by what is said by Ferishta and the Persian historians of the history of that time. Nothing can now, however, be more easily intelligible than the visit of Bahram Gaur to India when first attacked by the White Huns. His marriage with an Indian (? Gupta) princess of Canouge; the tribute or assistance claimed by Feroze and his successors on the Persian throne, are all easily explicable, on the assumption that the two nations were at that time engaged in a struggle against a common enemy."*

Soon, the empire of the Kuṣāṇas began to shrink under attack from the Hūṇas, who were controlling Bactria in 459 CE. Persia was ruled by the Sasanian king Hormizd III then, who confronted the Hūṇas. Hormizd III was backstabbed by his brother Piruz, who made a pact with the Hūṇas. Piruz killed Hormizd III and became the new ruler of the Sasanian dynasty. In 481 CE, a battle was fought between Piruz and the Hūṇas, in which Hūṇas initially lost, but Piruz chased them deep inside their territory and was surrounded. Piruz had to pay a ransom for his release and his son Kavadh was held hostage by the Hūṇas for three years.

After securing the release of his son Kavadh in 484 CE, Piruz attacked the Hūṇas with a huge army. Again, after initial victories, he was surrounded by enemy forces near Herat. The Sasinid army was wiped out in the battle and Piruz was killed by Khush-Newaz, the chief of Hūṇas. Balash was made the ruler for a short period between 484-488 CE. Balash was deposed by Kavadh with the help of an army provided by the Hūṇa king. Kavadh ruled till 496 CE, when he was ousted and Djamasp was made the ruler. In 498 CE, Kavadh became king again with the help of the Hūṇas. He ruled till 531 CE, when Khosrow I (Anushirvan the Just) ascended the throne. Khosrow I had a long reign of 48 years during which time he dealt a crushing blow to the Hūṇas.

6.2 An Emperor Par Excellence

In this chapter, we are exploring the relation between India and Persia during the invasion of Hephthalites or White Hūṇas. The central character during this period was the Persian emperor Anushirvan the Just. There have been only few rulers of such calibre in history. Let us learn more about him, who was the son of Kavadh, called Kobad in the following excerpt [5]:

> *"Kobad left several sons; but he appears always to have shown a decided preference for Nousheerwan; and that early sentiment must have every day gained strength, from observing the extraordinary wisdom and goodness of that prince's character. At his death, Kobad bequeathed his kingdom to this favourite son. The testament was committed to the principal mobud or high priest, and read by him to the assembled nobles of the empire, who immediately declared their cheerful submission to the will of their deceased sovereign; but Nousheerwan refused the proffered diadem, on the ground of his inability to reform the great abuses of the government. "All the principal offices, "he exclaimed, "are filled by worthless and despicable men; and who, in such days, would make a vain attempt to govern this kingdom according to principles of wisdom and justice. If I do my duty, I must make great changes; the result of these may be bloodshed; my sentiments toward many of you would perhaps alter; and families whom I now regard would be ruined. I have no desire to enter into such scenes: they are neither suited to my inclination nor to my character, and I must avoid them." The nobles could not deny the truth of what he said; and convinced for the moment of the necessity of a reform, they took an oath to support him in all his measures, to give implicit obedience to all his orders, and to devote their persons and property to his service, and that of their country.*
>
> *Satisfied by these assurances, Nousheerwan ascended the throne, and assembled all his court. He then made the following address: "The authority which I derive from my office is established over*

your persons, not over your hearts: God alone can penetrate into the secret thoughts of men. I desire that you should understand from this, that my vigilance and control can extend only over your actions, not over your consciences: my judgments shall always be founded on the principles of immutable justice, not on the dictates of my individual will or caprice; and when, by such a proceeding, I shall have remedied the evils which have crept into the administration of the state, the empire will be powerful, and I shall merit the applause of posterity."

The conduct of Nousheerwan was at first correspondent with his professions: but the moment he felt secure in his strength, he resolved to eradicate the baneful schism of Mazdak. The doctrine of this impostor has been already explained. His faith was at variance with the established worship of the kingdom; its fundamental tenet was the annihilation of all property: anarchy was its certain result; and a monarch like Nousheerwan required not the aid of that resentment which the insult to his mother had kindled, to induce him to adopt all means for the speedy destruction of so dangerous a belief. But the numbers of Mazdak's followers may have compelled him to use artifice; and we cannot altogether reject that account, which represents the just Nousheerwan as having been forced by attention to the safety of the state, to stoop to an unworthy stratagem in order to prevail on the impostor, and a number of his followers, to assemble near his palace, where, instead of meeting with that kind treatment which his promises had led them to expect, they were all put to death: but it is more probable, and much more consonant to the character of this monarch, to credit the relation, that a man complained of his wife having been taken from him by a disciple of Mazdak. The king desired the pretended prophet to command his follower to restore the woman; but the mandate of the earthly monarch was treated with scorn and contempt, when its effect was contrary to what was deemed a sacred precept. Noursheerwan, enraged at this bold opposition to his authority, ordered the execution of Mazdak, which was followed by the destruction of many of his followers, and the proscription of his delusive and abominable tenets.

Nousheerwan was indefatigable in his endeavour to promote the prosperity of his dominions: he ordered all bridges of every description which had fallen into decay, to be repaired: he directed many new edifices to be built; and we are told by his flattering historians, that every town and village within his kingdom which had been destroyed, was restored and repeopled. He also founded schools and colleges; and gave such encouragement to learned men, that philosophers from Greece resorted to his court. He divided his empire into four great governments: the first comprising Khorassan, Seistan, and Kerman: the second, the lands dependant upon the Cities of Isfahan and Koom; the provinces of Ghelan, Aderbijan, and Armenia: the third, Fars and Ahwaz ; and the fourth, Irak, which extended to the frontier of the Roman empire. The most excellent regulations were introduced for the management of these different governments; and every check established that could prevent abuse of power in the officers appointed for their administration: but the vigilance and justice of the monarch were the great source of the prosperity of his territories; and historians have added to his merit, when they have attributed a part of the success and glory of his reign to the extraordinary wisdom of his favourite minister, Abouzurg-a-Mihir, who was raised from the lowest station to the first rank in the kingdom, and the minister's virtues and talents have shed a lustre even on those of the great monarch, whose penetration discovered and whose confidence employed them.

The accounts given by eastern and western authors of the successes of Nousheerwan, in his invasions of the Roman empire, differ but very little: some of the former have falsely asserted, that he took an emperor of the Romans prisoner; and they have all, with a partiality which, in national historians writing of this monarch, seems almost excusable, passed over the few reverses which his arms sustained. But the disgraceful peace which Justinian purchased at the commencement of Nousheerwan's reign, the subsequent war, the reduction of all Syria, the capture of Antioch, the unopposed progress of the Persian monarch to the shores of the Mediterranean, his conquest of Iberia, Colchis, and the temporary establishment of his power on the banks of the Phasis, and on the shores of the Euxine, are facts not questioned by his enemies. They assert, however, that his genius, as a military leader, even when his fortune was at the highest, was checked by Belisarius, who was twice sent to oppose his progress; and whose success, considering his want of means, and the character of the court he served, was certainly wonderful.

In all the negotiations between the Emperor Justinian and Nousheerwan, the latter assumed the tone of a superior. His lowest servants were treated at the imperial court in a manner calculated to inflame the pride and raise the insolence of a vain and arrogant nation: and the impressions this conduct must have made, were confirmed by the agreement of the Roman emperor to pay thirty thousand pieces of gold; a sum which could be of no importance to Nousheerwan, but as it showed the monarch of the western world in the rank of his tributaries. In a second war with the Emperors Justin and Tiberius, Nousheerwan, who, though eighty years of age, still led his armies, experienced some reverses; but the perseverance and valour of the aged sovereign were ultimately rewarded by the conquest of Dara, and the plunder of Syria.

During these great successes over the Romans, the empire of Nousheerwan had been equally extended in other quarters. The countries beyond the Oxus, as far as Ferghana, all those to the Indus, some provinces of India, and the finest districts of Arabia, acknowledged the sway of the mighty monarch of Persia. …

Historians have dwelt on the magnificence of the courts which sought the friendship of Nousheerwan. The Emperors of China and India are the most distinguished. Their presents to the sovereign of Persia are described as exceeding in curiosity and richness any that were ever seen. Eastern monarchs delight to display their wealth and grandeur in the splendour of their embassies; but this conduct has in general a better motive than vanity. It is from the style of his equipage, the magnificence of his presents, and the personal deportment of an ambassador, that ignorant nations judge of the power and character of the monarch whom he represents; and to this cause we must refer the minute account which every eastern historian deems it his duty to give of the state and appearance, as well as the conduct, of the embassies he describes. …

Whatever success attended the endeavours of Nousheerwan to promote the happiness of his subjects, by the establishment of justice, there can be no doubt of his personal love of it. A Roman ambassador, sent to Ctesiphon with rich presents, when admiring the noble prospect from the windows of the royal palace, remarked an uneven piece of ground, and asked the reason why it was not rendered uniform. "It is the property of an old woman," said a Persian noble, "who has objections to sell it, though often requested to do so by our king; and he is more willing to have his prospect spoiled, than to commit violence." "That irregular spot, "replied the Roman, "consecrated as it is by justice, appears more beautiful than all the surrounding scene." But it would be endless to repeat the anecdotes preserved of Nousheerwan, who may certainly be considered as the greatest of Asiatic monarchs. The title of good and just cannot perhaps be given to any human being placed in such a situation, and in such an age; for, whatever may be his disposition, the monarch, whose will is law, who is compelled to repress rebellion, to retaliate attack, and to attain power over foreign nations in order to preserve his own in peace, must commit many actions at variance with humanity and justice; but, if we are to deny the claim of Noursheewan to those attributes with which eastern historians have clothed him, we must admit that his reign was glorious for his country; that he displayed, during a life protracted for more than eighty years, and a reign of forty-eight, all those great qualities which, by the concurring opinion of mankind,

> *have given fame to their possessors; and above all, that he was to the last hour of his life unconquered by prosperity. His firm and noble character resisted the influence of that luxury by which he was courted: he neither gave himself up to indulgence, nor permitted it in others; and the aged monarch was seen, shortly before his death, leading his troops to the attack of Dara, with as active and ardent a spirit as he had shown in his earliest enterprises."*

Anushirvan the Just was deeply interested in philosophy, and was a wise ruler. He said that to find out the truth, he not only examined the customs of his forefathers but of Romans and Indians too. He accepted what was reasonable and praiseworthy among them, and he did not reject any customs just because they belonged to others. Likewise, he did not accept the bad customs just because his forefathers followed them [6]. There was excellent contact with India. His chief physician went to India for spiritual learning and when he returned, he brought a copy of the Pañchatantra, which was translated in Persian as Kalila and Dimna. He also received presents from the Emperor of India [7]:

> *"The presents from the Emperor of India were equally magnificent. A thousand pounds weight of aloe wood. A vase, formed of one precious stone, and filled with pearls. On one side of this vase was engraven the figure of a lion; on the other, that of a young maiden, seven hands in height. Her eye-lashes fell on her cheeks; and the brilliancy of her eyes, increased by the fairness of her complexion, shone through them like lightning. The Indian monarch also sent to Nousheerwan a carpet, made of a serpent's skin, finer than any silk, and more beautifully speckled by the hand of nature than art could ever imitate."*

In the light of the information presented in this book, the Emperor of India at that time can be identified as Śilāditya VII. According to well established Indian traditions, Śilāditya VII married the daughter of the Persian emperor Anushirvan the Just. The aim of this marriage alliance was to check the growing power of the

Hūṇas, who were controlling vast areas in Central Asia bordering both Persia and India. We need to learn more about the rise and fall of the Hūṇas to better understand their impact on India.

6.3 The Barbaric Hūṇas

When we talk of the Hūṇas, it is generally assumed that they were of Mongol descent. This may not have been the case. The following two passages from the fourth volume of the 65-volume monumental work "The Universal History" published between 1747-1768 CE suggest that the Hūṇas and the Turks both came from the same stock of people:

> *"According to the Chinese historians, the Huns and Turks are the same people; who, at different times, went under those different names. They give them the appellations of Hyong-nu and Tu-ki-uk, that is, Huns and Turks; the first is that which they had before the Christian era ; the second, that which, a remnant of those Huns, re-established in Tartary, assumed afterwards; and say, that they dwelt in the neighbourhood of the great desert, extending from the country of Korea, in the east, to that of the Getes, in the west; which part of Tartary was their habitation from all antiquity." [8]:*

> *"The Huns were a considerable nation of Great Tartary; and had the dominion there more than 200 years before the Christian era. ... These Huns or Turks dwelt in tents, placed in carts, and removed from place to place, for the conveniency of pasture to feed their cattle; which supplied them with both food and clothing. They despised old people, and only set a value on the young, as more proper for war, which was their sole occupation. Their riches consisted in sheep and cattle; but chiefly in the number of slaves, taken in war. The skulls of their enemies served for cups to drink out of in their principal ceremonies." [9]:*

The above paragraph gives us a glimpse into the ways of the Hūṇas. We also see that they made their first appearance in the history books around 200 BCE. Soon afterwards they were knocking on the doors of the Imperial Gupta Empire. Fortunately, Emperor Skandagupta handed them a crushing defeat, and the feat was repeated again by Emperor Yaśodharmā after a few decades. The Hūṇas retreated, and we don't hear about them for a few centuries as India dealt with other invaders – the Śakas and the Kuṣāṇas -- who made significant inroads inside India. When the Hūṇas appeared again in the beginning of the fifth century, their appearance was somewhat different. Now they were called Hephthalites or White Hūṇas [10]:

> *"According to the Chinese writers, the White Huns first appeared in the countries on the Oxus in the beginning of the fifth century, when Shelun, the son of the Tsanyu (or Shanyu) of the Jwan-jrvan (or Yuan-Yuan), retired to the west with his brother. After defeating Payekhi, the king of the Hiungnu, he gave up the title of Tsanyu and assumed that of Kieu-teu-fa Khākān. In 410 A.D. he was defeated by the Wei Tartars, and died during his flight. His brother Hulu succeeded him, and was followed in 414 by his nephew Puluchin, who was killed by his cousin Tātān in 425. The new king began his reign by the invasion of the north-east provinces of Persia; but, being vigorously attacked by the Sassanian king Varahran V., he was defeated and killed near Merv in 428 A.D. His whole camp, with his queen, the Khātun, and his rich crown set with gems, all fell into the hands of the conqueror.*
>
> *Tātān was succeeded by his son Uti, who took the title of Solien Khan. He would appear to have been the real founder of the Ephthalite power, as he received a Chinese princess in marriage and gave his own sister to the Emperor of China. He carried on a nine years' war with Isdegerd II of Persia, from 443 to 451 A.D., and eventually, about 456, forced him to retire to his own dominions to the south of the Oxus. From this time the empire of the White Huns became very powerful until 554, when Solien-teu-fa Khan was defeated by Tumen, the "Grand Shahu" of the Turks. During this*

> *century of their prosperity the dominion of the White Huns was extended on all sides, until, as described by Sung-yun in 520, it embraced all the countries lying between Persia on the west and Khotan on the east to Tieh-li on the south."*

We saw in Chapter 3 that Kipunadha was the last Kuṣāṇa ruler, whose reign ended circa 475 CE. Around this time, the Hūṇas had become very powerful and their invasion of India dealt a death blow to the Kuṣāṇas. We can go one step further and identify the Hūṇa chief who was responsible for ending the Kuṣāṇa rule in India. We have the following information about the Hūṇas during the fifth century as described in "The Universal History" [11]:

> *"The country of Abtela, which signifies, in Persian, water of gold, takes its name from a people so called; who, some time before, had conquered it. The Greeks, corrupting the word, called them Nephtalites, Eutalites, and, more nearly, Ephtalites. They were denominated, by the Arabs, Hayātelah. According to Procopius, the Ephtalites were those called the white Huns: they seem to have been masters, for a time, of all Mawara'lnahr, or Great Bukharia; to which Abulfeda gives the name of Hayātelah. Dr. Hyde observes, that Heyāteleh was the title of the king of Katlān, a province in the eastern part of Mawara'lnahr: and Eutychius informs us, that Goshnawaz, king of Abtelah, who raised Firuz to the throne of Persia, about the year 465, was king of Balkh, and part of Khorasan; which shews, that the dominion of the Abtela had once been very extensive; though we may suppose their power to have been much reduced, at the time when Anushirwān conquered them."*

Based on the information presented in this chapter, we have compiled the list of Hūṇa chiefs in Table 6.2. It was the Hūṇa chief Goshnawaz, who was ruling over a vast empire circa 465 CE. This is also close to the final years of the Kuṣāṇa rule as described in Chapter 3. Thus it stands to reason that the Hūṇa chief Goshnawaz (Khush-Newaz) attacked India and ended the rule of the Kuṣāṇas. When the Kuṣāṇas lost to the Hūṇas, the results were devastating.

We can now turn to the archaeological proof of the devastation brought to India by the Hūṇas.

Table 6.2: The Hūṇa Khākāns (chiefs)

Name	Year known	Source	Notes
Shelun	circa 401 CE	Chinese	
Hulu	circa 410 CE	Chinese	
Puluchin	circa 414 CE	Chinese	
Tātān	circa 425 CE	Chinese	Killed by Bahram V
Uti/ Solien Khan	circa 425-456 CE	Chinese	Fought Yazdegerd II
Goshnawaz/ Khush-Newaz	circa 465 CE	Persian	Killed Piruz
Gollas	circa 530 CE	European	Sacked Vallabhī
Solien-teu-fa Khan	circa 554 CE	Chinese	Defeated by Tumen, Turk Khākān

6.4 The Urban Decay

According to modern history books, the rule of the Kuṣāṇas was followed by the rule of the Imperial Guptas. The age of the Imperial Guptas is considered the golden age of India. This was the age of unprecedented growth in prosperity, art and culture. However, the archaeological excavations present a completely different picture. When the cities are supposed to be flourishing, there is definitive sign of rapid decay. Here is a summary of the status of Indian cities during the third to fifth century of the Common Era according to archaeological findings [12]:

> *After third century of Common Era, there was rapid decay in urban centres of Punjab, Haryana and western Uttar Pradesh, for example Hastināpura and Mathurā. During Gupta age, cities were fast*

> *deteriorating in middle Gangetic plains, for example Śrāvastī, Kauśāmbī and Rājagīra. Conditions were similar in West Bengal and Odisha. Urban decay started in North India with the rise of the Imperial Guptas. The signs of urban decay in cities administered by Guptas are clear in cities such as Pāṭaliputra, Vaiśālī, Vārāṇasī, Kauśāmbī, Ayodhyā, Hastināpura and Mathurā.*

This should be shocking to students of Indian history and is a clear proof that the Imperial Guptas are misplaced in history. How can urban decay start with the rise of the Imperial Guptas, when the Gupta period is known as the Golden age of India? The ruins that archaeologists assign to the Gupta era do not belong to the Gupta era. What archaeologists have witnessed during the period of third to fifth century of Common Era is the decay of civilization under attack from the Hūṇas. When the Hūṇas finally conquered North India, they burned down cities. According to John Marshall, who was the Director-General of the Archaeological Survey of India from 1920-1928 CE, the fire that burnt Sirsukh in Taxila must have been huge judging from the quantity of burnt soil [13]. Marshall estimates that Sirsukh was burnt during the last quarter of the fifth century, which is the time period we have estimated for the end of the reign of the Kuṣāṇas. Ajram, about 15 km from Hoshiarpur in Punjab, was burnt twice, first by the Hūṇas and then many centuries later by Muslims [14]. Sanghol in Punjab and Kauśāmbī, present day Kosam in Uttar Pradesh, were also sacked by the Hūṇas [15].

We also have literary confirmation of the urban decay after the fall of the Kuṣāṇas. Hiuen Tsiang, who commenced his journey to India in 629 CE, notes that Pāṭaliputra was in ruins for a long time and gives the following description of Pāṭaliputra [16]:

> *"When the old capital of Kusumapura was changed, this town was chosen, and from the circumstance of the genii building the mansion of the youth the name henceforth of the country was Pāṭaliputra pura (the city of the son of the Pāṭali tree).*

> *To the north of the old palace of the king is a stone pillar several tens of feet high; this is the place where Aśoka (Wu-yau) rāja made "a hell." In the hundredth year after the Nirvāṇa of Tathāgata, there was a king called Aśoka (O-shu-kia), who was the great-grandson of Bimbiasāra-rājā. He changed his capital from Rājagṛha to Pāṭali (pura), and built an outside rampart to surround the old city. Since then many generations have passed and now there only remain the old foundation walls (of the city). The saṅghārāmas, Deva temples, and stūpas which lie in ruins may be counted by hundreds. There are only two or three remaining (entire). To the north of the old palace, and bordering on the Ganges river, there is a little town which contains about 1000 houses."*

In the wake of the attacks by the ruthless Hūṇas, life in North India was severely affected. Some cities were sacked by the Hūṇas, while others declined due to the disruption of the rule of law and trade activities. We have seen during the overview of Sasanian history that the Hūṇas had become so powerful during the last quarter of the fifth century and the first quarter of sixth century that they were not only dictating terms to the Persians but installing persons of their choice on the Persian throne. At the zenith of their power they had overrun western parts of North India as well. This has been stated by a European traveller named Cosmas Indicopleustes [17]:

> *"Cosmas Indicopleustes, who traded in the Red Sea about 535 AD, speaks of the Huns as a powerful nation in northern India in his days."*

It was a dark age of Indian history, and in this dark age a city stood as the beacon of hope for the Hindu-Jain civilization: the city of Vallabhī. In 525 CE, Vallabhī was ruled by emperor Śilāditya VII. Located close to the Arabian Sea, Vallabhī was engaged in maritime trading with the Persians. It was only natural for both of these empires to seek an alliance to counter the Hūṇas.

6.5 The Axis of Evil

It was discussed in Chapter 4 that Śilāditya VII married the princess of Persia, the daughter of Anushirvan the Just, in circa 541 CE. Soon afterwards, in circa 543 CE, Vallabhī was sacked by the Hūṇas in a surprise attack. The name of the Hūṇa Khākān who conducted this raid was Gollas. Cosmas Indicopleustes has given the following information about him [18]:

> *"In India further up the country, i.e., further north, are the White Huns. The king, named Gollas, tis said, goes forth to war with not less than 1,000 elephants, besides a great force of cavalry. This ruler tyrannizes over India. Once when he laid siege to a certain inland city of India, protected all round by water . . . his army drank up all the water, and he took the city."*

The description of an inland city protected all round by water is a good fit for the city of Vallabhī, located very close to the Arabian sea. Cosmas Indicopleustes was the author of "The Christian Topography" from which the above excerpt has been drawn. The surname "Indicopleustes" means the Indian navigator. Cunningham says in the article quoted above that Cosmas Indicopleustes travelled to India between 522-530 CE. However, this does not mean that the attack on Vallabhi took place before 530 CE. Cosmas Indicopleustes wrote the "The Christian Topography" in 547 CE [19]. He has mentioned that some 25 years had passed since the time when the Axumite king Elesboas was preparing for an expedition against the Homerites in Arabia. This event took place in 522 CE. Thus, Cosmas Indicopleustes was writing about an event that took place recently. The name of the Hūṇa Khākān Gollas given by Cosmas Indicopleustes is probably a variation of the word "Gula". We have seen that the name of the Hūṇa Khākān in 465 CE was Khush-Newaz. Since the Hūṇas were illiterate to begin with, it would have been natural for them to adopt the Persian language as they became civilized due to the close interaction with Persians. When the Hūṇas attacked Vallabhī,

Anushirvan the Just was busy on the western front of the Persian Empire. The Hūṇas took advantage of the situation and sacked Vallabhī in a surprise attack in 543 CE. After Anushirvan the Just came to know of this attack, he attacked the Hūṇas to seek revenge. We learn the following from the fourth volume of the "The Universal History" [20]:

> *"D'HERBELOT reports, from Mirkond, that Anushirwān having repulsed the Hiyātelah beyond the mountain Parapamisus, in his twelfth year, marched against the Khākān of the oriental Turks, who then reigned in the Transoxane provinces, and obliged him to sue for peace, as also to yield him one of his daughters in marriage. Eutychius relates this transaction with some variation: he tells us, that the Persian monarch, resolving to revenge on the Hiyatelah the injury done his grandfather Firūz, first makes an alliance with the great Khākān of the Turks, and acquaints him with his design; that then marching against the enemy, he overthrew them, and killed their king; by this means the country of Balkh, and the adjacent parts of Khorasān, were delivered up to him: after which he encamped in Fargāna and married the Khākān's daughter."*

Since Anushirvan the Just ascended the throne in 531 CE, the twelfth year of his reign would be in 542/543 CE. This is the year in which he first marched against the Hūṇas and killed their Khākān. We can identify this Hūṇas Khākān with Gollas as described above. After killing Gollas, Anushirvan marched against the Turks. The Turks were defeated and the Turk Khākān offered his daughter in marriage to Anushirvan as part of the treaty. The name of the Turk Khākān is given as Silzibulos by the Greeks and Sinjibu by the Arabs [21]. Turks used the title Khākān for the supreme ruler, while the title Khān was used for a sub-ordinate ruler [22].

It should be noted that the currently accepted view is that the battle between Anushirvan the Just and the Hūṇas took place much later than 543 CE, possibly in 557 CE or in the 560s. However, this goes against the Persian tradition that Hormizd IV, son of Anushirvan, was born to a Turkish princess [23], which is recorded in Shahnamah. Some historians doubt that Hormizd IV was the son of a Turkish princess as they consider the marriage of Anushirvan with the Turkish princess to have taken place in the seventh decade of the sixth century. Hormizd IV ruled between 579-590 CE, which is consistent with the marriage of Anushirvan the Just and the Turkish princess in the fifth decade of the sixth century.

The Hūṇas had their centre of power at Bactria, south of the Oxus (Amu Darya or Vankṣu), while the Turks controlled the territories north of the Oxus. The passage quoted above gives two scenarios: the first scenario has been discussed above. The second scenario is that Anushirvan the Just made a pact with Turk Khākān and then marched against the Hūṇas. We have reason to believe that the first scenario is the correct one. The support for this scenario comes from the inscription of the Gurjara king Jayabhaṭa IV. As discussed in the last chapter, Jayabhaṭa IV had inflicted a crushing defeat on the Tājikas who were occupying Vallabhī after sacking it. It is interesting that the invaders are called Tājika, which will imply the Turkish descent of the invaders. It thus stands to reason that in the aftermath of the alliance between Persia and Vallabhī, the Hūṇas and Turks also formed an alliance. When Anushirvan the Just was busy on the western front of his empire, the Hūṇas and Turks attacked Vallabhī and sacked it. In the aftermath of the attack on Vallabhī, Anushirvan attacked the Hūṇas, and killed their Khākān Gollas. As Anushirvan attacked the Turks and cut their access to Vallabhī, Jayabhaṭa IV found himself in a position where he could attack the remaining Hūṇas and Turks who were occupying Vallabhī. As the Hūṇa and Turk survivors fled, they regrouped with the Hūṇa survivors from the attack by Anushirvan. The regrouped Hūṇas tried to recover their strength and in a few months, after getting a fresh supply of recruits and arms, started on their usual campaign of loot and plunder. This time they planned to sack the western parts of North India. The invasion by these ruthless Hūṇas took place in 544 CE. Fortunately, India had a new hero to defend the motherland. An epic battle was fought at Korūr, and it fascinated the country so much that the memory of this epic battle got etched in the collective memory of the masses. We will discuss the hero of this epic battle in the next chapter.

Notes:

1. Skrine (1899): 22-29.
2. Analysis of Eastern Works (1838).
3. Fergusson (1876): 726.
4. http://www.cais-soas.com/CAIS/History/Sasanian/sasanid.htm.
5. Malcolm (1829): 107-118.
6. http://www.iranicaonline.org/articles/sasanian-dynasty.
7. Malcolm (1829): 115, footnote.
8. The Modern Part of a Universal History (1759): 7
9. The Modern Part of a Universal History (1759): 41
10. Evans et al. (1890).
11. The Modern Part of a Universal History (1759): 48.
12. Śarmā (1995): 225-227.
13. Śarmā (1995): 28.
14. Śarmā (1995): 174.
15. Śarmā (1995): 174.
16. Beal (1906b): 85-86.
17. Topographia Christiania, lib. Xi, p. 338, as quoted in The Encyclopaedia Britannica (1891): 790.
18. Evans et al. (1890).
19. http://www.tertullian.org/fathers/cosmas_00_2_intro.htm.
20. The Modern Part of a Universal History (1759): 49.
21. The Encyclopaedia Britannica (1888): 613.
22. Lacouperie (1887-1888)
23. Garthwaite (2005): 109.

śūrabāhūṣu loko ayam lambate putravat sadā।

tasmāt sarvāsvavasthāsu śūraḥ sammānamarhita।।

na hi śauryāt param kiñchit trilokeṣu vidyate।

śūraḥ sarvam pālayita sarvam śūre paritiṣṭhitam ।।

-- This world is always supported by the arms of the brave like a son (by his father). Therefore, a brave man is to be honoured under all circumstances. There is nothing existing in all three worlds, which cannot be obtained by bravery. The braves sustain all and all are dependent upon the brave.

- Mahābhārata, Śānti Parva 99.17-18

7. THE PROWESS OF THE PANTHERS

After the Hūṇas ran over the Kuṣāṇa Empire during the last quarter of the fifth century, North India was left without a central authority. The strength of Indian civilization during this period was that it was full of people proud of their heritage. It was not that they never fell, as everybody falls sometime or the other. The strength of Indians was that they rose with renewed vigour every time they fell. They were too proud to be ruled by invaders, and invaders assimilated into the culture realizing the the superior nature of the culture. In turn, these assimilated invaders became the vanguards in protecting Indian society from further invasions. Two empires rose to fill the vacuum that was created by the devastating blows received from the Hūṇas, those of the "Later Guptas" and the "Maukharis". It fell upon the Maukharis to defend India from the menace of the Hūṇas.

7.1 The Maukharis

The first three kings of the Maukhari line are known from the inscriptions of king Anantavarman. The Nāgārjunī hill cave inscription of Anantavarman gives the genealogy as follows [1]:

> *"Om! May the foot of (the goddess) Devī, fringed with the rays of (its) pure nails, point out the way to fortune, endowing with a (suitable) reward your state of supplication which is such as befits the expression of firm devotion; - (that foot) which, surpassing in radiance all the beauty of a full-blown waterlily, was disdainfully placed, with its tinkling anklet, on the head of the demon Mahishāsura.*
>
> *(Line 3.) There was a king, the illustrious* ***Yajñavarman****, possessed of greatness by celebrating copious sacrifices; renowned; possessed of fame as pure as the spotless moon; abode of (all) the dignity of one of the warrior caste; - who, though he was the foremost of all kings in respect of wisdom, (high) descent, liberality, and prowess, yet through modesty, was (like) an ocean which adheres to the natural state (of tranquility), (and) the calmness of which is never disturbed.*
>
> *(L. 5.) His son (was) the king* ***Śārdūlavarman****, who stretched out over the faces of the points of the compass, (as) an emblem of sovereignty, the renown that he had acquired in the occupation of war resembling (in its extensiveness) the great swollen ocean; who conquered (the stains of) this present age with (his) fame; who was illustrious; (and) who acquired, as it were, the glory of the kalpa-tree, by satisfying with rewards the wishes of (his) relatives and friends.*
>
> *(L. 7.) Of him, who was always possessed of infinite fame and renown, the son (is) he, pure of soul, (and) possessed of intellect animated with innate piety, who is known by the appellation of*

__Varman__ commencing with __Ananta__; by whom, desiring a shrine of religious merit that should endure as long as the sun, the earth, the moon, and the stars, this (image of) (the goddess) Kātyāyanī has been placed in (this) wonderful cave of the __Vindhya__ mountains.

(L. 9.) – He has given to (the goddess) Bhavānī, to be enjoyed up to the time of the destruction of all things, the charming village of … possessed of a great wealth of enjoyment,- the sin, impurity, mud, and blemishes of which are washed away by the pure waters of a great river;- which is filled with perfume by the breezes that agitate the priyaṃgu and vakula trees in (its) groves;- (and) from which the radiance of the sun is screened off by (this) lofty mountain."

According to the inscription the first three rulers of the Maukhari dynasty were: Yajñavarman, his son Śārdūlavarman, and Śārdūlavarman'son Anantavarman. Śārdūla, which means panther, was the most illustrious of them. Based on the location of their inscriptions, Barābar and Nāgārjunī caves in Gaya district in Bihar, they were ruling the area around Gaya in South Bihar. Since their inscriptions are undated, it is difficult to pinpoint the exact time period they ruled. It seems likely that they were feudatories of the later Kuṣāṇas. Based on the chronology developed in this book, this will place them in the fifth century, 400-475 CE. The Kuṣāṇas were uprooted by the Hūṇas in circa 475 CE. The Hūṇas were barbaric nomads, who left after plundering and ravaging the cities. This created opportunity for Maukharis to move west towards Uttar Pradesh.

We have a set of inscriptions of Maukharis from current day Uttar Pradesh giving their genealogy. These Maukharis do not refer to the three Maukhari rulers from Bihar discussed above and were most probably closely related, but they were not in the direct bloodline of Anantavarman. The Harahā stone inscription gives the initial genealogy of the new Maukhari line. This important inscription gives the following information [2]:

Verse 3: The Mukhara princes considered themselves to be the descendants of the hundred sons whom King Aśvapati got from Vaivasvata Manu.

Verse 4: Among the Mukhara princes, Harivarman was born for the welfare of the earth and was also known by the name of Jvālāmukha.

Verse 6: Ādityavarman was the son of Harivarman.

Verse 8: Īśvaravarman was the son of Ādityavarman.

Verse 11: Īśānavarman was the son of Īśvaravarman.

Verse 13: Īśānavarman conquered the lord of the Āndhras, who had thousands of rutting elephants; vanquished the Śūlikas, who possessed countless galloping horses; and caused the Gauḍas living on the seashore to stay confined within their realm.

Verse 15: Earth was sinking in the ocean shaken by storms of Kali. Īśānavarman forcibly held the broken boat of earth together by fastening it with the strings of his hundred-fold virtues.

Verse 16: Sūryavarman was the son of Īśānavarman.

Verse 21: Īśānavarman was ruling the earth in year 611.

Verse 23: The eulogy was written by Raviśānti, the son of Kumaraśānti and resident of Garggarakata.

The Harahā inscription is considered to be dated year 611, which is equivalent to 554 CE, counting from the beginning of Vikram era. The inscription was recorded by Sūryavarman, son of Īśānavarman, during the renovation of a Śiva temple. According to the Harahā stone inscription, the genealogy of this branch of Maukharis runs from father to son in the following order: Harivarman, Ādityavarman, Īśvaravarman, Īśānavarman, and Sūryavarman. In this dynasty Īśānavarman was the most powerful ruler, and he assumed the title of Mahārājādhirāja. Sūryavarman did not ascend the throne, and it was his brother Śarvavarman who became the ruler and assumed the title of Mahārājādhirāja, according to the Asirgadh copper seal inscription shown below [3]:

> *"(There was) the illustrious Mahārāja Harivarman, whose fame stretched out beyond the four oceans; who had other kings brought into subjection by (his) prowess and by affection (for him); who was like (the god) Chakradhara, in employing (his) sovereignty for regulating the different castes and stages of religious life; (and) who was the remover of the afflictions of (his) subjects. His son, who meditated on his feet, (was) the illustrious Mahārāja Ādityavarman, begotten on the Bhattārikā and Devī Jayasvāminī. His son, who meditated on his feet, (was) the illustrious Mahārāja Īśvaravarman, begotten on the Bhattārikā and Devī Harshaguptā. His son, who meditated on his feet, (was) the Mahārājādhirāja, the glorious Īśānavarman, begotten on the Bhattārikā and Devī Upaguptā. His son, who meditates on his feet, (is) the most devout worshipper of (the god) Maheśvara, the Mahārājādhirāja Śarvavarman, the Maukhari, begotten on the Bhattārikā and Mahādevī Lakshmīvatī."*

Śarvavarman was followed by Avantivarman, who was followed by Grahavarman. We will discuss the political condition during the reign of Avantivarman and Grahavarman in the next chapter. Right now, we will focus our attention on the dynasty of the Later Guptas, who became bitter rivals of the Maukharis in their quest for supremacy over North India during sixth century.

7.2 The Later Guptas

The initial genealogy of the Later Guptas is provided by the undated Aphsaḍ stone inscription of Ādityasena as described below [4]:

> *"Om! There was a king, the illustrious Krishṇagupta, who was like a mountain, in that (his) cities, like the slopes of a mountain, were*

crowded with thousands of elephants; in that he was attended by men of learning, as a mountain is inhabited by Vidyādharas; in that he was of good descent, as a mountain is possessed of excellent bamboos; (and) in that he was firm (and) lofty; (and) whose arm played the part of a lion, in bruising the foreheads of the array of the rutting elephants of (his) haughty enemies, (and) in being victorious by (its) prowess over countless foes.

(Line 1.) - Just as the full-moon, destitute of spots, the destroyer of the darkness, was produced from the ocean, so from him there was born a son, the majestic one, named the illustrious Harshagupta, who,--raining down a terrible flight of arrows from (his) firm bow that was bent with ease at the befitting proper time, (and) being gazed upon with copious tears by (his enemies) who, averse to the abode of the goddess of fortune being with (him, her) own lord, were stupified (at being unable to prevent it),-was (always) displaying a glorious triumph, the written record as it were of terrible contests, in the guise of the rows of the knots of hard callous places, caused by wounds from many weapons, on (his) chest.

(L. 3.) - His son was the illustrious Jīvitagupta (I.), the best among kings, who was a very-cold-rayed (moon) to (wither) the waterlilies that were the countenances of the women of (his) proud enemies. The very terrible scorching fever (of fear) left not (his) haughty foes, even though they stood on seaside shores that were cool with the flowing and ebbing currents of water, (and) were covered with the branches of plantain-trees severed by the trunks of elephants roaming through the lofty groves of palmyra-palms; (or) even though they stood on (that) mountain (Himālaya) which is cold with the water of the rushing and waving torrents full of snow. Even still his superhuman deeds are regarded with astonishment by all mankind, like the leap of (the monkey Hanumat) the son of the Wind from the side of (the mountain) Kośavardhana.

(L. 5.) - That king begat one son, by name the illustrious Kumāragupta, of renowned strength, a leader in battle; just as (the

god) Hara begat a son, (Kārttikeya) who rides upon the peacock;-by whom, playing the part of (the mountain) Mandara, there was quickly churned that formidable milk-ocean, the cause of the attainment of fortune, which was the army of the glorious Īśānavarman a very moon among kings, (and) which had for (its) spreading rows of waves the plantain-trees that were wantonly shaken to and fro by the roaring wind (caused by the marching of the troops), (and) had (its) rocks, that were the ponderous and mighty rutting elephants (of the forces), whirled round and round by the masses of water that were the rising dust (stirred up by the soldiers). Cherishing heroism and adherence to the truth, (even) in (the possession of) wealth, he went to Prayāga; (and there), honourably decorated with flowers, plunged into a fire (kindled) with dry cow-dung cakes, as if (simply plunging to bathe) in water.

(L. 8.) - The son of that king was the illustrious Dāmodaragupta, by whom (his) enemies were slain, just like the demons by (the god) Dāmodara. Breaking up the proudly stepping array of mighty elephants, belonging to the Maukhari, which had thrown aloft in battle the troops of the Hūṇas (in order to trample them to death), he became unconscious (and expired in the fight); (and then, waking again in heaven and) making a choice among the women of the gods, saying "(this one or that) belongs to me," he was revived by the pleasing touch of the waterlilies that were their hands. He, (while he was) king, gave away in marriage a hundred daughters of virtuous Brāhmans endowed with many ornaments and with youth, (and) dowered with agrahāra-grants.

(L. 10.) - From him there was a son, the illustrious Mahāsenagupta, the leader, among brave men; who in all the assemblages of heroes acquired a (reputation for) valour (that stood) in the foremost rank;-whose mighty fame, marked with the honour of victory in war over the illustrious Susthitavarman, (and) [white], as a full-blown jasmine-flower or waterlily, or as a pure necklace of pearls pounded into little bits (?), is still constantly sung on the banks of (the river) Lohitya, the surfaces of which are (so) cool, by the Siddhas in pairs,

when they wake up after sleeping in the shade of the betel-plants that are in full bloom.

(L. 11.) - As (the god) Mādhava, whose feet are graced by the attentions of (the goddess) Śrī, (was born) from Vasudeva, so from him there was (a son), the illustrious Mādhavagupta, finding pleasure only in prowess, whose feet were graced by the attentions of the goddess of fortune. He being remembered in the foremost rank . . . ; being the leader of those who acquire renown in war; (and) being a very store-house of goodness, the best of those who excel in the collection and bestowal of riches, the natural home of wealth, truth, and learning, (and) a firm bridge of religion,-there is no one on the earth . . . who is (as) worthy to be praised by virtuous people, (as he was). He also, (like the god), carried a discus in the palm of (his) hand; to him also belonged a bow made of horn, and a pleasing sword (which was employed) for the destruction of (his) enemies (and) the happiness of his friends; (and), when the slaughter of (his) foes had been achieved, . . . was averted by him; . . . people did obeisance . . . "(My) mighty enemies have been slain by me in battle; there remains nothing more for me to do,"-thus he, the hero, determined in his mind; (and then) with the desire to associate himself with the glorious Harshadeva . . .

(L. 15.) - His son was the illustrious one, named Ādityasena, the best among kings, whose scimetar was sullied with a thick coating of dust in the shape of the pearls from the temples of the lordly elephants of (his) enemies that were split open (by it), . . . Maintaining the supreme renown, that (his) perfect praise, coming from . . . (and) rising from the destruction of (his) enemies, is worthy to be lauded in the presence of all wielders of the bow,-a continuous line of blessings . . . Cleaning with the edge of the silken cloth of a banner, (used) under the excuse of (wiping away) sweat in battle, (his) sword that was stained with the rut (of the elephants slain by him), and was covered with sand in the shape of the minute fragments of the pearls (from their foreheads) through . . . that was broken to pieces, . . . the destruction of rutting elephants, in the

course of which many swarms of bees, led into a mistake by the copious fragrant juice that trickled forth, were attracted by their perfume. . . . in battle which is full of terrible and repulsive frownings . . . (he) is accustomed to laugh in a charming manner in the gatherings of (his) favourites and servants. His [wife], truthfully constant to (her) lord; performing penance with the excellent qualities of (her) mouth (?); . . . laughter . . . Being . . . (and) being the greatest cause of the destruction of the power of all (his) enemies, (and) being possessed of his own mighty prowess, even when he is full of weariness produced by the fatigue of drawing (his) sword forth (from its scabbard) and (dealing) blows (with it), . . . the foreheads of rutting elephants in battle, [he is verily] a guardian of the world, by whose white umbrella the whole circuit of the earth is covered. He, the king, has had both (his) gleaming arms increased in bulk by splitting open the temples of rutting elephants in war; he has a halo of fame, [acquired] by destroying the power of many enemies; the darting fire of the prowess of (his) feet has had thrown into it (to feed it) the locks of hair on the tops of the heads of all (other) kings; he is possessed of fortune; (and) he has a pure and celebrated reputation (acquired) by honourable behaviour in war.

(L. 23.) - This best of temples has been caused to be made, on account of (the god) Vishṇu, by him, the king, whose very great fame, (of) this (kind that has been described), white as the orb of the autumn moon (and) conferring renown on the (whole) circle of the world, was for a long time made angry by him through (his) desire for (her) association with (his) wealth, and then, becoming more wonderful than ever, went, forsooth, through the enmity natural to the condition of rival wives, to the other side of the ocean (in order to dwell there far away).

(L. 24.) - By his mother, the Mahādevī Śrīmatī, a religious college has been caused to be built, resembling a house in the world of the gods, (and) has been given by herself in person to religious people.

(L. 25.) - By the queen, the illustrious Konadevī, the dear wife of that same king, in the performance of an excellent penance, there has been caused to be excavated a wonderful tank, the waters of which are eagerly drunk by people; which is full of drifting and glistening spray, resembling in lustre a shankha-shell, or the moon, or crystal; (and) in the waves of which, driven to and fro by the motion of the alligators, the birds disport themselves and the large fishes play about.

(L. 26.) - As long as a digit of the moon [remains] on the head of (the god) Hara, (and) (the goddess) Śrī on the breast of Vishṇu, (and) (the goddess) Sarasvatī . . . in the mouth of Brahman; as long as the earth [remains] on a hood of (Śesha) the king of serpents; and as long as there is lightning in the interior of a cloud,--so long shall the king Ādityasena display here (in these works) (his) dazzling fame!

(L.27.) - (This) eulogy, (written in) beautiful letters, [has been composed, or engraved] by Sūkshmaśiva, (a native of) the Gauḍa (country), who is thoroughly religious (and) very intelligent."

According to the Aphsad stone inscription of Ādityasena mentioned above, the genealogy of the Later Guptas runs from father to son in the following order: Kṛṣṇagupta, Harṣagupta, Jīvitagupta I, Kumāragupta, Dāmodaragupta, Mahāsenagupta, Mādhavagupta, and Ādityasena. The rest of the genealogy of the Later Guptas starting from Madhavagupta is given in the Deo-Baranark inscription of Jivitagupta II, which is shown below [5]:

"Reverence to . . . Hail! From the victorious camp, possessed of shouts of victory acquired by the three constituents of power, (and) invincible through (its) equipment of great ships and elephants and horses and foot-soldiers, (and) situated near the fort of Gomatikoṭṭaka:-

(Line 2.) - (There was) . . . the illustrious Mādhavagupta. His son, who meditated on his feet, (was) the most devout worshipper of the Divine One, the glorious Ādityasenadeva, begotten on the

Paramabhaṭṭārikā the queen, the Mahādevī, the glorious Śrīmatīdevī.

(L. 3.) - His son, who meditated on his feet, (was) the most devout worshipper of (the god) Maheśvara, the Paramabhaṭṭāraka, Mahārājādhirāja, and [Parameśvara], the glorious Devaguptadeva, begotten on the Paramabhaṭṭārikā, the queen, the Mahādevī, the glorious Koṇadevī.

(L. 4.) - His son, who meditated on his feet, was the most devout worshipper of (the god) Maheśvara, the [Paramabhaṭṭāraka], Mahārājādhirāja, and Parameśvara, the glorious Vishṇuguptadeva, begotten on the Paramabhaṭṭārikā, the queen, the Mahādevī, the glorious Kamaladevī.

(L. 5.) - His son, who meditates on his feet, the most devout worshipper of . . . the Paramabhaṭṭāraka, Mahārājādhirāja, and Parameśvara the glorious Jīvitaguptadeva (II.),-[begotten] on the Paramabhaṭṭārikā, the queen, the Mahādevī, the glorious Ijjādevī,- being in good health, [issues a command] to the herdsmen, Talāvāṭakas, messengers, makers of boundaries, . . . Rājaputras, Rājāmātyas, . . . Mahādaṇḍanāyakas, Mahāpratihāras, . . . Kumārāmātyas, Rājasthānīyas, Uparikas, . . . Chauroddharaṇikas, Dāṇḍikas, Daṇḍapāśikas . . . of the village of Vāruṇikā, which lies in the . . . in the Nagara bhukti, (and) . . . belonging to the Vālavi vishaya, (and) to . . . the village of Kiśoravāṭaka (?), which was laid out by . . . and to those who subsist on the favour of Our feet, and to the neighbours, headed by the Brāhmaṇs, (and) to the Mahattaras, . . .

(L. 12.) - By the Bhojaka Sūryamitra, belonging to (the establishment of) the divine (god) the holy and sacred Varuṇavāsin, who was requested . . . the above-mentioned [village] . . . together with . . . and the village, &c., was formerly bestowed by the Parameśvara, the glorious Bālādityadeva, by (his) own charter, . . . the divine (god) the holy and sacred Varuṇavāsin, . . . by restoration

to the Bhojaka Haṃsamitra, and by those who presided at different times, viz. the Parameśvara, the glorious Śarvavarman . . . [to] the Bhojaka Ṛshimitra . . . by the Parameśvara Avantivarman. In accordance with this practice . . . assent to its enjoyment by the Bhojaka Durdharamitra was given, by the grant of a charter, by the Mahārājādhirāja and Parameśvara . . . and it is now enjoyed by him.

(L. 17.) - "Therefore I [now announce] that it is assented to . . .; such is (my) command to all people. . . . the altar of (the god) Varuṇavāsin; after that, there is given . . . with the udranga and the uparikara, with (the proceeds of fines for) the ten offences, the five . . .

With the aid of the Deo-Baranark inscription, the complete genealogy of the Later Guptas runs from father to son in the following order: Kṛṣṇagupta, Harṣagupta, Jīvitagupta I, Kumāragupta, Dāmodaragupta, Mahāsenagupta, Mādhavagupta, Ādityasena, Devagupta II, Viṣṇugupta, and Jīvitagupta II. Now that we are familiar with the genealogies of both Maukharis and Later Guptas, let us try to understand how these two dynasties battled for supremacy to rule over North India.

7.3 The Battle for Supremacy

Table 7.1 shows the list of the Maukhari and Later Gupta rulers along with some important points of their reigns. Towards the end of the fifth century, the Kuṣāṇa Empire has been decimated by the Hūṇas. In the power vacuum that was created, two powers rose to fill that vacuum, and these were the dynasties of the Later Guptas and the Maukharis. The Later Gupta king Harṣagupta tried to expand westward by attacking Vallabhī, but was repelled by the combined power of Vallabhī rulers and the Gurjaras. This restrained the ambitions of the Later Guptas and they tried to enhance their influence by entering into marriage alliances with the Maukharis.

Table 7.1: The Maukharis and Later Guptas

Later Guptas	**Notes**	**Maukharis**	**Notes**
Kṛṣṇagupta	Founder	Harivarman	Founder
Harṣagupta	Attacked Vallabhī	Ādityavarman	
Jīvitagupta I		Īśvaravarman	Fought Āndhras
Kumāragupta	Fought Īśānavarman	Īśānavarman	Mahārājādhirāja, defeated Āndhras and Śūlikas, checked the Gauḍas
Dāmodaragupta	Fought Maukharis	Śarvavarman	Mahārājādhirāja
Mahāsenagupta	Defeated Susthitavarman	Avantivarman	Parameśvara
Devagupta I		Grahavarman	
Mādhavagupta	Sought friendship of Harṣadeva		
Ādityasena	Mahārājādhirāja		
Devagupta II	Mahārājādhirāja		
Viṣṇugupta	Mahārājādhirāja		
Jīvitagupta II	Mahārājādhirāja		

Mahārāja Ādityavarman was married to Devī Harṣaguptā, and Mahārāja Īśvaravarman was married to Devī Upaguptā, who gave birth to Mahārājādhirāja Īśānavarman. The cordial relations between the Later Guptas and the Maukharis soon turned into bitter rivalry when the Maukharis, under the rule of Īśānavarman, started the campaign to unite all of North India under their rule.

Īśānavarman was the first Maukhari ruler to assume the imperial title of Mahārājādhirāja. His military successes are listed in the Harahā stone inscription, where it is stated that Īśānavarman defeated the Āndhras and the Śūlikas, and confined the Gauḍas within their boundaries. Obviously, the Gauḍas were also becoming powerful and had designs to expand their empire. The imperial ambitions of Īśānavarman brought him in direct conflict with the contemporary Later Gupta ruler Kumāragupta. The fight continued during the reign of Later Gupta ruler, Dāmodaragupta. The Later Guptas lost both times and they had to recognize the sovereignty of the Maukharis.

Mahāsenagupta had to fight Susthitavarman, who was the ruler of Kāmarūpa, under the aegis of the Maukharis. The ancient kingdom of Kāmarūpa was located in present day Assam, and at its peak included parts of Bengal, Bhutan and Bangladesh as well. Modern historians have wondered how Mahāsenagupta, ruler of Malwa, went to fight Susthitavarman, when he had to cross territories held by Maukharis in order to do so. It can be explained when we understand that the Later Guptas simply chose to tell partial truths to maintain their dignity. The Deo-Baranark inscription of the Later Gupta emperor Jivitagupta II quoted above clearly mention Maukhari emperors -- Śarvavarman and Avantivarman as Parameśvara or Supreme Lord. This means that Magadh was under the control of the Maukhari emperors Śarvavarman and Avantivarman, as Deo-Baranark is a village in South Bihar. The acceptance of Maukhari sovereignty by the Later Guptas is also corroborated by the marriage of Mahāsenagupta's sister with the Puṣyabhūti king Ādityavardhana, grandfather of Harṣavardhana. Since the Puṣyabhūtis were allies of the Maukharis, this marriage could not have taken place without the approval of the Maukhari emperor, which in turn implies that Mahāsenagupta had accepted Maukhari sovereignty.

Obviously, the state of affairs was not palatable to some of the close relatives of the Later Gupta rulers. They were simply aghast by the surrender of sovereignty of the Later Guptas by Mahāsenagupta. The result was a coup by Devagupta I, who usurped the Later Gupta kingdom. Mahāsenagupta was worried about the safety of his sons, and he sent them to his brother-in-law Ādityavardhana for their safety. According to Bāṇa, Kumāragupta and Mādhavagupta were companions of Rājyavardhana and Harṣavardhana, while according to the Aphsaḍ stone inscription of Ādityasena, Mādhavagupta was desirous of the company of Harṣadeva. The literary and inscriptional evidence support each other in this case. We will discuss the aftermath of these events in the next chapter on the Puṣyabhūti dynasty. For now, we have covered the background to discuss the epic battle, which broke the backbone of Hūṇa power to such an extent that they did not remain a significant threat to India after this engagement.

7.4 The Battle of Korūr

The Battle of Korūr has been mentioned by Al-Biruni in the following passage [6]:

> *"The epoch of the era of Śaka or Śakakāla falls 135 years later than that of Vikramāditya. The here-mentioned Śaka tyrannised over their country between the river Sindh and the ocean, after he had made Āryavarta in the midst of this realm his dwelling-place. He interdicted the Hindus from considering and representing themselves as anything but Śakas. Some maintain that he was a Śūdra from the city of Almanshūra; others maintain that he was not a Hindu at all, and that he had come to India from the west. The Hindus had much to suffer from him, till at last they received help from the east, when Vikramāditya marched against him, put him to flight and killed him in the region of Karūr, between Multān and the castle of Lonī. Now this date became famous, as people rejoiced in the news of the death of the tyrant, and was used as the epoch of an era, especially*

by the astronomers. They honour the conqueror by adding Śrī to his name, so as to say Śrī Vikramāditya. Since there is a long interval between the era which is called the era of Vikramāditya and the killing of Śaka, we think that that Vikramāditya from whom the era has got its name is not identical with that one who killed Śaka, but only a namesake of his."

Fergusson made the following comments in 1876 regarding this passage by Al-Biruni [7]:

"It seems impossible to apply this narrative to any events happening in the first century B.C., not to mention the inherent absurdity of Vicramaditya establishing an era 56 B.C., and then 135 years after wards defeating the Saka king on the banks of the Indus. If it meant anything, it might point to the origin of the Saka era, not that of Vicramaditya.

Turning from this to the 'Raja Tarangini,' we find the following passages in Troyer's translation:-... (passages in French)

Before going further, it may be as well to point out what appears to be a fair inference from the above. That the first Vicramaditya, the friend of Pratapaditya, was so near in date to the second - he, in fact, appears to have been his grandfather - as to be confounded with him, and to have the name of Sakari applied to him, which in fact belonged to his grandson, the real destroyer of the Sakas.

My conviction is, that these paragraphs refer to one and the same event; and, assuming that the battle of Korur was fought 544 - the year before Vicramaditya sent Matrigupta to be his viceroy in Kashmir - what I believe happened was this: Some time after 750, when the Hindus were remodelling their history and their institutions, so as to mark their victory over the Buddhists, they determined on establishing two eras, which should be older than that of the Buddhists, A.D. 79, and for this purpose instituted one, ten cycles of sixty years each, before the battle of Korūr, and called it by the name of the hero of that battle, the most illustrious of their history; the other ten centuries, or 1000 years before the same date, and called it by the name of his father, Sri Harsha - a title he himself often bore in conjunction with his own name - the first consequently dated for 56 B.C., the second from 456. It need hardly be added that no Sri Harsha existed in the fifth century B.C., any more than a Vicramaditya in the first. ... If this view of the matter can be sustained, the advantage will be not only that the date of the battle of Korūr, and of the expulsion of the Sakas, Hunas, Yavanas, &c., from India will be fixed with mathematical precision in 544, but that one of the greatest mysteries connected with the history of the period will be cleared up, and the revival of the Hindu religion relegated to a much later period. If, on the other hand, it can be shown that this view of the matter is not tenable, we shall lose these advantages, but it will require a great deal more than that to prove that Vicramaditya, or any Hindu king, reigned in the first century B.C."

Fergusson made similar statements in another paper published in 1880 [8]. Max Müller then made the following comments in 1883 on the hypothesis proposed by Fergusson [9]:

"It has long been an open secret, however, among all who are interested in Indian coins and inscriptions, that there is absolutely no documentary evidence whatever for the existence of such a king Vikramāditya in the first century B.C. But the puzzle has always been, how the belief in such a king, living in the first century B.C., and in all his wonderful achievements, could have arisen, and this puzzle has at last been solved, I believe, by what I may be allowed to call the architectonical genius of Mr. Fergusson.

I do not mean to say that all difficulties which beset that period of Indian Chronology have been removed by him, but I cannot help thinking that in the main his solution will turn out to be correct. Mr. Fergusson tries to prove that what is called the era of Vikramāditya, 56 B.C., was a date arrived at by taking the date of the great battle of Korur, in which Vikramāditya, i.e. Harsha of Uggayini, finally defeated the Mlekkhas, 544 A.D., and by throwing back the beginning of the new era 6 X 100 (or 10 X 60) before that date, i.e. 56 B.C. By a similar process, i.e. by adding 10 X 100 years, another chronological era, called the Harsha era, was fixed at 456 B.C., though it never seems to have come into actual use.

This certainly seems very plausible. We should thus understand why much that was said originally of the Vikramāditya of the sixth century A.D. was reflected on the purely nominal Vikramāditya of the Vikrama era, 56 B.C., the inventor of the era being projected 600 years before his actual reign, a period when there is really no monumental, numismatic, or historical evidence of the existence of any such king.

It has been said that there is as yet no other evidence for this battle of Korur (Kurukshetra?) besides Albiruni's statement. But Albiruni does not invent battles. He tells us what he was told, and he may sometimes have misunderstood what he was told. But in our case the chronological side of the argument is too strong to be set aside by mere general suspicions and surmises, though, no doubt, it would have to yield to contemporaneous evidence which should make a great battle against foreign invaders at that time and in that place impossible. Besides, the statements of Tārānāth as to Harsha's victory near Multan, though no doubt very modern, cannot be due to mere accident."

Max Müller also gave the following information regarding the Battle of Korūr in the footnotes:

"This battle of Korur may be the same as that of Multan, mentioned by Tārānāth, 'Sri Harsha abolished the teaching of the Mlekkhas by massacring them at Multan.' Asaṅga and Vasubandhu were his contemporaries; his predecessor was called Gambhirapaksha, his successor Sila." [10]

> *"The same date 466 Saka = 544 A.D. is mentioned in Śatrungaya Māhātmya as the beginning of Vikramāditya's reign; Kern, Preface, p. 15, on the authority of Wilford."* [11]

Based on the evidence of Al-Biruni and Śatrunjaya Māhātmya, an epic battle was fought in 544 CE at a place called Korūr, which was located close to current day Multan in Pakistan. The original name of Multan was Mūlasthāna, which means "place of origin". There was a famous Sun temple at Mūlasthāna. Muslim rulers kept it as a bargaining chip and threatened to destroy it if any Hindu ruler planned to attack them to take back the area originally belonging to Hindus. Hindu rulers backed down under such threat. This Sun temple was totally destroyed by Mahmud of Ghazni in 1026 CE.

We have seen that the Hūṇas were the most devastating force during the fifth and sixth century of the Common Era. The Persian and Indian civilizations both were fighting for survival against these barbarians from Central Asia. So, chronologically the Hūṇas were the attacking force during the Battle of Korūr. We also know from the Aphsaḍ stone inscription of Ādityasena that the Hūṇas suffered a humiliating defeat at the hands of Maukharis. Thus, the hero of the epic battle at Korūr was a Maukhari king. The Maukhari king who inflicted a crushing defeat on the invading Hūṇas can then be identified as Īśānavarman as he was the first ruler in the dynasty to assume the title of "Mahārājādhirāja", and naturally would have been called upon to confront the Hūṇas.

We have a small problem here, however. In the Harahā stone inscription, supposedly written in 554 CE, Īśānavarman is shown conquering the Āndhras and the Śūlikas, but the inscription is silent about conquering the Hūṇas. If Īśānavarman had defeated the Hūṇas in 544 CE, this victory would certainly be mentioned in the Harahā stone inscription, if the inscription was written in 554 CE. If the Harahā stone inscription does not mention the defeat of the Hūṇas by the Maukharis, then most probably it had not taken place at the time of writing of the inscription. However, the date of 544 CE for the Battle of Korūr and the rout of the Hūṇas is tantalizingly close to the known date of Īśānavarman, and he is the most likely hero of this battle. The answer to this problem comes from the book "The Maukharis" [12]:

> *"It was suggested, however, that atirikta which means 'increased' also means 'redundant' or 'superfluous', in which case eleven years would have to be subtracted from six hundred, giving us the date of the inscription as 589."*

It now seems likely that the date of the Harahā stone inscription is 11 less than 600 or year 589, rather than 11 more than 600 or year 611. If the date of the Harahā stone inscription is corrected to year 589, it would become equivalent to 532 CE and the epic battle with the Hūṇas would still be 12 years away. Meanwhile, Īśānavarman would be expanding his empire and growing in strength to defend the kingdom from the Hūṇas. Based on the foregoing discussion and information presented in previous chapters, we are now in a position to develop the revised chronology of the Later Guptas and Maukharis.

7.5 Timeline

Table 7.2 shows the proposed chronology of the Maukharis along with the currently accepted chronology. The chronology has been adjusted to be consistent with two important dates of Īśānavarman's reign: one, he was reigning when the Harahā stone inscription was written in 532 CE and two, the Battle of Korūr was fought under his leadership in 544 CE.

Table 7.2: Maukhari chronology

Kings	Modern Chronology	Proposed Chronology
Yajñavarman		c. 430-445 CE
Śārdūlavarman		c. 445-460 CE
Anantavarman		c. 460-475 CE
Harivarman	510-550 CE [13]	c. 480-495 CE
Ādityavarman		c. 495-510 CE
Īśvaravarman		c. 510-525 CE
Īśānavarman	c. 550-576 CE [14]	c. 525-550 CE
Śarvavarman	c. 576-580 CE [14]	c. 550-575 CE
Avantivarman	c. 580-600 CE [14]	c. 575-600 CE
Grahavarman	600-605 CE [13]	c. 600-606 CE

Since beginning this work on the reconstruction of India's history, one puzzle has been to figure out who was the patron of the renowned astronomer Āryabhaṭa. It is a matter of great intellectual satisfaction that we now have an answer to this question. It could not be but that great astronomers like Varāhamihira and Āryabhaṭa needed great patrons of science to flourish. In the case of Varāhamihira, we have seen in "India after Alexander" that his patron was the great emperor Yaśodharmā Vikramāditya. Let us now therefore identify the patron of Āryabhaṭa. Āryabhaṭa has given information about his birth in Āryabhaṭīya, which has been translated to mean that Āryabhaṭa was 23 years old in the year 3600 of the Kali era. It is thus believed that Āryabhaṭa wrote the Āryabhaṭīya in 499 CE and he was born in 476 CE. However, commentator Someśvara (11th century) had interpreted the relevant verse to mean that Āryabhaṭa was born 23 years after 3600 years of Kali era had passed [15]. This will place the birth of Āryabhaṭa in 522 CE. Also, it is believed that Āryabhaṭa did his work at Pāṭaliputra, current day Patna. This is based on a wrong identification of the city "Kusumapura", which was another name for Kānyakubja, present day Kanauj instead of Patna. Kusumapura means the city of flowers, and Kanauj is still famous for the fragrances made there from flowers. Since the Maukharis were ruling from Kānyakubja, a close look at Table 7.2 shows that Āryabhaṭa's patron was Mahārājādhirāja Īśānavarman, the destroyer of the Hūṇa hordes and the saviour of India.

For the Later Gupta chronology, we need to consider another piece of evidence. This evidence is the dated Shahpur stone image inscription of Ādityasena. The Later Gupta rulers starting with Ādityasena obtained sovereignty after the death of Harṣavardhana and assumed the title of Mahārājādhirāja. The Shahpur stone image inscription has been described as follows by Fleet [16]:

> *"The inscription refers itself to the time of Ādityasena, of the family of the Guptas of Magadha. Its date, in numerical symbols, is the year sixty-six, on the seventh (?) day of the bright fortnight of the month Mārga, i.e. Mārgaśira or Mārgaśīrsha (November-December). The era is not specified; but from the known facts of Ādityasena's history, it is that of Harshavardhana of Kanauj, commencing A.D. 606 or 607; and the result for this date, therefore is A.D. 672-73. The inscription is one of solar worship; and the object of it is to record, in the first place, some grant, the details of which are illegible in line 1; and, in the second place, the installation of the image by the Balādhikṛta Sālapaksha, in, apparently, the agrahāra of Nālanda."*

Since Ādityasena's father Mādhavagupta was given protection by Harṣavardhana, it seems reasonable that Ādityasena would have used the era started by Harṣavardhana. Thus the known date of Ādityasena is 672 CE, assuming that Harṣa era started in 606 CE. Another chronological marker is that Harṣagupta attacked Vallabhī in 500 CE as discussed in Chapter 5. Also, Kumāragupta fought Īśānavarman and Dāmodaragupta fought a Maukhari ruler, which could be either Īśānavarman or his son Śarvavarman. We will assume that it was Śarvavarman. Based on these considerations, the revised chronology of the Later Guptas is shown in Table 7.3.

Table 7.3: Later Gupta chronology

Kings	Modern Chronology	Proposed Chronology
Kṛṣṇagupta	490-505 CE [17]	c. 480-495 CE
Harṣagupta	505-525 CE [17]	c. 495-510 CE
Jīvitagupta I	525-540 CE [17]	c. 510-525 CE
Kumāragupta	540-560 CE [17]	c. 525-550 CE
Dāmodaragupta		c. 550-575 CE
Mahāsenagupta	575-601 CE [17]	c. 575-600 CE
Devagupta I		c. 600-606 CE
Mādhavagupta		
Ādityasena	650-675 CE [17]	c. 650-675 CE
Devagupta II	675-700 CE [18]	c. 675-700 CE
Viṣṇugupta	700-725 CE [18]	c. 700-725 CE
Jīvitagupta II	725 CE [13]	725 CE

The battle for supremacy between the Later Guptas and the Maukharis led to many intrigues, and to the rise of a great emperor, who will be the focus of our attention next.

Notes:

1. Fleet (1888): 226-228.
2. Śāstri (1917-18).
3. Fleet (1888): 219-221.
4. Fleet (1888): 200-208.
5. Fleet (1888): 213-218.
6. Sachau (1910): 6.
7. Fergusson (1876): 745-747.
8. Fergusson (1880).
9. Max Müller (1883): 281-283.
10. Max Müller (1883): 282, Footnote 1.
11. Max Müller (1883): 282, Footnote 2.
12. Pires (1934): 76.
13. Śrivāstava (2007): 452-453.
14. Majumdar et al. (1997): 70.
15. Dāji (1865).
16. Fleet (1888): 208-210.
17. Sen (1999): 247-248.
18. Cunningham (1882): 166.

nābhiṣeko na saṃskārah siṃhasya kriyate vane|

vikramārjitasattvasya svayameva mṛgendratā||

-- Neither coronation nor consecration is performed for the lion in the forest. Lion gains the right (to rule the jungle) because of his own prowess.

- A Sanskrit Proverb

8. THE ROAR OF THE LIONS

The fight for supremacy between the Later Guptas and the Maukharis entangled another dynasty called the Puṣyabhūti dynasty in its web. The genealogy of the Puṣyabhūti dynasty is given in the Madhuban Copper Seal inscription of Harṣavardhana as follows [1]:

"(Line 1) Om. Hail!

From the great Royal residence of victory, (furnished) with boats, elephants and horses – from Kapitthikā:-

(There was) the Mahārāja Naravardhana, begotten of Vajriṇīdevī, his son, who meditated on his feet, (was) the devout worshipper of the Sun, the Mahārāja Rājyavardhana [I.].

Begotten on Apsarodevī, his son, who meditated on his feet, (was) the devout worshipper of the Sun, the Mahārāja Ādityavardhana.

Begotten on Mahāsenaguptādevī, his son, who meditated on his feet, (was) the devout worshipper of the Sun, the Parambhaṭṭāraka Mahārājādhirāja Prabhākaravardhana, whose fame crossed the four oceans; before whom other kings bowed down on account of his prowess and out of affection for him; who wielded his power for the due maintenance of the castes and orders of life, (and) who, like the sun, relieved the distress of the people. Begotten on the queen of spotless fame Yaśomatī, his son, who meditated on his feet, (was) the devout worshipper of Sugata (Buddha)- like Sugata solely delighting in the welfare of others - the Parambhaṭṭāraka Mahārājādhirāja Rājyavardhana [II.], the tendrils of whose bright fame overspread the whole orb of the earth; who appropriated the glory of Dhanada, Varuṇa, Indra and the other guardian (deities) of the world; who gladdened the hearts of suppliants by many donations of wealth and land acquired in righteous ways, (and) who surpassed the conduct of former kings.

He in battle curbed Devagupta and all the other kings together, like vicious horses made to turn away from the lashes of the whip. Having uprooted his adversaries, having conquered the earth, having acted kindly towards the people, he through his trust in promises lost his life in the enemy's quarters.

(L. 7.) His younger brother, who meditates on his feet, the devout worshipper of Maheśvara (Śiva)- like Maheśvara taking compassion on all beings- the Parambhaṭṭāraka Mahārājādhirāja Harsha issues this command to the Mahāsūmantas, Mahārājas, Dauḥsādhasādhanikas, Pramātāras, Rājasthānīyas, Kumārāmātyas, Uparikas, Vishayapatis, regular and irregular soldiers, servants and others assembled at the village of Somakuṇḍakā, which belongs to the Kuṇḍadhānī vishaya in the Śrāvastī bhukti, and to the resident people-

(L. 10.) Be it known to you! Having ascertained that this village of Somakuṇḍakā was held by the Brāhmaṇa Vāmarathya on the strength of a forged charter, I therefore have broken that charter

and taken (the village) away from him, and, for the increase of the spiritual merit and fame of my father, the Parambhaṭṭāraka Mahārājādhirāja Prabhākaravardhanadeva, of my mother, the Parambhaṭṭārikā Mahādevī, the ... Yaśomatīdevī and of my revered eldest brother, the Parambhaṭṭāraka Mahārājādhirāja Rājyavardhanadeva have given in the ... of a donation (to Brāhmaṇs), as an agrahāra, extending to its proper boundaries, with the udraṅga, together with all income that might be claimed by the king's family, exempt from all obligations, as a piece taken out of the district (to which it belongs), to follow the succession of sons and sons' sons, for as long as the moon, the sun and the earth endure, according to the maxim of bhūmichchhidra - to the Bhaṭṭa Vātasvāmin, who is of the gotra, of Sāvaṃi and a student of the Chhandogas, and the Bhaṭṭa Śivadevasvāmin who is of the gotra of Vishṇuvṛddha and a fellow-student of the Bahvṛchas. Knowing this, you should assent to this, and the resident people, being ready to obey my commands, should make over only to these two, the tulya-meya, the share of the produce, payments in money and other kinds of income, as they may be due, and should render service to them. Moreover:

(L. 16.) Those who profess (to belong to) the noble line of our family and others should approve of this donation. Of fortune, unstable as lightning and a bubble of water, donations and the preservation of others' fame are the (real) fruit.

By deeds, thoughts and words one should do good to the living. This Harsha has declared to be the very best way of earning religious merit.

(L. 17.) The dūtaka in this matter is the Mahāparamātāra Mahāsāmanta, the illustrious Skandagupta. And by order of the great officer in charge of the office of records, the Sāmanta Mahārāja Īsvaragupta, (this was) engraved by Garjara.

The year 20 5 Mārgaśīrsha-vadi 6."

According to this inscription, the genealogy of the Puṣyabhūti dynasty ran from father to son in the following order: Naravardhana, Rājyavardhana (I), Ādityavardhana, Prabhākaravardhana, and Rājyavardhana (II). After Rājyavardhana (II), his brother Harṣavardhana ascended the throne. The Sonpat Copper Plate inscription starts the genealogy with King Rājyavardhana (I) and continues as above [2]. Ādityavardhana married the Later Gupta princess Mahāsenaguptā, sister of Mahāsenagupta. Since Ādityavardhana did not assume the title Mahārājādhirāja, which signifies sovereignty and his kingdom was adjacent to the Maukharis, we can conclude that Ādityavardhana was a subordinate ruler under the Maukharis. Also, to fight the Hūṇas at the Battle of Korūr near Multan in Pakistan, Īśānavarman would have to cross the kingdom of Thanesar. Thus Ādityavardhana could not have married Mahāsenaguptā, sister of Mahāsenagupta, without the blessing of the Maukhari monarch. After his father Dāmodaragupta died fighting the Maukharis, Mahāsenagupta accepted Maukhari sovereignty. As a test of his loyalty, Mahāsenagupta had to fight Susthitavarman, ruler of Kāmrūpa, under the aegis of the Maukharis. After the death of Harṣavardhana, the Later Gupta ruler Ādityasena became sovereign and assumed the title of Mahārājādhirāja. From Ādityasena to Jīvitagupta II, all Later Gupta rulers assumed the title of Mahārājādhirāja. Keeping his enhanced prestige in mind, the Later Gupta ruler Ādityasena in his Aphsaḍ stone inscription tells that his grandfather Mahāsenagupta defeated Susthitavarman, ruler of Kāmrūpa, on the banks of Lauhitya (Brahmaputra river), but fails to mention that he did it under the banner of the Maukharis.

Prabhākaravardhana was the first ruler of the Puṣyabhūti dynasty to assume the title of Mahārājādhirāja. Prabhākaravardhana has been called "a lion to the Hūṇa deer" by Bāṇa in the Harṣacharita. Prabhākaravardhana's daughter Rājyaśrī was married to Maukhari ruler Grahavarman. In 606 CE, Grahavarman was killed by the Later Gupta ruler Devagupta, and Rājyaśrī was imprisoned. Rājyavardhana defeated Devagupta and killed him, but was treacherously murdered by the Gauḍa king Śaśāṅka. Under these tragic conditions, Harṣa had to accept the throne of Thanesar as well as Kanauj. Harṣa conquered most of North India and ruled till 647 CE. He was not able to conquer South India, as his move was checked by the Chalukya ruler Pulakeśina II.

It is considered by modern historians that the history of Kanauj after Harṣa is completely dark till the reign of Yaśovarman. The evidence from Nepal suggests that the kingdom went back to the Maukharis after Harṣa died issueless. This makes perfect sense as Harṣa had received the kingdom of Kanauj from the Maukharis. The evidence from Nepal is as follows [3]:

> *"The Nepāl inscription, which mentions the name of Aditya Sena, is a long record of Raja Jaya Deva, bearing the date of Samvat 153 Kartika Sudi 9, or A.D. 606+153 = 759. Of Siva Deva, the father of Jaya Deva, there are two inscriptions, dated in Samvat 119 and S. 143, or A.D. 725 and 749. Of this prince Jaya Deva's inscription gives the following important notice:-*
>
> *That prince respectfully took illustrious Vatsā Devi to be his queen, as if she were Fortune, her the daughter of illustrious Bhoga Varman, who was the crest jewel of the illustrious Varmans of the valorous Maukhari race, and who by his glory put to shame (all) hostile kings, and the grand-daughter of great Aditya Sena, the illustrious lord of Magadha.*
>
> *From this account we get the following genealogy, with the approximate dates:-*
>
> *A.D. 660. - Aditya Sena.*
>
> *„ 690. - daughter married Bhoga Varman Maukhari.*
>
> *„ 720. - Vatsā Devi married Siva Deva of Nepāl 725-749.*
>
> *„ 750. - Jaya Deva, A.D. 759.*

> *It will be observed that the date here assigned to Aditya Sena agrees with that already derived from the Shāhpur inscription. I should, however, mention that Pandit Bhagwān Lāl reads the Shāhpur date as 88 instead of 55, which would bring Aditya Sena down to 606+88 = 694 A.D. I cannot, however, agree with this reading as both the figures of the date are common Bengali fives."*

There is no reason for Śivadeva and Jayadeva to use the Harṣa era having a start date of 606 CE as the empire of Harṣavardhana did not extend to Nepal. Śivadeva and Jayadeva were using the Mānadeva era prevalent in Nepal, which started in 576 CE. Accordingly, the known dates of Śivadeva are 695 CE and 719 CE, and the known date of Jayadeva is 729 CE. Bhogavarmā, the Maukhari ruler, was married to the daughter of Ādityasena, the Later Gupta emperor. Śivadeva, the ruler of Nepal, was married to Vatsadevī, the daughter of Bhogavarmā. Jayadeva was the son of Śivadeva and Vatsadevī. Jayadeva married Rājyamatī, the daughter of Śrī Harṣadeva, the ruler of Gauḍa, Oḍra and Kaliṅga [4]. Since Bhogavarmā was married to the daughter of Ādityasena, he can be considered to have ruled at the same time as Devagupta II, son of Ādityasena. Based on the preceding discussion and the discussion of the Maukharis and Later Guptas in the previous chapter, the proposed chronology of the Maukharis, Later Guptas and Puṣyabhūtis is shown in Table 8.1.

The Puṣyabhūti dynasty started with the rule of Naravardhana during the second quarter of the sixth century. Possibly, Rājyavardhana (I) fought under Īśānavarman during the Battle of Korūr. In recognition of his bravery, he was made a king by Īśānavarman. From then onwards, the fortunes of Puṣyabhūti dynasty kept on rising. Though the backbone of the Hūṇas was broken during the Battle of Korūr, they still remained as a minor irritant for a long while. After the Battle of Korūr, the Hūṇas were cut off from their roots and lost their destructive power. They established a locality called Hūṇa Maṇḍala and were routinely defeated by Hindu rulers. Prabhākaravardhana defeated the Hūṇas when they sought to probe the borders. Later, when he was old, he sent his son Rājyavardhana (II) to crush the Hūṇas. When Rājyavardhana (II) returned after his victorious campaign, his father had already passed away.

Table 8.1: Maukhari, Later Gupta and Puṣyabhūti chronology

Maukharis	**Later Guptas**	**Puṣyabhūtis**
Harivarman c. 480-495 CE	Kṛṣṇagupta c. 480-495 CE	
Ādityavarman c. 495-510 CE	Harṣagupta c. 495-510 CE	
Īśvaravarman c. 510-525 CE	Jīvitagupta I c. 510-525 CE	Naravardhana c. 525-545 CE
Īśānavarman c. 525-550 CE	Kumāragupta c. 525-550 CE	Rājyavardhana (I) c. 545-560 CE
Śarvavarman c. 550-575 CE	Dāmodaragupta c. 550-575 CE	Ādityavardhana c. 560-580 CE
Avantivarman c. 575-600 CE	Mahāsenagupta c. 575-600 CE	Prabhākaravardhana c. 580-606 CE
Grahavarman c. 600-606 CE	Devagupta I c. 600-606 CE	Rājyavardhana (II) 606 CE
	Mādhavagupta	Harṣavardhana 606-647 CE
	Ādityasena c. 650-675 CE	
Bhogavarmā c. 675-700	Devagupta II c. 675-700 CE	
	Viṣṇugupta c. 700-725 CE	
	Jīvitagupta II 725 CE	

After Rājyavardhana (II) was treacherously murdered by the Gauḍa king Śaśāṅka, Harṣa ascended the throne. The Harṣa era commemorates the accession of Harṣa Vikramāditya to the throne in 606 CE. Modern history knows of Harṣa Vikramāditya as Harṣa Śīlāditya. Vikramāditya and Śīlāditya are synonyms. Harṣa Vikramāditya is considered to have converted to Buddhism, based on the evidence of Hiuen Tsang. There is no evidence for this based on Indian sources. Harṣa Vikramāditya was a devout Śaiva, as described in the Madhuban Copper Seal inscription. After conquering most of North India, Harṣa tried to conquer South India, but was stopped by Pulakeśina II, a Chālukya monarch. We will discuss the rise of the Chālukyas next.

Notes:

1. Kielhorn (1902-03).
2. Fleet (1888): 231-232.
3. Cunningham and Garrick (1883): 80.
4. Regmi (1983): 236.

sthirā vaḥ santvāyudhā parāṇude vīlū uta pratiṣkabhe |

yuṣmākamastu taviṣī paniyasī mā martyasya māyinaḥ | |

-- Let your weapons stay unyielding to drive away the enemies and stay strong to stop their march. Let your strength be praiseworthy, not those of the deceiving people.

- Ṛgveda 1.39.2

9. THE CHILDREN OF HĀRITI

According to Indian history books, the Chālukya dynasty was established at the beginning of the sixth century. In this chapter, we will go deeper into the origins of the Chālukya dynasty to rediscover their roots. We can start with the mythical account of the origins of Chālukyas, as summarized by Fleet [1]:

> *"The mythical account of the origin of the name Chalkya, Chalikya, and Chalukya, the etymology of which has not yet been satisfactorily explained, is that the founder of the race sprang from the spray of a water-pot (chulka, chuluka, chaluka), when Hāriti, who wore five tufts of hair on his head, was pouring out a libation to the gods. The probability is that the oldest and original form was Chalkya, and that the other forms were created by the use of pronunciative vowels. The Chalukyas belong originally to the Somavamsa, or lunar race; and, like the early Kadambas, they claim*

to belong to the Mānavya gotra and to be 'of the sons of Hāriti'. It is suggested by Mr. Rice, that they borrowed these details of descent from the Kadambas, as being the most powerful and important family supplanted by them in Western India. But this can hardly be the case; for, these same details are given in the earliest known Chalukya inscription, the Khedā or Kaira grant of Vijayarāja, dated Saka 394 (A.D. 472-3), which was engraved before the Chalukyas left the northern part of this Presidency and, travelling southwards, came in contact with the Kadambas. The kuladevatā, or family-god, of the Chalukyas was Vishnu; and the principal emblem that the seals of their grants and their coins always bear is a boar, derived from one of the incarnations of Vishnu. But, in spite of this fact, in early times they displayed a considerable amount of tolerance in matters of religion, and patronised the Jain and Saiva, equally with the Vaishnava, faiths. And in the later generations they devoted themselves almost entirely to the Saiva religion, particularly in the linga form of worship.

The early tradition of the family is that fifty-nine kings of this dynasty reigned at Ayodhyā, and after them sixteen more over the region of the south, by which must be meant the northern part of the Dekkan immediately to the south of Ayodhyā. There was then a temporary obscuration of their power, which was restored in the person of Jayasimha I.

No inscriptions of the time of Jayasimha I., also called Jayasimharāja and Jayasimhavallabha, are as yet known to exist. Should any be hereafter discovered, they will probably carry back the genealogy to still earlier times; for the directions of the Sanskrit lawyers, followed in nearly all these records, are, that the genealogical portion of the grant must give the name of at least three generations. At present the name of Jayasimha I. is the earliest 'historical name in this dynasty that we possess."

As described above, the Chālukyas derived their name from "Chuluka" or curved/cupped palm to hold water. They had another version of this myth in which their progenitor sprang from the water of oblation held in the "Chuluka" of Brahmā as follows [2]:

> *"The inscription, which is of the time of Vikramāditya VI., deduces the genealogy from Vishnu, through Brahmā, who was born in the water-lily that grew out of Vishnu's navel, Manu, Māndavya, and Harita, to Hāriti-Panchasikha, from whose water-pot the Chalukyas sprang as stated above. —Bilhana, the Vidyāpati or Chief Pandit of Vikramāditya VI. , gives a somewhat different account, and says (Vikramānkadevacharita, I., 31-58) that, when Brahmā was engaged in the morning ceremonies on the bank of the river of the gods, Indra came and represented to him that the inhabitants of the earth were becoming so indifferent about religion that it seemed as if all sacrifice to the gods would soon cease, and asked him to create a hero to destroy the enemies of religion. Brahmā turned his eyes, full of meditation, upon his water-pot, from which there then sprang forth a warrior, clothed in golden armour proof against all weapons, who was dedicated by Brahma to the destruction of the enemies of the gods. He attained pre-eminence over all the kings of the earth; and by him there was founded a family, of which Hārita came to be considered the ādi-pums or 'first progenitor,' and in which Mānavya was born, who humbled the pride of his enemies,…"*

Now that we have presented the accounts of the mythical origins of Chālukyas, let us get an overview of the current understanding of the history of the Chālukyas. For this, we will follow the most famous inscription of the Chālukya dynasty, the Aihole Inscription, which is important for many reasons. Besides giving the genealogy of the Chālukyas up to Pulakeśina II, it also gives the date of inscription in the Śaka era. It also provides the time elapsed since the Mahābhārata war till the writing of the inscription. The Aihole inscription of Pulakeśina II is as follows [3]:

"(Verse 1.) Victorious is the holy Jinendra--he who is exempt from old age, death and birth--in the sea of whose knowledge the whole world is comprised like an island.

(V. 2.) And next, long victorious is the immeasurable, wide ocean of the Chalukya family, which is the birth-place of jewels of men that are ornaments of the diadem of the earth.

(V. 3.) And victorious for very long is Satyāśraya, who in bestowing gifts and honours on the brave and on the learned, both together on either, observes not the rule of correspondency of number.

(V. 4.) When many members of that race, bent on conquest, applied to whom the title of Favourite of the Earth had at last become appropriate, had passed away,-

(V. 5.) There was, of the Chalukya lineage, the king named Jayasimha-vallabha, who in battle-where horses, footsoldiers and elephants, bewildered, fell down under the strokes of many hundreds of weapons, and where thousands of frightful headless trunks and of flashes of rays of swords were leaping to and fro--by his bravery made Fortune his own, even though she is suspected of fickleness.

(V. 6.) His son was he who was named Ranarāga, of divine dignity, the one master of the world, whose superhuman nature, (even) when he was asleep, people knew from the pre-eminence of his form.

(V. 7.) His son was Polekeśin, who, though endowed with the moon's Beauty, and though the favorite of Fortune, became the bridegroom of Vātāpipurī.

(V. 8.) Whose path in the pursuit of the three objects of life the kings on earth even now are unable to follow; and bathed by whom with the water of the purificatory rite, when he performed the horse-sacrifice, the earth beamed with brightness.

(V. 9.) His son was Kirtivarman, the night of doom to the Nalas, Mauryas and Kadambas, whose mind, although his thoughts kept

aloof from others' wives, was attracted by the Fortune of his adversary.

(V. 10.) Who, having secured the fortune of victory by his valour in war, being a scent-elephant of a king, of great strength, at once completely broke down the multitude of the broad kadamba trees-the Kadambas.

(V. 11.) When his desire was bent on the dominion of the lord of the gods, his younger brother Mangaleśa became king, who by the sheets of dust of his army of horse, encamped on the shores of the eastern and western seas, stretched an awning over the quarters.

(V. 12.) Who in that house which was the battle-field took in marriage the damsel, the Fortune of the Kaṭachchuris, having scattered the gathering gloom, (viz.) the array of elephants (of the adversary), with hundreds of bright-rayed lamps, (viz.) the swords (of his followers).

(V. 13) And again, when he was desirous of taking the island of Revati, his great army with many bright banners, which had ascended the ramparts, as it was reflected in the water of the sea appeared like Varuṇa's forces, quickly come there at once at his word (of command).

(V. 14.) When his elder brother's son, named Polekeśin, of a dignity like Nahusha's, was coveted by Fortune, and finding his uncle to be jealous of him thereat, had formed the resolution to wander abroad as an exile,-

(V. 15.) That Mangaleśa, whose great strength became on all sides reduced by the application of the powers of good counsel and energy gathered by Him, abandoned, together with the effort to secure the kingdom for his own son, both that no mean kingdom of his and his life.

(V. 16.) Then, on the subversion of that rule encompassed by the darkness of enemies, the whole world grew light again, invaded as it were by the lustrous rays of His irresistible splendour. Or when was

it that the sky ceased to be black like a swarm of bees with thundering clouds, in which flashes of lightning were dancing like banners, and the edges of which were crushed in the rushing wind?

(V. 17.) When, having found the opportunity, he who was named Appāyika, and Govinda approached with their troops of elephants to conquer the country north of the Bhaimarathi, the one in battle through His armies came to know the taste of fear, while the other at once received the reward of the services rendered by him.

(V. 18.) When He was besieging Vanavāsi, which for a girdle has the rows of haṃsa birds that sport on the high waves of the Varadā as their play-place, and which by its wealth rivalled the city of the gods, that fortress on land, having the surface of the earth all around covered with the great sea of his army, to the looker-on seemed at once converted into a fortress in the water.

(V. 19.) Although in former days they had acquired happiness by renouncing the seven sins, the Gaṅga and Ālupa lords, being subdued by His dignity, were always intoxicated by drinking the nectar of close attendance upon him.

(V. 20.) In the Konkaṇas the impetuous waves of the forces directed by Him speedily swept away the rising wavelets of pools-the Mauryas.

(V. 21.) When, radiant like the destroyer of Pura, He besieged Purī, the Fortune of the western sea, with hundreds of ships in appearance like arrays of rutting elephants, the sky, dark-blue as a young lotus and covered with tiers of massive clouds, resembled the sea, and the sea was like the sky.

(V. 22.) Subdued by His splendour, the Lāṭas, Mālavas and Gūrjaras became as it were teachers of how feudatories, subdued by force, ought to behave.

(V. 23.) Harsha, whose lotus-feet were arrayed with the rays of the jewels of the diadems of hosts of feudatories prosperous with unmeasured might, through Him had his mirth (harsha) melted away

by fear, having become loathsome with his rows of lordly elephants fallen in battle.

(V. 24.) While He was ruling the earth with his broad armies, the neighbourhood of the Vindhya, by no means destitute of the lustre of the many sandbanks of the Revā, shone even more brightly by his great personal splendour, having to be avoided by his elephants because, as it seemed, they by their bulk rivalled the mountains.

(V. 25.) Almost equal to Indra, He by means of all the three powers, gathered by him according to rule, and by his noble birth and other excellent qualities, acquired the sovereignty over the three Mahārāshṭrakas with their nine and ninety thousand villages.

(V. 26.) Through the excellencies of their householders prominent in the pursuit of the three objects of life, and having broken the pride of other rulers of the earth, the Kaliṅgas with the Kosalas by His army were made to evince signs of fear.

(V. 27.) Hard pressed (pishṭa) by Him, Pishṭapura became a fortress not difficult of access; wonderful (to relate), the ways of the Kali age to Him were quite inaccessible!

(V. 28.) Ravaged by Him, the water of Kunāla--coloured with the blood of men killed with many weapons, and the land within it overspread with arrays of accoutred elephants-was like the cloud-covered sky in which the red evening-twilight has risen.

(V. 29.) With his sixfold forces, the hereditary troops and the rest, who raised spotless chowries, hundreds of flags, umbrellas, and darkness, and who churned the enemy elated with the sentiments of heroism and energy, He caused the splendour of the lord of the Pallavas, who had opposed the rise of his power, to be obscured by the dust of his army, and to vanish behind the walls of Kāñchipura.

(V. 30.) When straightway He strove to conquer the Cholas, the Kāverī, who has the darting carps for her tremulous eyes, had her current obstructed by the causeway formed by his elephants whose

rutting-juice was dripping down, and avoided the contact with the ocean.

(V. 31.) There He caused great prosperity to the Cholas, Keralas and Pāṇḍyas, he being the hot-rayed son to the hoar-frost--the army of the Pallavas.

(V. 32.) While He, Satyāśraya, endowed with the powers of energy, mastery and good counsel,--having conquered all the quarters, having dismissed the kings full of honours, having done homage to gods and Brahmans, having entered the city of Vātāpī- is ruling, like one city, this earth which has the dark-blue waters of the surging sea for its moat;

(V. 33.) (Now) when thirty (and) three thousand and five years besides, joined with seven hundred years, have passed since the Bhārata war;

(V. 34.) And when fifty (and) six and five hundred years of the Śaka kings also have gone by in the Kali age;

(V. 35.) This stone mansion of Jinendra, a mansion of every kind of greatness, has been caused to be built by the wise Ravikīrti, who has obtained the highest favour of that Satyāśraya whose rule is bounded by the three oceans.

(V. 36.) Of this eulogy and of this dwelling of the Jina revered in the three worlds, the wise Ravikīrti himself is the author and also the founder.

(V. 37.) May that Ravikīrti be victorious, who full of discernment has used the abode of the Jina, firmly built of stone, for a new treatment of his theme, and who thus by his poetic skill has attained to the fame of Kālidāsa and of Bhāravi!"

According to this inscription, early Chalukya kings ruled in the following order: Jayasiṃha, his son Raṇarāga, Raṇarāga's son Pulakeśina I, Pulakeśina I's son Kirtivarman I, Kirtivarman I's younger brother Mangaleśa, and then Pulakeśina II, who was the son of Kirtivarman I and nephew of Mangaleśa. Pulakeśina II has been called Satyāśraya in Verse 3 of this inscription. The biggest accomplishment of Pulakeśina II was to stop the advance of North Indian emperor Harṣavardhana. The Aihole inscription was written in 556 Śaka era or 634 CE. The inscription also states that at the time of writing, 3735 years had passed since the Mahābhārata war. Thus, at that time it was believed that the Mahābhārata war took place in 3102 BCE, keeping in mind that there was no 0 CE and 1 CE followed 1 BCE.

The Aihole inscription starts the genealogy of early Chālukya kings, starting from Jayasiṃha. The question is whether this Jayasiṃha was the founder of the Chālukya Dynasty. To address this question, we have compiled the list of Chālukya rulers along with the years they ruled, as shown in Table 9.1. As we can see, modern history does not accept the existence of any Chālukya ruler in the fifth century.

Table 9.1: Currently accepted Chālukya chronology [4]

King	Regnal period
Jayasiṃha	c. 500-520 CE
Raṇarāga	520-535 CE
Pulakeśina I	535-566 CE
Kirtivarman I	566-597 CE
Mangaleśa	597-610 CE
Pulakeśina II	610-642 CE
Vikramāditya I	655-681 CE
Vinayāditya	681-696 CE
Vijayāditya	696-733 CE
Vikramāditya II	733-747 CE
Kirtivarman II	747-757 CE

Let us negate this view by producing epigraphic evidence of the existence of a Chālukya ruler called Pulakeśina in the fifth century. Since other Chālukya rulers had the same name as Pulakeśina, this had created a lot of confusion among the early researchers of this dynasty. The early rulers of the Chālukya Dynasty have been hidden in the closets of history as certain facts were too inconvenient to fit in the jig-saw puzzle manufactured by modern historians. Let us therefore get those inconvenient truths out of the closet and try to give the early Chālukya rulers their proper place in history. Among the evidence for the rule of the Chālukyas in fifth century is a Chālukya inscription published by Professor Dowson in 1865 CE [5]:

> *"In that royal capital, the city of victory, . . . extensive as the expanse of the sky when clear from clouds at the approach of summer, illustrious for the numerous gem-like virtues of its various men, a solace to the sorrows of kings, who sought its refuge, and, like the great ocean, intent upon the maintenance of its depth and permanence, there was in the family of the Chālukyas, who were of the Mānavya stock, sons of Hārīti, and worshippers of the feet of Swāmī Mahāsena, a king named Jaya Sinha, whose fame was purer than a lotus under the beams of the moon when it comes forth to the sky from behind a mass of rain clouds. His son was Śrī Buddha Varmma Rājā, heroic in battle, dear as the sun, whose might . . . who was a continuous current of prosperity, and a thunderbolt piercing the dark clouds of his powerful foes. His son was Śrī Vijaya Rājā Sarvva, a hero unequalled in the earth, whose fame had tasted the waters of the four oceans, who was equal in dignity with Kuvera, Varuna, Indra, and Yama, a fortunate monarch who with his own arm (had scattered) the hosts (of his enemies), by whose great might the whole neighbouring region was subdued, in whom duty, wealth, and love were not inimical to each other, whose heart was bowed with the exceeding great joy . . . who was always devoted to the cherishing of his people, who was compassionate to the poor, and . . . who granted rewards as they were desired, and respectfully reverenced the feet of his parents. He (Śrī Vijaya Rājā Sarvva) announces to all governors of provinces, chief men of districts, heads of villages, and others (as follows) : Be it known to*

you that we have granted, with the pouring out of water, in the full moon of Vaisākha, for the increase of the merit and fame of ourself and our parents, to the general body of priests and students belonging to the Kaṇwa school of the Vājasaneya (division of the Yajur-veda) in the town of Jambusara, for the performance of the Bali, Charu, Vaiswadeva, Agnihotra, and other rites, the village of Pariyachasa . . . belonging to the province of Kāshākula, with the water-courses and all things standing thereon, free from all rights to forced labour for cutting and hewing . . . and into which the entrance of cheats and outcasts is interdicted, to be enjoyed for all time, as long as the sun, moon, sea, and earth shall endure, by the sons, grandsons, and descendants (of the following Brahmans) :-

Wherefore, having reflected that the world is (as frail) as the pith of a reed, bamboo or plantain—that enjoyment is as transitory as a wave of the ocean, that fortune is as unsteady as the leaves of the holy -fig tree agitated by a strong wind, and youth like water on the flowers of the blooming mimosa—let future proprietors of our own or any other race who are desirous of reaping the rewards of gifts of land, which confer a general benefit, respect and maintain this our grant. That ignorant man, with a mind shrouded in thick masses of darkness, who shall seize it, or shall abet the seizure of it, shall be guilty of the five great sins. And it has been said by the holy Vyāsa, the compiler of the Vedas:—

1. Sixty thousand years the giver of land dwells in heaven, but he who resumes or approves the resumption shall dwell the same number of years in hell.

2. Those who seize a grant of land are verily born (again) as black serpents dwelling in dry hollow trees in the arid forests of the Vindhya.

3. By Sagara and many other kings the earth has been enjoyed, and whoever at any time has possessed the earth has enjoyed its produce.

4. Strenuously guard, O Yudhishṭhira ! land granted afore time to the twice-born; for better than the gift (itself) is the conservation thereof, O best of rulers.

5. Gifts, productive of fame, have been granted in this world by former rulers for the sake of religion - these are like the unconsumed flowers of an offering - what honest man then would take them back again?

Written on the full moon of Vaiśākha, in the year three hundred and ninety-four, under the direction of Nanna Vāsāpaka, by Khuddaswāmī, the minister charged with the affairs of peace and war. Samvatsara 394, Vaiśākha-suddha. Engraved by Kshatriya Matṛ-sinha."

According to this inscription, the founder of the Chālukya Dynasty was Jaya Siṃha, who was followed by his son Buddha Varmā, who in turn was followed by his son Vijaya. The inscription was written when king Vijaya was ruling, and is dated Samvatsara 394. This is a huge problem for the accepted chronology as modern historians can think of only two options for the era used in this inscription: Vikrama era or Gupta/Ballabhī era. The Vikrama era makes the date of inscription as 337 CE and the Gupta/Ballabhī era makes it 713 CE, with the former making it too early and the latter too late. The obvious solution is that the intended era is the Śaka era, which will make the date of inscription as 472 CE. This, however, is an uncomfortable situation for modern historians as this is tantamount to accepting the existence of an earlier Śaka era, which was so much older than the Śaka era of 78 CE that over time Śaka had become equivalent to Samvatsara, both meaning year. One of the scholars trying to piece together the fragments of the early Chālukya history was Kāshināth Trimbak Telang, who wrote the following in 1875 CE regarding the era used in the inscription quoted above [6]:

"But before we can obtain any answer to this inquiry, it is necessary to take a review of the information which we do possess. Now the main facts regarding the Chālukya kings after the Śaka year 895 may be taken to be settled with reasonable certainty. At any rate the present paper is not concerned with them. But in spite of the great and fruitful labours of Sir Walter Elliot and others, we can scarcely be said to be yet in full possession of the facts regarding the earlier Chālukyas. Sir Walter Elliot himself, to whom we are indebted for the best part of the information which we possess about this dynasty, implies that the period before the Śaka year 895 is not well authenticated, expressly mentions "difficulties" and "improbabilities" attaching to the statements of the inscriptions in his possession, and endeavours to escape from these "difficulties" and "improbabilities" by what Mr. Fergusson describes, - and, I may add, justly describes - as a "violent adjustment." This is in 1836. In 1858 Sir Walter returns to the subject, and still speaks of "chronological obscurity" which he "hopes to clear up hereafter," but which, I own, appears to me to have remained nearly as dark at the end of his paper as at the beginning. He gives a fresh list of the Chālukya kings, about which it is to be noted, that it contains two very important modifications of statements contained in the previous list, without any explanation of those modifications. Meanwhile in 1844 Professor Bāl Gangādhar Shāstri, and in 1851 Sir LeGrand Jacob (then Major Jacob), had published in the Journal of our Society several copperplates of Chālukya princes, and made out their own lists from them, differing in some respects both from Sir Walter's original list of 1837 and from his amended list of 1858. In 1864 Professor Dowson appears on the scene, but he too still notes "deficiencies," still points out "discrepancies," still complains of "the loose and varying nature of the genealogies." Next comes Mr. Fergusson, who, although he does not, like his predecessors, add to the raw material available, proposes a new mode of working it up, so to speak; sets aside Sir Walter Elliot's "violent adjustment;" substitutes in its stead the theory of a "mislection or wilful alteration;" and makes rather short work of Professor Dowson's

suggested additions to Elliot's list. Lastly, in 1870, our late learned Vice-President Dr. Bhāu Dājī brings forward an inscription, assigning to one of the most eminent of the Chālukya kings a date quite irreconcileable with that which is given in Elliot's amended list, and which has been pronounced by Mr. Fergusson to be "fixed within very narrow limits."

It must, I take it, be at once admitted, that this looks very much like a hopelessly tangled web. Yet until it is unravelled, our knowledge of the early Chālukyas must be held to be, in great measure, imperfect. Mr. Fergusson's suggestion, indeed, with reference to the inconvenient Buddha Varma and Vijaya Rāja of Professor Dowson's plate, namely, that they should be referred to a different branch of the Chālukya family, would, if employed in all similar difficulties, place the several threads separately in our hands to re-arrange them afresh as we please. But that suggestion, I confess, appears to me equivalent to cutting the knot, not untying it. Dr. Bhāu Dājī, in his paper just referred to, promised us "the fullest notes" upon the Chālukya among other dynasties. But, unfortunately, his recent lamented death has deprived us of the benefit of his acuteness and extensive information in these matters.

Upon the best consideration that I have been able to give to the subject, I am bound to say, that I have not succeeded in hitting on any mode of reconciling all the published statements of copperplates and inscriptions regarding the Chālukyas. I will endeavour, however, to evolve some order out of at least one part of the chaos. And let us first take the earliest document available for our present purpose, namely, that translated by Professor Dowson. That document purports to bear the date - Vaisakha Suddha of the Saṃvatsara 394. Professor Dowson takes this to mean the Saṃvat or Vikrama year 394, equivalent to 338 A.C., and thus raises a factitious difficulty which, be it said with all deference to the learned Professor, does not exist. The notion that the word Saṃvatsara necessarily indicates that the so-called Vikrama era is referred to has been, I believe, attacked on various occasions, and

> *may now be safely taken to be exploded. Saṃvatsara is a common name for 'year,' and refers to no particular era whatever. Even the word Saṃvat - the word now-a-days employed to designate the Vikrama era - is not by any means confined to that sense. And in the Amarnath inscription deciphered by Dr. Bhāu Dājī, we have the expression - which is very noteworthy in this connexion - of Śaka Saṃvat. Professor Dowson, indeed, at the very beginning of his paper, after saying that "some doubt has hitherto been felt as to the era in which these plates are dated," goes on to ask - "Was the 'samvatsara' that of Vikramāditya or that of Ballabhi? - holding apparently that any other era but these two is out of the question. I cannot concur in this opinion. And in the particular case before us, the undoubted and indubitable fact that the other known grants of the Chālukya dynasty which bear any date are expressly dated in the Śaka Kāla, should lead us, I think, not only to discard both of Professor Dowson's alternatives, but to accept the one to which he does not even refer, namely, that the plate is dated in the Śaka era. If that is so, the year 394 of this plate must be taken to be the Śaka year, equivalent to 472 A.C. Professor Dowson has also given the name of the grantor in his plate as Vijaya Rāja Sarva, which, on the face of it, is rather an odd name. But the oddity is the result of an inadvertence on the part of the learned Professor. In the copperplate itself, of which he has luckily published a facsimile, the name is much less singular, being simply Vijaya Rāja. And now mark the results to which these rectifications lead. Taking the Śaka year 411 given by Captain Jervis's copperplate to be the correct date of Pulakeśi I., the Vijaya Rāja of Professor Dowson's plate may fairly be placed immediately before Pulakeśi."*

We can now add another name to the list of the three early Chālukya rulers -- that of Pulakeśina who was ruling in the Śaka year 411 or 489 CE. This date of the Śaka year 411 for Pulakeśina was so frustrating to colonial era historians that they proposed to substitute it with some other convenient year. Fergusson wrote the following in 1873 CE [7]:

"All this is bad enough, and renders inscriptions per se nearly useless for the purpose of fixing the dates of buildings or events; but it would be a fearful aggravation of the case, if, besides the difficulties attaching to the initial date, it should turn out that, either from negligence or design, the dates in the inscriptions were so falsified that they could not be depended upon. I have recently been led to suspect that this is the case in more instances than one; and it seems so important that it should be ascertained whether this is so or not, that I request you will allow me an opportunity of laying the case before your readers. The first case I wish to refer to, is the well-known copper-plate grant of Pulakeśi I. of the Chālukya dynasty, dated in 411 Śaka, or 489 A.D. This was first brought to the notice of the learned by Sir Walter Elliot, in the 4th volume of the Journal of the Royal Asiatic Society, p. 7, et seqq.; but even at that early date he saw the difficulty of reconciling this date with the circumstances narrated in the inscription, and therefore proposed (page 12) to substitute Śaka 610 for Śaka 411.

When I wrote on the subject in 1869 (J. R. A. S., new series, volume IV. p. 92), this appeared to me too violent a correction, and I suggested substituting 511 for 411; and if the facts are as stated in the inscription, and Pulakeśi I. was the grandfather of Pulakeśi II., which I see no reason for doubting, some such correction as this seems indispensable, but not to a greater extent than 100 years."

The problem with the date of the Śaka year 411 is that it is unambiguous. It is equivalent to 489 CE and there is no scope for fudging it. Prima facie, the evidence is clear that there was a Chālukya king Pulakeśina ruling in 489 CE. Since the historians were not willing to accept this date, they made the outrageous suggestion to modify the date itself.

Telang has mentioned that a copper plate in the possession of Professor Eggeling was dated in the Śaka year 534 and states that to be the third year of Satyāṣraya's reign [6]. Thus Satyāśraya started his reign in 610 CE. According to the Aihole inscription,

Satyāśraya was another name of Pulakeśina. Telang has also quoted an inscription according to which Śaka 532 (610 CE) was the twentieth year of another king's rule [6]. Thus the Chālukya king preceding Pulakeśina Satyāśraya ascended the throne in AD 591. This Chālukya king can be identified with Mangaleśa. Based on the discussion so far, the revised chronology of the main branch of Chālukya rulers is shown in Table 9.2.

Table 9.2: Revised Chālukya chronology

Accepted Chronology [4]		**Proposed Chronology**	
		Jayasiṃha I (Jayabhaṭa I Vītarāga)	c. 435-455 CE
		Buddha Varmā	c. 455-470 CE
		Vijaya Rāja	c. 470-485 CE
		Pulakeśina I	c. 485-500 CE
Jayasiṃha	c. 500-520 CE	Jayasiṃha II	c. 500-520 CE
Raṇarāga	520-535 CE	Raṇarāga	520-535 CE
Pulakeśina I	535-566 CE	Pulakeśina II	535-566 CE
Kirtivarman I	566-597 CE	Kirtivarman I	566-591 CE
Mangaleśa	597-610 CE	Mangaleśa	591-610 CE
Pulakeśina II	610-642 CE	Pulakeśina III Satyāśraya	610-642 CE
Vikramāditya I	655-681 CE	Vikramāditya I	655-681 CE
Vinayāditya	681-696 CE	Vinayāditya	681-696 CE
Vijayāditya	696-733 CE	Vijayāditya	696-733 CE
Vikramāditya II	733-747 CE	Vikramāditya II	733-747 CE
Kirtivarman II	747-757 CE	Kirtivarman II	747-757 CE

Based on the inscriptional evidence shown in this chapter that Vijaya Rāja was ruling in 472 CE (Samvat 394), his grandfather Jayasiṃha I would be ruling around 450 CE. The find place of the aforementioned inscription was Kheda (Kaira) in Gujarat, which was under the rule of Gurjaras at that time, as shown in Chapter 5. The Gurjara ruler at that time was Jayabhaṭa I Vītarāga. The founder of the Chālukya dynasty was Jayasiṃha, which raises the possibility that Jayasiṃha and Jayabhaṭa I Vītarāga were the same person. Bhaṭa means a soldier, and could have been later replaced by Siṃha, which means "lion" to enhance his prestige. We can then entertain the possibility that Jayabhaṭa I was of an enterprising nature and ventured south in search of new territory to conquer after handing the reigns to his son Dadda II. This would mean that the Gurjaras were the ancestors of the Chālukyas.

In the seventh century, when the power of the Chālukyas was rising, another force was rising in a far away land that would crush everything in its path. In the closing chapter of this book, we will take a look at the rise of this force that would pose the most formidable challenge that the ancient civilization of India had faced since its origin.

Notes:

1. Fleet (1882): 17-18.
2. Fleet (1882): 17, footnote 2.
3. Kielhorn (1900-01).
4. Śrivāstava (2007): 660.
5. Dowson (1865).
6. Telang (1875).
7. Fergusson (1873).

śreyānsvadharmo viguṇaḥ paradharmātswanuṣṭhitāt |

svadharme nidhanam śreyaḥ paradharmo bhayāvahaḥ ||

-- Our own Dharma is better even if imperfect compared to the Dharma of others even if perfect. It is praiseworthy to die following one's own Dharma as the Dharma of others is to be afraid of.

- Gītā 3.35

10. THE FALL OF PERSIA

When the reign of Harṣavardhana was coming to an end, a powerful ideology was developing in a faraway land. Soon, it was going to reach the borders of India. Before this ideology could make an impact on the fabulously rich land of India, it had to overcome a major hurdle, and that was the empire of Persia.

10.1 When the Curtain Falls

We have explored the interaction between Indian rulers and the rulers of the last pre-Islamic dynasty of Persia, the Sasanian dynasty, at various points in this book. When the curtains fell on the Sasanian dynasty, a great civilization came to an end and with the end of the the Sasanian dynasty the Indian civilization came face to face with a new challenge. The dying days of the Sasanian dynasty and the travails of its last emperor Yezdijird have been described by Sir John Malcolm in his classic work, "The History of Persia" in the following words [1]:

"The reign of Yezdijird has obtained celebrity, from having been that in which the ancient empire of Persia was subverted by a band of naked lizard-eaters; for such was the contemptuous appellation formerly used by their vain neighbours, when they mentioned the tribes of Arabia. No common cause could have produced such a revolution: Persian historians are alike disposed, from superstition and from patriotism, to deem it one of the greatest miracles by which God has manifested the truth of the Mahomedan religion. Those who take a worldly view of this great event, will discover, that a monarchy, like that of Persia, enervated by luxury, distracted by internal divisions, exhausted by foreign wars, and bending to its fall from age and weakness, was ill calculated to resist the enthusiastic robbers of Arabia; who, fired by the double hope of present and future enjoyment, rushed like an overwhelming torrent on the nations around them. But, before the progress of this great work of destruction is narrated, it will be necessary to say a few words on the country, character, and religion, of that extraordinary race by whom it was effected.

Though there are several lofty ranges of mountains in the peninsula of Arabia, the greatest part of that celebrated country consists of level, sandy, and arid plains, which can support but few inhabitants. We may judge of this whole extensive tract by our knowledge of Yemen, or Arabia the Happy. The few cultivated spots, the thinly scattered groves, and the small though pure streams of this province, could only be deemed delightful by men whose eyes were unaccustomed to vegetation, who seldom found shade to protect them from the scorching rays of a meridian sun, and whose thirst was usually allayed by the brackish water of the desert. The inhabitants of the peninsula are an original and unmixed race. They boast that their country has never been conquered; and we have no record of the whole being subject to a foreign yoke: but the Romans, at one period, possessed a part of Arabia; and Yemen and some adjoining provinces have been often over run, and at times been tributary to Persia. That the monarchs of that country, and the emperors of Rome, did not pursue their conquests till they subdued the deserts of Arabia, may have arisen from other causes than a dread of the courage of its roving inhabitants. Independence is the certain and just reward of all who consent to a life of privation and hardship. Deserts and mountains have ever been the sanctuaries of the free and brave; and those who are content to inhabit them, are seldom exposed to attack: for ambition, only greedy of wealth and grandeur, could derive little gratification from the possession of a country, where no labour could render the fields fruitful, and no time could make the inhabitants slaves.

The Arab is not very robust, but he is well formed and active, and, from habit and education, careless of danger, and insensible to fatigue. His mind is quick rather than intelligent; and his character is at once marked by an extreme of credulity and of enthusiasm. He is allied in all his pleasures and fatigues to the horse and camel of his desert; and these animals appear to have obtained a superiority over their own species, from being elevated into the companions of their masters.

The Arabs in former days worshipped the sun and planets; but they were latterly distracted by n variety of religions: some continued in the faith of their fathers; others adopted the Jewish or Christian tenets. These differences in belief, added to other causes, had long rendered their country a scene of contention and weakness. But the doctrine of Mahomed prevailed almost as soon as it was promulgated; and that extraordinary man lived to see his faith acknowledged over all Arabia. That the religion which he taught contained some of the noblest and most sublime tenets, is as true as that these were taken from the purest of all sources. But it had in its very origin the character of violence; and, while it taught one great, all powerful, and merciful Creator, and called on the idolatrous Arab to renounce his plurality of gods for a better worship, it offered, as the reward of his conversion and obedience, the complete gratification of all his desires. The goods of this world, and every earthly enjoyment, were the pious prize for the valour of the faithful soldier who drew his sword against infidels; and if he fell, a paradise was provided, and he was promised perpetual youth, amid scenes where palaces of gold and rubies, virgins of never-fading beauty, clear streams, and sweet-scented groves, were to afford him eternal bliss.

This religion, which proclaimed war against the property of all who did not receive it, was well adapted to the principles and habits of those to whom it was first addressed. One of its most remarkable features was the great indulgence which it granted to the strongest of all the sensual passions. By this indulgence, it enabled those who had wealth or power to confirm if not to establish usages which placed a great portion of the females of the countries where Mahomedanism was introduced, in a condition little above that of slaves, and this alone perpetuated, if it did not create, an insuperable obstacle to the progress of civilization.

This appears to be the general character of that religion by which the enthusiastic Arabs were kindled. Their ardent minds received with delight doctrines, which at once elevated the soul, fired the imagination, and gratified the passions. The zeal and ardour of converts were not likely to seek other causes for the success of their arms, than the divine origin of that faith which they had embraced; and the tenets of Mahomed were calculated to give victory to his followers. The meed of superior piety was the reward of distinguished courage; and in the early days of this religion, the hero alone was deemed worthy of Paradise.

The first attack made by the Arabs on the Persian empire was during the reign of the Caliph Omar, who commanded one of his generals, Abou-Obeyd, to cross the Euphrates. The force employed must have been small, as we find it opposed by two detachments of two thousand men each; one commanded by Jyan, the other by Roostum-Ferokhzad. The Persians were afterwards reinforced by a corps under a general called Jalenous, and took post on the east of the Euphrates, where they were attacked by Abou-Obeyd. The action was furious; but the Arabian chief lost it by his imprudent courage. He observed a white elephant in the centre of the Persian host; and towards this animal, which he deemed the object of their superstition, he fought his way with irresistible valour, and with one blow of his scimetar struck off his trunk. Maddened by pain, the furious animal rushed upon the rude assailant, and trampled him to atoms. The Arabs, dispirited by the fate of their leader, fled in confusion: numbers were slain in the action; more were drowned, as the bridge on the Euphrates, which they had crossed, was broken down. The few that survived retreated to Salabeh, a place on the west bank of the river, and informed Omar of what had happened. The caliph reinforced them: they advanced under Jereer-Ben-Abdullah into Irak; but were again encountered and defeated by Mehran, the general of Pooran-dokht. The celebrated Durufsh Kawanee, or apron of the blacksmith Kāwāh, which had been the royal standard of Persia for so many ages, was displayed in both these battles, and was for the last time propitious to Persia. Encouraged by success, Mehran ventured on another action, but was defeated and slain, and his dispirited troops fled in dismay to Madain. The Persians attributed their bad success to the incompetency of their powerless sovereigns. Ruler after ruler was dethroned and murdered, until the elevation of Yezdijird, which seems to have given a momentary hope to the falling nation. His first measure was to send an envoy to Saad-ben-Wakass, the leader whom the caliph had appointed to the chief command of his forces against Persia; and Saad, in compliance with the request communicated through this person, sent a deputation to Madain, consisting of three old Arab chiefs. When these were seated in the presence of Yezdijird, that monarch addressed himself to the principal person among them, whose name was Shaikh Maghurah, in the following words:—

"We have always held you in the lowest estimation. Arabs hitherto have been only known in Persia in two characters; as merchants and as beggars. Your food is green lizards; your drink, salt water; your

covering, garments made of coarse hair. But of late you have come in numbers to Persia; you have eaten of good food, you have drunk of sweet water, and have enjoyed the luxury of soft raiment. You have reported these enjoyments to your brethren, and they are flocking to partake of them. But not satisfied with all the good things you have thus obtained, you desire to impose a new religion on us, who are unwilling to receive it. You appear to me like the fox of our fable, who went into a garden where he found plenty of grapes. The generous gardener would not disturb him. The produce of his abundant vineyard would, he thought, be little diminished by a poor hungry fox enjoying himself; but the animal, not content with his good fortune, went and informed all his tribe of the excellence of the grapes, and the good nature of the gardener. The garden was filled with foxes; and its indulgent master was forced to bar the gates, and kill all the intruders to save himself from ruin. However, as I am satisfied you have been compelled to the conduct which you have pursued from absolute want, I will not only pardon you, but load your camels with wheat and dates, that, when you return to your native land, you may feast your countrymen. But be assured, if you are insensible to my generosity, and remain in Persia, you shall not escape my just vengeance."

The firm, and pious envoy heard unmoved a speech at once displaying the extreme of pride and of weakness. "Whatever thou hast said," replied Shaikh Maghurah, "concerning the former condition of the Arabs, is true. Their food was green lizards; they buried their infant daughters alive; nay, some of them feasted on dead carcasses and drank blood; while others slew their relations, and thought themselves great and valiant, when by such an act they became possessed of more property; they were clothed with hair garments; knew not good from evil; and made no distinction between that which is lawful and that which is unlawful. Such was our state. But God in his mercy has sent us, by a holy prophet, a sacred volume which teaches us the true faith. By it we are commanded to war against infidels, and to exchange our poor and miserable condition for wealth and power. We now solemnly desire you to receive our religion. If you consent, not an Arab shall enter Persia without your permission; and our leaders will only demand the established taxes which all believers are bound to pay. If you do not accept our religion, you are required to pay the tribute fixed for infidels; should you reject both these propositions, you must prepare for war."

Yezdijird was still too proud to attend to such degrading conditions. The embassy was dismissed; and the war renewed with all the vigour of which the declining empire was capable. The Persian army was commanded by Roostum Ferokhzad, who endeavoured to avoid a general action; when at last compelled to fight, he was defeated with immense loss. Almost the whole Persian army, which, we are told, was one hundred thousand strong, fell in the celebrated battle of Kudseah; in which Mahomedan authors assert, that the Arabs lost only three thousand men. The booty was great; but the inhabitants of the desert were yet ignorant of its value. I will give any quantity of this yellow metal for a little white, was an exclamation made after the battle by an Arabian soldier, who desired to exchange gold, which he had never before seen, for silver, which he had learned to appreciate. But what gave its chief importance to this action, was the capture of the famous Durufsh-e-Kawanee, the royal standard of the Persian empire; an event deemed both by Arabians and Persians a certain presage of the result of the war. Yezdijird, when he heard of this great defeat, fled to Hulwan with all the property he could carry. Saad-ben-Wakass, after taking possession of Madain, pursued him; and sent his nephew, Hashem, to attack a body of troops which had arrived from Shirwan and Aderbijan. This force took shelter in the fort of Jelwallah, where they were attacked and made prisoners. On learning this, Yezdijird left his army, and fled to Rhe. Hashem advanced to Hulwan, which he soon reduced. The city of Ahwaz, which appears to have been a place of great importance at this period, was also taken by the Arabs ; thence Saad marched by the caliph's order to Amber; but finding that situation unhealthy he halted his army at Koofa,—a place which soon afterwards acquired celebrity. The foundations of Bussorah were laid in the same year by the Arab chief, Alabah Ghuzwan.

Saad-ben-Wakass, who continued to govern all that part of Persia which he had conquered from his fixed camp or rather new City of Koofa, was recalled by Omar, on account of a complaint made against him by those under his rule; and Omar Yuseer was appointed his successor. Yezdijird, encouraged by the removal of a leader whom he so much dreaded, assembled an army of one hundred and fifty thousand men from Khorassan, Rhe, and Hamadan; and placing it under the command of Firouzan, the bravest of the Persian generals, resolved to put the fate of his empire at issue on one great battle.

The caliph, when he heard of these preparations, ordered reinforcements to be sent to his army in Persia from every quarter of his dominions; and committing the whole to the chief command of Noman, he directed him to exert his utmost efforts to destroy forever the impious worship of fire. The Arabian force assembled at Koofa, and thence marched to the plains of Nahavund, on which the Persians had established a camp, surrounded by a deep entrenchment. During two months these great armies continued in sight of each other, and many skirmishes were fought. The Persian general appearing determined not to quit his position, the zeal of the leader of the faithful became impatient of delay. He drew up his army in order of battle, and thus addressed them: "My friends! Prepare yourselves to conquer, or to drink of the sweet sherbet of martyrdom. I shall now call the Tukbeer three times: at the first you will gird your loins; at the second mount your steeds; and at the third point your lances, and rush to victory or to Paradise. As to me," said Noman, with a raised and enraptured voice, "I shall be a martyr! When I am slain, obey the orders of Huzeefah-ebn-Aly-Oman."

The moment he had done speaking, the first sound of the Tukbeer (Allah-Akbar, or God is great,) was heard throughout the camp. At the second all were upon their horses; and at the third, which was repeated by the whole army, the Mahomedans charged with a fury that was irresistible. Noman was slain, as he predicted; but his army gained a great and memorable victory. Thirty thousand Persians were pierced by their lances; eighty thousand more were drowned in the deep trench by which they had surrounded their camp. Their general, Firouzan, with four thousand men, fled to the hills; but such was the terror on one side and the confidence on the other, that he was pursued, defeated, and slain by a body of not more than a thousand men.

The battle of Nahavund decided the fate of Persia, which now fell under the dominion of the Arabian caliphs. Yezdijird protracted for several years a wretched and precarious existence. He first fled to Seistan, then to Khorassan, and lastly to Merv. The governor of that city invited the Khakan of the Tartars to take possession of the person of the fugitive monarch. That sovereign accepted the offer; his troops entered Merv, the gates of which were opened to them, by the treacherous governor, and made themselves master of it, in spite of the desperate resistance of the surprised but brave and enraged inhabitants. Yezdijird escaped on foot from the town during the confusion of the contest. He reached a mill eight miles from Merv, and entreated the miller to conceal him. The man told him he owed a certain sum to the owner of the mill, and that, if he paid the debt, he should have his protection against all pursuers. The monarch agreed to this proposal; and, after giving his rich sword and belt as pledges of his sincerity, retired to rest with perfect confidence. But the miller could not resist the temptation of making his fortune by the possession of the rich arms and robes of the unfortunate prince, whose head he severed from his body with the sword he had received from him, and then cast his corpse into the water-course that turned the mill. The governor of Merv, and those who had aided him, begun in a few days to suffer from the tyranny of the Khakan, and to repent of the part they had acted. They encouraged the citizens to rise upon the Tartars; and not only recovered the city, but forced the Khakan to fly with great loss to Bokharah. A diligent inquiry was made after Yezdijird, whose fate was soon discovered. The miller fell a victim to popular rage; and the corpse of the monarch was embalmed and sent to Istakhr, to be interred in the sepulchre of his ancestors. This prince, who appears to have been as weak as he was unfortunate, sat upon the throne only nine years; that being the period from his elevation to the battle of Nahavund. He was the last sovereign of the House of Sassan, a family which governed Persia during four hundred and fifteen years; and their memory is still cherished by a nation whose ancient glory is associated with the names of Ardisheer, Shahpoor, and Nousheerwan. ...

After the flight of Yezdijird, the leaders of the caliph's armies soon overran the whole of Persia from the Euphrates to the Oxus, destroying, with bigot fury, all that was useful, grand, or sacred. A great portion of the conquered, preferring the abandonment of their religion to oppression or death, adopted the faith of their new masters; while those, who were unable to endure the scene, fled self-banished into a distant land."

10.2 The Persian Genocide

When the zealots of a new religion overran Persia, Persians were left with essentially four choices -- escape from Persia, death, life under an extremely oppressive regime, or adoption of a new religion. Under these circumstances, most of those willing to live in Persia were left with no choice but to accept the new religion, especially when tens of thousands of Persians were slaughtered or hanged to serve as an example to those who refused to convert. As is the case in Indian history, Persian history too has been sanitized to show that the new religion spread in Persia by peaceful means due to its superiority. Facts are otherwise and must be presented because history must be an account of what has actually happened instead of make-belief and lies.

Persia had a highly advanced civilization at that time, and due to the intellectual achievements of its people the Persian language and culture formed the backbone of the Arabic civilization after the conversion of Persia to the Islamic faith. The conversion of Persians began with mass scale executions and destruction of their knowledge base which was considered useless by the conquerors. For a detailed discussion, readers are referred to an article by Dr. Daryoush Jahanian [2]. We will present some examples for illustrative and summary purposes only.

Persians had a huge library at the city of Ctesiphon. Ctesiphon was located about 30 km from Baghdad in Iraq and was the capital of the Sasanian Empire. The Arab commander Saad ibn-e Abi Waqqas wrote to Mullah Omar about what to do with the library at Ctesiphon. Mullah Omar replied that if the books contradict the Koran they were blasphemous, and if they conformed to Koran they were not needed. In either case they were to be destroyed. The books were then either burnt or thrown in the Euphrates. Similarly, the splendid library at Alexandria was burned down when Egypt was defeated and captured by Muslims. In India, the Nalanda University received the same fate at the hands of Bakhtiyar Khilji. In Persia, other libraries located in Ray and Khorasan met the same fate along with the University of Gondishapour. The subjugation of Persians involved the destruction of their knowledge base, mass executions, mass enslavement, destruction of their places of worship, and imposition of the economically debilitating Jizya tax.

The mass execution of Persians has been sanitized from Persian history, but it still resides in the collective memory of the Zoroastrians who managed to hang on to their faith despite the overwhelming odds. Arab commander Yazid-ibn-e Mohalleb was responsible for beheading so many Persians at Gorgan that it is reported the flowing blood could turn a water-operated mill. In the Mazandran province 12,000 Persians were hanged following the order by the same commander. According to an estimate, nearly

400,000 Persian civilians were massacred by the Arabs [2]. Actual numbers may be higher and careful research can provide us more information about the massive slaughter of Persians and the destruction of their civilization.

10.3 A Home Away from Home

When Persia was overrun by zealots of a new faith, most of the Persians were left with no choice but to accept the new religion. A small group of Zoroastrians chose not to do so and fled from the reaches of their tormentors in search of a safe place to practice their ancestral religion. Their search for a safe place to practice their religion finally brought them to Sanjan in the Valsad district of Gujarat in India, a country where religious conversion by force was unknown till that point in time. The heroic saga of this small group of people, who are called Pārsī in their adopted land, has been described in vivid detail by Dosabhoy Framjee in his fascinating book "The Parsees: Their History, Manners, Customs, and Religion" [3]:

> *"The remnant of that mighty and flourishing race of people who inhabited Persia centuries before the Christian era, and whose dominion, in. its most prosperous period, reached as far as the Persian Gulf and Indian Ocean on the south, the rivers Indus and Oxus on the east, the Caspian Sea and Caucasian Mountains on the north, and the deserts of Lybia and the Mediterranean on the west, whose grandeur, magnificence, and glory were unequalled by any nation of ancient times; whose kings were at once the most powerful of monarchs, and the wisest and most beneficent of rulers; that remnant is known in India under the designation of Parsees, a name which they derive from their original country, Pars or Fars. That province, called by the Greeks, Persis, contained the chief city of the empire, and the most splendid of the royal palaces, and from it the whole kingdom gained its name. Of the remnant of the ancient Persians now found in Western India, and chiefly in Bombay,*

where they form a most numerous and respectable class of the population, it is proposed to give in this publication a short history.

To enter upon the history of the ancient Persians, the ancestors of the Parsees, would be foreign to the subject; the public have already been put in possession of all the facts that are, or probably can be, known concerning them. Suffice it to say, that with Yezdezird, the forty-fifth king in the descent of the race of Kaimurs, ended the ancient Persian monarchy. The neighbouring and wealthy empire of Persia presented too tempting a prize to the fanatic and ambitious spirit, evoked by Mahomed, to remain long unmolested, and in the middle of the seventh century of the Christian era, the Arab sword invaded Persia, under Caliph Omar. In a fierce and well-contested battle with the Persians at the village of Nahavand, about fifty miles from the ancient city of Ecbatana, the fate of the empire was decided. The Persian army, numbering fifteen thousand fighting men, was defeated with great slaughter. Yezdezird, abandoning his kingdom as lost, fled the country; and, after wandering in solitude and disguise for a period of ten years, was at last treacherously slain by a miller, to whom the secret of his identity had been confided. This event occurred A.D. 651, and thus ended the dynasty of the Sussanian Kings of Persia, and the monarchy founded by Kaikhoshru, the Cyrus the Great of the Greeks. With the overthrow of the monarchy every vestige of Persian magnificence disappeared, and the empire with its glories, became the inheritance of the Mahomedans, whose supremacy in the newly conquered kingdom was at once established.

History has faithfully drawn the character of the Mahomedan conquerors wherever they have appeared, and has traced their footsteps in characters of blood. Toleration in religion is unknown to the haughty, uncivilized barbarian believers in the Koran. Bigotry is the highest virtue demanded of the Mahomedan, and one which secures for him favour in the eyes of his prophet and his God, and takes him by the shortest route to a place in heaven. Thus on the conquest of Persia, the Mahomedan soldiers of the Caliphat of

Bagdad traversed the length and breadth of the country, presenting the alternative of death or the Koran, and compelling the conquered nation to accept the one or the other. By these oppressive and cruel means, a hundred thousand persons are said to have daily abjured the faith of their forefathers; and the fire-temples and other sacred places were destroyed or converted into mosques. Under such rulers, almost the whole Zoroastrian population of Persia embraced the faith of Islam, and nearly every trace of the religion of Zoroaster was obliterated.

Historians have noted that the effect of the Mahomedan conquest (for to call it conversion would be simply ridiculous) was greatly demoralizing to the people. The ancient Greeks have borne testimony to the character for truth of their Persian contemporaries, while modern writers have denounced the Persians of our own times as a nation of liars. Such of the followers of Zoroaster as preferred obeying the dictates of their conscience, to freeing themselves from the persecution of their rulers by accepting the Koran, abandoned their homes, and fled to the mountainous districts of Khorassan, where for a time they succeeded in evading the pursuit of their terrible foe. For about a hundred years they remained in Khorassan in the unmolested enjoyment and practice of their religion. But persecution at last reached them even in those remote districts, and they were once more compelled to fly from the enemies of their faith, and a considerable number emigrated to the little island of Ormus, at the mouth of the Persian Gulf.

Their stay at this retreat was, however, but of short duration. They were yet within the reach of their cruel persecutors, and rather than fall into the hands of the fanatic, impious devs (devils) they at last determined to relinquish forever the land of their forefathers, and to remove to a country where they might hope to live in tranquillity, and in the enjoyment of their social and religious rights. Acting upon this determination, they sought an asylum in the country of the Hindoos, and are said to have engaged at Ormus several vessels for their transport, and placing their wives and children on board they set sail towards the distant shores, of India. It is impossible to suppose that this was the only exodus of the Persians from the land of their fathers. That several emigrations took place at successive periods, as the flame of the fanatic zeal and persecuting spirit of the Mahomedans burned more or less brightly, can hardly be doubted. Various meagre and unsatisfactory traditions exist concerning the tide of emigration, the manner in which it was effected, and the total number of those who left the shores of the Gulf. Whatever information is now in our possession, and is to any extent reliable, is gleaned from a work entitled Kissah-i-Sanjan, which was compiled in the year 1599, by one Behram a Zoroastrian resident of Nowsaree, from the traditions extant in his time. According to that writer, the first port in Hindostan at which the earliest refugees arrived was Div or Diew, a small island in the Gulf of Cambay, lying to the south-west of the peninsula of Kattiwar. Here it is said they disembarked and took up their residence for nineteen years, at the expiration of which period they quitted Diew to find another place of adoption. The causes which led to this migration have not been satisfactorily explained; but the following mysterious passage relating to the event is to be found in Behram's work: - "An aged Dastoor (high priest) reading the tablets of the stars, made an augury that it behoved them to depart from that place, and seek out another abode. All rejoiced at his words, and sailed swiftly towards Guzrat."

That misfortunes never come singly was literally fulfilled in the case of this outcast people, for hardly had they lost sight of land when a severe storm overtook the little fleet, and deprived them of all hope. Rather than abandon the faith they had inherited from their fathers, they had voluntarily made themselves exiles for ever from the land that gave them birth, and were now at the mercy of strangers for a home, and now at the mercy of the treacherous deep in seeking more friendly shores. What wonder then that the little band, confused and in despair, were ready to believe that they were the sport of merciless fate. But, though sick at heart, their better sense does not seem to have entirely forsaken them. In their helplessness they called to mind Him who is the author of all good, the Preserver, Supporter and Cherisher of the poor and the distressed, and who never fails to listen to the supplications of the humble and meek.

To rescue them from the impending danger, they are said to have offered up the following prayer to the throne of the Most High. "O wise God, come to our assistance in this jeopardy; and we pray to Thee to deliver us from the impending danger. O glorious God, we beseech Thee to gladden our hearts by removing these difficulties with which we are now surrounded. On Thy goodness, O Lord, we fully depend, and hope that the storm which has overtaken us will soon be over through Thy Divine Grace. As long as we have hopes of Thy aid, O God, we tremble not at this calamity. We have implicit faith in Thee, as the hearer of those who cry to Thee. Deliver us, therefore, O Merciful Providence, from this trouble, and lead us to the right path, that we may escape from this sea to the shores of India, and we promise, O Lord, to kindle on high the flame sacred to Thee in grateful remembrance of thy kindness and protection."

We may suppose that their prayer was heard, for the storm abated and a gentler gale carried them in safety to Sanjan about twenty five miles south of Damaun, where they landed about the year A.D. 717. The territory of Sanjan was then under the rule of a wise and liberal chief named Jadao Rana. A Dastoor or high priest of the Parsees was accordingly sent to the Rana with fitting presents, in order to obtain from him the terms of their landing. The Dastoor, a venerable old man, on approaching the Rana blessed him, and having explained the reasons which caused the Parsees to relinquish their native country, and detailed their vicissitudes and sufferings, requested to be allowed to reside in the city of Sanjan. It is said, that the Prince, struck with the warlike and hardy appearance of the men who came as refugees to his court, had some fear for the safety of his throne and country, and before granting the desired permission requested the chief priest to explain to him the secret of their affairs and the nature of their faith.

During their stay at Diew, the Parsees acquired a knowledge of the language, religion, manners and customs of the Hindoos, and were enabled to answer the inquiries of the Rajah so satisfactorily that no opposition was made by him to their making Sanjan their place of abode and their adopted country. The learned among the Parsees prepared sixteen schlokes or disticlies, and in these they briefly described the tenets of their religion and their mode of worship. As it will doubtless interest the European reader to know what those schlokes contained, they are given entire, though they must not be supposed to give a complete abstract of the Parsee faith.

1st. We are worshippers of Hormuzd (Supreme Being) and the sun and five elements.

2nd. We observe silence while bathing, praying, making offerings to fire, and eating.

3rd. We use incense, perfumes, and flowers in our religious ceremonies.

4th. We are worshippers of the cow.

5th. We wear the sacred garment, the sadrā or shirt, the kusti or cincture for the loins and the cap of two folds.

6th. We rejoice in songs and instruments of music on the occasion of our marriages.

7th. We ornament and perfume our wives.

8th. We are enjoined to be liberal in our charities, and especially in excavating tanks and wells.

9th. We are enjoined to extend our sympathies towards males as well as females.

10th. We practise ablutions with gaomutra, one of the products of the cow.

11th. We wear the sacred girdle when praying and eating.

12th. We feed the sacred flame with incense.

13th. We practise devotion five times a day.

14th. We are careful observers of conjugal fidelity and purity.

15th. We perform annual religious ceremonies on behalf of our ancestors.

16th. We place great restraints on our women after their confinements.

The reader is here cautioned against supposing the foregoing to be the fundamental principles of the Parsee religion. The Parsees are not the idolatrous people which the preceding dogmas would lead one to suppose, and ample opportunity will be given to the reader of forming an opinion as to the true religion of the Parsees in subsequent pages of this work. It is necessary here to state frankly, that the first refugees of our faith in India played the part of dissemblers and that the distiches appear to have been framed with the view of gaining the favour of the Hindoo Rajah. While allusion is made therein to many minor ceremonies, which are no more the essentials of Zoroastrianism than of Christianity, yet because of their approximating to certain ceremonies of the Hindoos, prominence is given to them, while silence is preserved regarding those doctrines on which the religion of Zoroaster is really based.

The Parsee refugees had sufficient opportunities of learning at Diew, how jealous the Hindoos are of association with people of other castes, from the dread of contamination fatal to themselves. Followed as they had been by continual misfortunes, and cast upon the world without country or home; the Parsees could not but be anxious to obtain, even at a great sacrifice, a landing place for themselves and their families. Bearing this in view, it is possible that they answered the inquiries of the Hindoo Rajah in such a form as to win his good opinion. They concealed from the Prince all that would have appeared extraordinary or offensive to him and his subjects, and supplied, in place thereof, ceremonies which had an origin exclusively Hindoo.

The device succeeded; and the people found favour in Jadao Rana's eyes, and permission was given them to reside in his city, on condition of their adopting the language of the country, and ceasing to speak that of their forefathers. They were also required to dress their females in the Indian fashion, to wear no armour, and to perform the marriage ceremonies of their children at night, in conformity with the practice of the Hindoos. The exiles had but two alternatives—to accept these conditions, or to return to their ships; and rather than become once more wanderers on the face of the earth, they chose the former course, and rested in the land of the Rajah. On being directed to occupy any vacant ground they pleased, they selected a large tract of waste land in the immediate vicinity of Sanjan.

After a long series of hardships endured for many years, the exiles had at last found a resting place, and might expect repose and happiness. Every one now betook himself to his profession, and their settlement which, but a short time before, was a sterile desert, became converted into a populous and thriving city. Neither did the Parsees forget Him who had assisted them in their day of trouble. They remembered the vow which they had made to "kindle on high the flame sacred to Him," in grateful memory of their deliverance from the hand of death, and they embraced the earliest opportunity of intimating to the Rajah their intention of building, with his permission, a fire-temple in Sanjan, in fulfilment of the solemn vow which they had made. As the Hindoos themselves hold fire in veneration, not only was the desired permission at once accorded, but every assistance was rendered to further the object. The fire temple was, however, wholly and exclusively constructed by the Parsees themselves, the Rajah merely supplying various articles which would expedite the great work. A few years witnessed the completion of the temple (A.D. 721), and saw the sacred fire kindled on its altar in accordance with the rights of the Zoroastrian religion.

For about three hundred years after their landing in Sanjan, the Parsees are said to have lived in peace and quietness. At the end of that period their number was greatly increased. Many of them had emigrated with their families to Surat, Nowsari, Broach, Variao, Ukleser and Cambay, places now easily recognised on the map of Guzerat. Two hundred years more rolled on and no records are left of the Parsees that are worth noting beyond the fact that they chiefly occupied themselves wherever they were located in agricultural pursuits. They seem ever to have lived amicably with the Hindoos; for during this long period of five centuries there is no tradition of any misunderstanding between the strangers and the children of the soil.

About the year A.D. 1507, the Parsees of Sanjan are said to have greatly distinguished themselves by their valor in assisting their Raja against the aggression of a Mahomedan chief, Sultan Mahomed Begada, who was residing at Ahmedabad. This chief was surnamed Begada from his having conquered the two hill forts of Joonagud and Champanir. While at the latter place, he formed a design for subverting the independence of Sanjan, and soon after collected a large army under a skilful general named Aluf Khan to effect this object.

The Mahomedan general, with thirty thousand men, arrived before Sanjan, and the Hindoo monarch, conscious of the insufficiency of his resources to cope with the hardy soldiers of the enemy trembled for his crown and country. He solicited the assistance of the Parsees, and summoning them to his presence addressed them as follows: - "My ancestors exalted you and lavished favours upon your people, and it behoves you in this my difficulty to show your gratitude, and to exert yourself on my behalf, and lead the way in battle." The Parsees were not unmindful of their obligations to the former rulers of Sanjan and at once undertook to defend the country which had so hospitably welcomed their forefathers to its shores. To the address of the Rajah they replied. "Fear not, O Prince, on account of this army: all of us are ready to scatter the heads of thy foes and will fight as long as a drop of blood remains in our veins. In battle we never give way; not one man of us will turn his back though a millstone were dashed at his head."

In adopting this resolve the Parsees were not unmindful of the persecutions sustained by their ancestors, and they determined that the Mahomedan invaders should be repelled at any sacrifice. The cause of the Hindoo monarch was their own; they knew that if the army of the Sultan was successful their religion would again be periled, and a second persecution of their faith instituted. Notwithstanding the oath they had taken never to bear arms, they considered that in this extremity they were fully justified in drawing the sword to defend the territories of the Hindoo Rajah, and a force of fourteen hundred Zoroastrians, under the leadership of one Ardeshir was immediately added to the Hindoo army.

This accession to his force caused the Raja to take courage; every preparation was made for the impending struggle, which was to decide the fate of his kingdom, and a fierce battle is said to have ensued, a few miles beyond Sanjan. Sword, javelin, and arrow did their deadly work, and many fell on both sides. In the thick of the battle the Hindoos were unable to keep their ground against the furious onslaught of the Mahomedans, and fled the field. The noble band of Persian allies, however, was not dismayed. They were fighting for their faith and for their homes, and the interests involved in the issue of the contest made them regardless of their lives. Their brave leader, Ardeshir, heroically led them on, and attacking the enemy furiously, broke their ranks, and threw them into confusion. The whole force was discomfited, and Aleef Khan fled, leaving Ardeshir and his little band masters of the field.

The Mahomedan armies in India have generally been successful over those of the Hindoos, from the hardy and warlike character of their soldiers. This defeat of thousands of their number, which was rendered more humiliating, from the fact of its having been caused by a handful of strangers, was more than their proud spirits could endure. Aluf Khan raised reinforcements, and again appeared in the field. Ardeshir emboldened by success was not, however, to be daunted, and he addressed the Hindoo Rajah in the following spirited terms. "Oh, Prince, the enemy has appeared in greater numbers than before. They are a hundred to our one, but behold our courage. We will either yield our lives, or take those of our foes, and

> *in this resolve may God befriend us, since he always removes our difficulties.*
>
> *In the battle that followed, Ardeshir was engaged in single combat with a Mahomedan chief of note. The gallant Parsee general hurled him from his horse, and killed him with his sword. Aluf Khan, it is said, witnessing the scene became furiously excited, and led on in person a heavy charge against the Parsees. The two armies joined in battle, and blood flowed in torrents. Fortune did not favour the allies on this occasion. A dart struck the Parsee leader, who fell headlong from his saddle, and as is the case with all Oriental nations, the army having lost its chief hesitated and gave way, and was completely routed by the enemy. The Hindoo prince is also said to have fallen in this battle. Aluf Khan was now master of Sanjan, and the Parsees soon found it impossible to call that place any longer their home."*

It is one of the great ironies of life that good people face overwhelming challenges in their struggle to keep their good faith and work. However, it is also true that goodness never dies no matter the overwhelming nature of the challenges. A fire might destroy a forest, but a little sapling or seed will take root and the forest will grow again. It may not be as grand as the old forest, but in this new forest the memories of the old forest will survive. In the wake of the devastation wrought on the Persians by the brutal onslaught of Alexander, a small group of Magi priests came to India to seek a new life and in time gave us one of the greatest astronomers of India, Varāhamihira, who adorned the court of Emperor Vikramāditya. When Vallabhī was sacked by Central Asian barbaric nomads, a Persian princess escaped the attack to preserve the royal line. She gave birth to Guhāditya, in whose lineage great warriors and proud sons of the soil such as Bappa Rawal, Maharana Pratap and Kshatrapati Shivaji were born, who kept fighting the invaders to keep the native civilization alive. In the wake of the near total devastation of Persian culture by the brutal Arabs, a small group of Zoroastrians, called Pārsī in the adopted land, came to India to seek a new life and in time have made enormous contributions to enrich Indian civilization. The numerically small Pārsī community in India now faces the danger of extinction due to falling birth rates. It would be a tragic end if that were to be so.

We have now arrived at the end of the narrative and reconstruction of ancient Indian history. In the course of the three volumes, we have explored the connection between the two sister civilizations of ancient times, Indian and Persian, both magnificent and heroic. They both suffered devastating blows from the same forces during the course of history, be it the Greeks, the Central Asians or the Arabs. Sadly, the ancient Persians could not survive the Arab onslaught. They gave a good fight, as we have seen, but ultimately their efforts fell short. The fate of the ancient Indian civilization still hangs in the balance.

The fact that ancient Indian civilization still survives is not a testimony of the peaceful nature of the invaders, which is the picture modern historians have sought to paint and sold successfully till now. It is a history of unparalleled violence and oppression and a story of fearless people who chose to follow the path of their ancestors in spite of the overwhelming challenges. Led by the fearless Rajputs, Hindus successfully defended their country for several centuries from the onslaught of the new breed of invaders, a feat that is unparalleled in history. The indomitable spirit of the fearless Rajputs is the stuff of legends that every Hindu should know and employ to dispel the perception, created by modern historians, that Hindu rulers were weak. When Hindus fell, it was not because they were not brave, but due to a series of unfortunate events coupled with the complacency that fearless Rajputs had developed by defeating these invaders time and again over the centuries. They showed mercy to the invaders when they won, but invaders were ruthless when they got the chance to return and wage war again. Modern history books teach us that Rajputs fell because they were not united. In fact, the Rajputs were so brave that they defeated the invaders even fighting alone. The problem was that they were fighting battles bound by the framework of their codes of honour.

Perhaps, soon, we may narrate the tales of the unparalleled bravery of the fearless Rajputs, if time and grace are on our side. For now, we believe that we have presented enough evidence to historians to seriously reconsider what is being taught as the history of ancient India.

Notes:

1. Malcolm (1829): 133-146.
2. Daryoush Jahanian, "The history of Zoroastrians after Arab invasion; Aliens in their homeland", http://www.cais-soas.com/SAIS/History/Post-Sasanian/zoroastrians_after_arab_invasion.htm#_ftn1.
3. Framjee (1858): 1-20.

BIBLIOGRAPHY

Agnihotry, V. K. (Chief Editor). (2010). Indian History. 26th edition. Mumbai, India: Allied publishers.

Analysis of Eastern Works – No. 1 - The Rozat al Sofa. (1838). The Asiatic Journal and Monthly Register for British and Foreign India, China and Australasia – New Series, Vol. XXVI: 228-237.

Beal, S. (1906a). Si-Yu-Ki: Buddhist Records of the Western World, Volume I. London, UK: Kegan Paul, Trench, Trubner and Co Ltd.

Beal, S. (1906b). Si-Yu-Ki: Buddhist Records of the Western World, Volume II. London, UK: Kegan Paul, Trench, Trubner and Co Ltd.

Bhandarkar, R.G. (1871-74). Transcript and Translation of a Copper plate grant of the Fifth Century of Christian era. The Journal of the Bombay Branch of the Royal Asiatic Society, 10: 19-30.

Bhandarkar, R.G. (1872). A Tāmba Patra or Ancient Copper Plate Grant from Kāthiāwād. Indian Antiquary, 1: 14-18.

Bhandarkar, D. R. (1902). A Kushana Stone Inscription and the Question about the Origin of the Śaka Era. The Journal of the Bombay Branch of the Royal Asiatic Society, 20: 269-302.

Bühler, G. (1875). A grant of King Dhruvasena I of Valabhi. The Indian Antiquary. 4: 104-106.

Bühler, G. (1876). Grants from Valabhi. The Indian Antiquary, 5: 204-212.

Bühler, G. (1878a). Additional Valabhi Grants, Nos. IX-XIV. The Indian Antiquary, 7: 66-86.

Bühler, G. (1878b). The Umetā Grant of Dadda II. The Indian Antiquary, 7: 61-66.

Bühler, G. (1882). Valabhi Grants. The Indian Antiquary, 11: 305-309.

Bühler, G. (1888). Gurjara Inscriptions, No. III: A New Grant of Dadda II or Prasantaraga. The Indian Antiquary, 17: 183-201.

Cunningham, A. (1871). The Ancient Geography of India. London, UK: Trubner and Co.

Cunningham, A. (1882). Report of Tours in Bihar and Bengal in 1879-80. Volume 15. Calcutta, India: Printed by the Superintendent of Government Printing.

Cunningham, A. and Garrick, H. B. W. (1883). Report of Tours in North and South Bihar, in 1880-81. Volume 16. Calcutta, India: Printed by the Superintendent of Government Printing.

Dāji, B. (1865). Brief notes on the age and authenticity of the work of Āryabhaṭa, Varāhamihira, Brahmagupta, Bhaṭṭotpala, and Bhāskarāchārya. Journal of the Royal Asiatic Society of Great Britain & Ireland, New Series, Volume the First: 392-418

Dāji, B. (1872). The ancient Sanskrit Numerals in the Cave Inscriptions, and on Sah-coins, correctly made out; with remarks on the era of Śālivāhana and Vikramāditya. Journal of Bombay Branch of Royal Asiatic Society, 8: 225-233.

Daniélou, A. (2003). A brief history of India. Rochester, Vermont, USA: Inner Traditions International.

Dowson, J. (1865). Art. X. – Translations of Three Copper Plate Inscriptions of the Fourth Century, A.D., and Notices of the Chālukya and Gurjjara Dynasties. Journal of the Royal Asiatic Society of Great Britain and Ireland, New Series, Volume the First: 247-286.

Evans, J., Head, B. V., and Grueber, H. A. (1890). Later Indo-Scythians.Ephthalites, or White Huns. The Numismatic Chronicle and Journal of the Numismatic Society, Third Series, Vol. X: 243-293.

Falk, H. (2001). The yuga of Sphujiddhvaja and the era of the Kuṣāṇas. Silk Road Art and Archaeology, 7, 121-136.

Fergusson, J. (1870). Art. II. – On Indian Chronology. Journal of the Royal Asiatic Society of Great Britain and Ireland, New Series, Volume the Fourth: 81-137.

Fergusson, J. (1873). On Indian Dates. Indian Antiquary, 2: 93-94.

Fergusson, J. (1876). History of Indian and Eastern Architecture. London, UK: John Murray.

Fergusson, J. (1880). Art. IX.- On the Saka, Samvat, and Gupta Eras. A Supplement to his paper on Indian Chronology. Journal of the Royal Asiatic Society of Great Britain and Ireland, New Series, Volume the Twelfth: 259-285.

Fleet, J. F. (1882). The Dynasties of the Kanarese Districts of the Bombay Presidency from the Earliest Historical Times to the Muhammadan Conquest of A.D. 1318. Bombay, India: Printed at the Government Central Press.

Fleet, J. F. (1888). Corpus Inscriptionum Indicarum, Vol. III: Inscriptions of the Early Guptas. Calcutta, India: Government of India, Central Publications Branch.

Framjee, D. (1858). The Parsees: Their History, Manners, Customs, and Religion. London, UK: Smith, Elder and Co.

Garthwaite, G. R. (2005). The Persians. Malden, MA, USA: Blackwell Publishing.

Jarrett, H.S. (1891). Ain-I-Akbari by Abul Fazl Allami, Vol. II, Book 3. Calcutta, India: Asiatic Society of Bengal.

Jayaswal, K.P. (1933). Epigraphia Indica, Vol. XX (1929-30): 71-89.

Kielhorn, F. (1900-01). Aihole Inscription of Pulikesin II, Saka-Samvat 556. Epigraphia Indica, 6: 1-12.

Kielhorn, F. (1902-03). Madhuban Plate of Harsha; The year 25. Epigraphia Indica, 7: 155-160.

Konow, S. (1923). Acta Orientalia, 1: 14-26, as quoted by Sethna, K. D. (1989). Ancient India in a New Light. New Delhi, India: Aditya Prakashana, page 474.

Lacouperie, T. D. (1887-1888). Khan, Khakan, and Other Tartar Titles. The Babylonian and Oriental Record, 2: 269-278.

Loeschner, H. (2008). Notes on the Yuezhi – Kushan relationship and Kushan chronology. Oriental Numismatic Society: 1-28.

Majumdar, R.C., Pusalker, A.D. and Majumdar A.K. (Editors). (1997). The History and Culture of the Indian People, Volume III: The Classical Age. 5th Edition. Mumbai, India: Bharatiya Vidya Bhavan.

Majumdar, R.C., Pusalker, A.D. and Majumdar A.K. (Editors). (2001). The History and Culture of the Indian People, Volume II: The Age of Imperial Unity. 7th Edition. Mumbai, India: Bharatiya Vidya Bhavan.

Malcolm, J. (1829). The History of Persia. Vol. 1. London, UK: John Murray.

Maṇḍalik, R. S. V. N. (1875). Art. XII. – Śālivāhana and Śālivāhana Saptaśatī. The Journal of the Bombay Branch of the Royal Asiatic Society, 10: 127-138.

Max Müller, F. (1883). India, what can it teach us?. London, UK: Longmans, Green, and Co.

McCrindle, J. W. (1877). Ancient India as Described by Megasthenes and Arrian. London, UK: Trubner & Co.

Middleton, J. (2015). World monarchies and dynasties. New York, USA: Routledge.

Mirashi, V.V. (editor). (1955a). Corpus Inscriptionum Indicarum, Vol. IV: Inscriptions of the Kalachuri-Chedi era. Part 1. New Delhi, India: Archaeological Survey of India.

Mirashi, V.V. (editor). (1955b). Corpus Inscriptionum Indicarum, Vol. IV: Inscriptions of the Kalachuri-Chedi era. Part 2. New Delhi, India: Archaeological Survey of India.

Pargiter, F. E. (1913). The Purana Text of the Dynasties of the Kali Age. London, UK: Humphrey Milford and Oxford University Press.

Pires, E. A. (1934). The Maukharis. Madras, India: B.G. Paul & Co.

Prichard, J. C. (1844). Researches into The Physical History of Mankind. Third Edition. Volume IV. London, UK: Sherwood, Gilbert, And Piper.

Regmi, D. R. (1983). Inscriptions of Ancient Nepal. New Delhi, India: Abhinav Publications.

Sachau, E. C. (1910). Alberuni's India. Vol. 2. London, UK: Kegan Paul, Trench, Trubner & Co. Ltd.

Sahāya, P. J. (1893). The Samvat Era. The Imperial and Asiatic Quarterly Review, New Series, 5 (9-10): 363-369.

Śarmā, R. (1995). Bhārata ke Prāchina Nagaroṃ kā Patana (in Hindi). New Delhi, India: Rājakamala Prakāśana.

Śāstri, H. (1917-18). Haraha Inscription of the reign of Isanavarman [Vikrama Samvat] 611. Epigraphia Indica, 14: 110-120.

Sen, S. N. (1999). Ancient Indian History and Civilization. Second Edition. New Delhi, India: New Age International Publishers.

Shastri, A.M. (Editor). (1999). The Age of the Satavahanas. Vol. I. New Delhi, India: Aryan Books International.

Sircar, D.C. (1971). Studies in the Geography of Ancient and Medieval India. Second Edition. Delhi, India: Motilal Banarsidass.

Skinner, M. C. (2005). Kalinga: Reconstructing a Regional History from the Sixth Century BCE to the First Century BCE. Master of Arts Thesis: University of Hawaii.

Skrine, F. H. (1899). The Heart of Asia: A History of Russian Turkestan and the Central Asian Khanates from the Earliest Times. London, UK: Methuen & Co.

Śrivāstava, K.C. (2007). Prāchina Bhārata kā Itihāsa tathā Sanskṛti (in Hindi). 11th edition. Allahabad, India: United Book Depot.

Sykes, W. H. (1841). Art. XIV.—Notes on the Religious, Moral, and Political State of India, before the Mahomedan Invasion, chiefly founded on the Travels of the Chinese Buddhist Priest, Fa Hian, in India, A.D. 399, and on the Commentaries of Messrs. Remusat, Klaproth, Burnouf, and Landresse. Journal of the Royal Asiatic Society of Great Britain and Ireland, 6: 248-450.

Telang, K. T. (1875). Art. X. - A New Chālukya Copper Plate; with remarks. The Journal of the Bombay Branch of the Royal Asiatic Society. 10: 348-367.

The Encyclopaedia Britannica: A Dictionary of Arts, Sciences, and General Literature, Volume XVIII. (1888). New York, USA: Henry G. Allen and Company.

The Encyclopaedia Britannica: A Dictionary of Arts, Sciences, and General Literature, Volume XII. (1891). Chicago, USA: R.S. Peale Company.

The Hindoos. Volume II. (1835). London, UK: Charles Knight.

The Modern Part of a Universal History, From the Earliest Account of Time, Vol. IV. (1759). London, UK: Published by S.

Richadson, T. Osborne, C. Hitch, A. Millar, John Rivington, S. Crowder, P. Davey and B. Law, T. Longman, and C.Ware.

Thomas, E. (1858). Essays on Indian Antiquities, historic, Numismatic, and Paleographic of the late James Prinsep to which are added his Useful Tables, illustrative of Indian history, chronology, modern coinage, weights, measures, etc. Volume II. London, UK: John Murray.

Tod, J. (1920). Annals and Antiquities of Rajasthan or the Central and Western Rajput States of India. Edited with an introduction and notes by William Crooke. Volume 1 (Original Dedication of the First Volume: June 20, 1829). Oxford, UK: Oxford University Press.

Waldman, C. and Mason, C. (2006). Encyclopedia of European Peoples. New York, USA: Facts on File, Inc.

INDEX

Abul Fazl, 44, 72-73

Ādityasena, 134-152, 157-160

Al-Biruni, 144-48

Alexander, 3, 25, 43, 201

Anantavarman, 131-132, 150

Āndhra, 6, 133, 142, 143, 148

Aṅga, 18, 24

Ardashir, 37-39, 45, 110

Ardeshir, 200, 201

Arjuna, 18

Arrian, 19

Āryabhaṭa, 150, 151

Aśoka, 19, 21, 94, 124

Bahram, 39-47, 102, 108-112, 122

Bālāditya, 55, 62, 65, 73, 74, 94, 95, 140

Bappa Rawal, 49, 63, 70, 201

Buddha, 17, 18, 35, 36, 155

Buddha Varmā, 171, 173, 175, 178

Chālukya, 16, 78, 80, 91-95, 161-179

Chanḍaśrī Śātakarṇi, 7, 8, 12

Chaṣṭana, 4, 9-12

Cunningham, 15, 20, 80, 93, 125

Cyrus Śaka era, 4

Cyrus the Great, 4, 192

Dadda 74, 77-96, 179

Dāmodaragupta, 136, 139-43, 151, 152, 157, 160

Dantapura, 17, 18

Devānāmpriya Priyadarśī, 6, 21, 94

Dharasena, 53, 54, 56, 62-65, 79, 83, 91-96

Dhruvasena, 55, 57, 62-65, 73, 74, 91-95

Framjee, 191

Gautamīputra Śātakarṇi, 4-9, 63

Gollas, 122, 125-127

Govinda, 167

Grahavarman, 134, 142, 150, 158, 160

Guhāditya, 65, 66, 201

Gurjara, 63, 67, 74, 76-99, 127, 141, 178, 179

Hāla, 7, 8

Hāriti, 162-64

Hephthalite, 113, 120

Hiuen Tsiang, 15, 35, 73, 74, 91, 123

Falk, 33, 35

Harṣa era, 147, 151, 159, 161

Harṣagupta, 90, 91, 96, 135, 141, 151, 152, 160

Harṣavardhana, 73, 74, 78, 80, 86, 87, 91, 143, 144, 151, 154, 157-160, 170, 180

Hūṇa, 37, 73, 90, 96, 99, 110-113, 119-128, 130- 132, 136, 141, 144, 148, 149, 151, 157, 159, 160

Imperial Gupta, 21, 34, 46, 111, 120, 122, 123

Indraprastha, 5

Indus Valley Civilization, 36

Īśānavarman, 133-136, 142-43, 148-151, 157-160

Jayabhaṭa, 76-99, 127, 134, 178

Jayadeva, 159

Jaya Siṃha, 173

Jivitagupta II, 139, 143

Justinian, 115, 116

Kalhaṇa, 33

Kali era, 150

Kālidāsa, 169

Kaliṅga, 15-26, 159, 168

Kanaksen, 50, 51, 64, 65

Kaniṣka, 4, 33-36, 45-47

Kannauj, 44

Kānyakubja, 151

Kārdamaka Śaka, 9-12

Kātyāyana, 13

Khākān, 103-105, 110, 120, 122, 125-127

Khāravela, 21-26

Khosrow, 72, 98, 99, 110-112

Khush-Newaz, 112, 121, 122, 125

Konow, 25

Korūr, 72, 99, 128, 144-149, 157-159

Kumāragupta, 135, 139, 141-144, 151, 152, 160

Kumāragupta I, 6, 21

Kuṣāṇa, 4, 26, 28, 32-34, 37, 45-47, 90, 102, 109, 111, 112, 120-23, 130, 132, 141

Kuṣāṇa era, 34

Later Gupta, 90, 96, 131, 134, 139-144, 149-152, 154-160

Magadha, 19, 23, 24, 26, 36, 151, 158

Mahābhārata, 16-20, 130, 164, 170

Mahāmeghavāhana, 21, 25

Mahāsenagupta, 136, 139, 141-144, 152, 157, 160

Maitraka, 52

Mānadeva era, 159

Mangaleśa, 94, 95, 166, 169, 170, 177, 178

Maukhari, 90, 131-136, 141-43, 148-52, 154-60

McCrindle, 19, 20

Megasthenes, 18, 19

Mihirakula, 3

Mūlasthāna, 148

Nāgārjuna, 5

Nanda, 19, 23-26

Noshirwān the Just, 72

Oḍra, 159

Pahlava, 2, 3

Parthian, 28-32, 102

Pāṭaliputra, 123, 150

Pliny, 16-18, 20, 42

Prabhākaravardhana, 155-160

Pratihāra, 76

Pratiṣṭhāna, 4, 5, 12

Prayāga, 136

Prinsep, 44

Ptolemy, 9, 12, 17, 19

Pulakeśina, 78, 93-95, 158, 161, 164, 169, 170, 176-178

Puruṣapura, 36

Rājagṛha, 23, 124

Rājyaśrī, 157, 158

Rājyavardhana, 144, 154-61

Rudradāman, 9-12

Rudrasena, 10-11

Śaka era, 4-9, 33, 35, 63, 64, 70, 72, 77-81, 86, 87,

95, 97, 164, 170, 173, 176

Śakasthāna, 3

Samudragupta, 21

Sanjan, 191-201

Sasanian, 37, 42, 45, 46, 72, 98, 102, 109-112, 124, 180,190

Śaśāṅka, 158, 161

Sātavāhana, 4-13, 63, 64

Scythian, 2, 3

Shahpour, 37-39

Śilāditya, 51, 53, 56, 58-74, 94-99, 118, 124, 125

Sisodia, 49, 50, 67, 70, 71, 73

Śivaśrī Pulumāvi, 7, 12

Skandagupta, 120

Sogdiana, 32

Someśvara, 150

Sphujidhvaja, 33

Srikakulam, 18

Susthitavarman, 136, 142, 143, 157

Tājika, 97-99, 127

Tiastenes, 9, 12

Vallabhī, 49, 51, 63-74, 80, 86-99, 122, 124-27, 141, 142, 151, 201

Vallabhī era, 63, 64, 70

Vaṅga, 18

Varāhamihira, 3, 4, 150, 201

Vasubandhu, 147

Vasudeva, 34, 44-47, 102, 109, 111

Vijayasen, 51, 64, 65

Vikramāditya, 1, 3, 5, 144-150, 161, 201

Vikramāditya, Chalukya, 93-95, 164, 170, 178

Vikrama era, 4, 77, 147, 173, 175

Wilford, 148

Yaśodharmā, 1, 3, 120, 150

Yaśovarman, 158

Yavanajātaka, 33-34

Yezdijird, 181-89

Yué-Chi, 29-32

ABOUT THE AUTHOR

Dr. Raja Ram Mohan Roy earned his undergraduate degree in Metallurgical Engineering from Indian Institute of Technology, Kanpur and Ph.D. in Materials Science and Engineering from The Ohio State University, USA. He moved to Canada as a Postdoctoral Fellow. Raja has conducted research and development in the areas of Extractive Metallurgy and Materials Processing for twenty years. He has co-authored 40 research papers that have been published in peer-reviewed journals and proceedings of international symposia. He has co-edited the book "Innovative Process Development in Metallurgical Industry."

Raja has always had a fascination for ancient Indian civilization. Through his writings, Raja hopes to contribute towards the continuity and understanding of his civilization and, in the Indic tradition, repay the debt to his ancestors for their contributions and their sacrifices.

www.ingramcontent.com/pod-product-compliance
Lightning Source LLC
Chambersburg PA
CBHW051752040426
42446CB00007B/332
* 9 7 8 0 9 6 8 4 1 2 0 8 4 *